The
BIG BOOK OF
Song Lyrics
BY

JOHN KANIECKI

Dedicated to my beloved:

My wife: *Sylvia*

Copyright © 2023 John Kaniecki
All rights reserved.
ISBN: 9798868062612

Lovely Ladie$

Bargain Price

(WRITTEN FOR MILEY CYRUS)

From the first two weeks of November 2020.

Star Light Lover

On The Corner (Under The Street Lamp)

Momma's Tears (Florence's Song)

Madonna Maybe

Zeppelin Lady (The Wind Blows)

Sylvia's Sorrows

In The Dark

Pop Singer Pop Song

Late Night Call

On The Run (Mare's Melody)

Fantasy

She's The Poetry

Train To Tomorrow

Lovely Ladies Bargain Price

Starlight Lover

Sunny days are spent in funny ways
He who says repent always pays
A coin in the jukebox to play a cover
Singing a song of my sweet starlight lover

Starlight lover you're a burning fire
Rising in the sky taking me higher
Your light your love the heat of my desire
Starlight lover you're all I require

The spaceman was chasing paradise
Fools spurn even the best advice
Annoyed in the void seeking secrets untold
You never have the winning hand if you fold

Starlight lover you're a burning fire
Rising in the sky taking me higher
Your light your love the heat of my desire
Starlight lover you're all I require

Venus dances with Mars in the eve
Love is yours if you just believe
Infinity is still small for number two
Take my hand understand dreams sometimes come true

Starlight lover you're a burning fire
Rising in the sky taking me higher
Your light your love the heat of my desire
Starlight lover you're all I require

A kiss sweet miss it's a start
Bliss is a blessing don't depart
Starlight lover you're living art
Paint your picture on my heart

Engines roar we ascend in the sky
I'm sure my friend love cannot die
With all your might hold tight love is revealing
Forever is a word more than a feeling

Starlight lover you're a burning fire
Rising in the sky taking me higher
Your light your love the heat of my desire
Starlight lover you're all I require

On The Corner (Under The Street Lamp)

See my sweetie standing a statue numb
Long ago she stopped singing we shall overcome
Between the sin and heroine so cuts the knife
Sometimes the living don't even know life

See her on the corner under the street lamp
The rains are eternal forever wet and damp
A lonely letter never finding her stamp
See her on the corner under the street lamp

Stars play guitars seeking another thrill
Sharks circle sharp teeth smiling expecting the kill
If you got the pay you'll be going all the way
But if you bluff then hey what could she say?

See her on the corner under the street lamp
The rains are eternal forever wet and damp
A lonely letter never finding her stamp
See her on the corner under the street lamp

Some fine ladies have a very high price
In the bars in the slums some are won throwing dice
Either way I say they welcome the naked truth
From dirty old men or the tender youth

See her on the corner under the street lamp
The rains are eternal forever wet and damp
A lonely letter never finding her stamp
See her on the corner under the street lamp

She dreams little more than fantasy
In her screams too much reality
A wounded warrior a fatality
A statistic a lost technicality

The sun always rises in the new day
For a better tomorrow I silently pray
Working girls are the mirror of the working class
See the pimps a massive pain in the ass

See her on the corner under the street lamp
The rains are eternal forever wet and damp
A lonely letter never finding her stamp
See her on the corner under the street lamp

Momma's Tears (Florence's Song)

True love is something beyond romance
True love always means taking a chance
For life is uncertain after I do
And the sky and the sea are forever blue

Momma why are you crying if I can be bold
I'm a weeping for the lies your father told
He promised me diamonds the price I was sold
But now I have nothing except days making me old

Flo put her dreams for another day
I'll be a lawyer I heard her say
Dear Ted said that things would work out that way
Sadly some debts are never to repay

Momma why are you crying if I can be bold
I'm a weeping for the lies your father told
He promised me diamonds the price I was sold
But now I have nothing except days making me old

Her hopes shattered caught inside a lie
Pondering wondering the reason why
Dawn finally shined after the long night
Sometimes the answer is you're in the right

Momma why are you crying if I can be bold
I'm a weeping for the lies your father told
He promised me diamonds the price I was sold
But now I have nothing except days making me old

Hell has a fire which always burns
Devils have lessons the child learns
You spend a life caught in the maze
The confusing agony of the early days

Florence fought but the battle was vain
I was the victim going insane
I know in my soul that mother was right
But bitter and evil so was the fight

Momma why are you crying if I can be bold
I'm a weeping for the lies your father told
He promised me diamonds the price I was sold
But now I have nothing except days making me old

Madonna Maybe

Reality and fantasy merge in the night
Sin showing skin she can do more than just bite
Spotlight burns Madonna maybe turns around
Magical music makes a miraculous sound

Madonna maybe do we ever know
Hey there baby the wind will blow
On the dance floor see her go go go
Madonna maybe she's a one-gal show

Silicone and microphone say what is real
Anything you can't earn you could try to steal
Photo shot getting hot simmering in the steam
Wide awake give and take life is a merry dream

Madonna maybe do we ever know
Hey there baby the wind will blow
On the dance floor see her go go go
Madonna maybe she's a one-gal show

She sold her soul but who's to say
Surrendering control she earns her pay
For every saint lies a rugged cross
Madonna maybe crazy on the loss

Eyes of envy green as the money coming in
The game of fame is the same you play to win
Sell soul and heart to top the chart at number one
Around the bend comes the end evening is done

Madonna maybe do we ever know
Hey there baby the wind will blow
On the dance floor see her go go go
Madonna maybe she's a one-gal show

As the pressure mounts she counts on the drugs and booze
Easy to please me they say just never lose
Somewhere between here and there everything went wrong
She sings to paupers and kings but it ain't her song

Madonna maybe do we ever know
Hey there baby the wind will blow
On the dance floor see her go go go
Madonna maybe she's a one-gal show

Zeppelin Lady (The Wind Blows)

Titanium chromium steel tell me what is real
Man and woman doubling down on the ultimate ideal
Full fantasy the dream in the highest extreme
Tenderly young the song is sung in the glimmering moon beam

Zeppelin lady floating in the sky
Zeppelin lady soaring in your high
Zeppelin lady hear your lover's sigh
The wind blows baby that's the reason why

Stairways to heaven they go on without any end
Everybody loves you but you ain't got a single friend
Turn the page plant the flower rock and roll can't die
Hear it in the words the wind blows baby that's the reason why

Zeppelin lady floating in the sky
Zeppelin lady soaring in your high
Zeppelin lady hear your lover's sigh
The wind blows baby that's the reason why

Laying down the electric led eating up the bread
Hear the wisdom in the words in the words we left unsaid
Lucifer ascends quoting cryptic cosmic verse
In the garden we made our sacred vows for better or worse

Zeppelin lady floating in the sky
Zeppelin lady soaring in your high
Zeppelin lady hear your lover's sigh
The wind blows baby that's the reason why

Aaah Aaah Aaaaah the circle is in spin
Aaah Aaah Aaaaah it feels good this sin
Rock and roll heavy metal we live to defy
The wind blows baby that's the reason why

Rust never sleeps the promises we keep remain deep
The good Lord in immense hunger watches his sheep
Our rock and roll road from blues to yellow to red
Embers in the ashes a flickering never to be dead

Zeppelin lady floating in the sky
Zeppelin lady soaring in your high
Zeppelin lady hear your lover's sigh
The wind blows baby that's the reason why

Sylvia's Sorrow

She was sunshine mighty fine
An angel of glory divine
Rising in the east headed west
She was Sylvia simply the best

Now we sing a song of Sylvia's sorrow
Everyone has to accept tomorrow
Comes a time there's nothing left to borrow
Now we sing a song of Sylvia's sorrow

My tears they wet my guitar
A final twinkle of the star
Goodbye on the tip of my tongue
I can't believe in forever young

Now we sing a song of Sylvia's sorrow
Everyone has to accept tomorrow
Comes a time there's nothing left to borrow
Now we sing a song of Sylvia's sorrow

Memories I laugh and cry
Even dreams have a time to die
The final line in the fine show
A sad song of Sylvia's sorrow

Now we sing a song of Sylvia's sorrow
Everyone has to accept tomorrow
Comes a time there's nothing left to borrow
Now we sing a song of Sylvia's sorrow

Hey babe in your day you were the rage
The part you played they turned the page
Now take a bow as you walk off the stage
If God is kind find another age

Freedom that's your final part
A moment before you depart
Alive you survive in my art
Almighty God how you broke my heart

Now we sing a song of Sylvia's sorrow
Everyone has to accept tomorrow
Comes a time there's nothing left to borrow
Now we sing a song of Sylvia's sorrow

In The Dark

Good girl by day but dark is the night
Ask her I say because she just might
Angels and demons they both got wings
Love's a song that everybody sings

Things go bump bump bump in the dark
Feel for your treasure hit the mark
Kiss me sweetly we're about to embark
Things go bump bump bump in the dark

Secrets whispered hear a lover's sigh
Truth is fine but she'll accept a lie
Give in to win please don't call it sin
Toke a smoke and then do it again

Things go bump bump bump in the dark
Feel for your treasure hit the mark
Kiss me sweetly we're about to embark
Things go bump bump bump in the dark

Hold on real tight it's all that I got
Pain can bite you know the fire burns hot
Ashes to ashes so goes the way
But deep in the dark I'll have my day

Things go bump bump bump in the dark
Feel for your treasure hit the mark
Kiss me sweetly we're about to embark
Things go bump bump bump in the dark

Lovers and friends it never ends
Lost at all cost the story bends
In the dark the night is alive
In the dark it's how I survive

Close your eyes to see midnight fury
We got the time but I like to hurry
In the dark words they redefine
In the dark baby your soul is mine

Things go bump bump bump in the dark
Feel for your treasure hit the mark
Kiss me sweetly we're about to embark
Things go bump bump bump in the dark

Pop Singer Pop Song

Hey baby maybe but you gotta look the part
We got silicone and makeup a work of art
Sing me a line all will be fine simply divine
If you ain't a perfect ten we'll accept a nine

Pop singer she got a pop song
Pop singer she sings a pop song
In the dream of scream they sing along
Pop singer she got a pop song

We'll hire a writer who pours blood into the ink
You'll have backup singers but you can just lip sync
Sex appeal is the deal pretend that you are real
Life is a show but even so you can still steal

Pop singer she got a pop song
Pop singer she sings a pop song
In the dream of scream they sing along
Pop singer she got a pop song

Coke or booze you can choose the wages of your sin
Party through the night but the show goes on again
If we're making money then you can go to hell
Lovers and friends but who just pretends we can't tell

Pop singer she got a pop song
Pop singer she sings a pop song
In the dream of scream they sing along
Pop singer she got a pop song

Fantasy is what they see in you
How's the deal when dreams come true
Pop singer pop song the chosen few
Life's a mystery where's a clue?

Jet planes and jewels fools telling stories built on sand
Welcome to the machine come clean and understand
The best of the blessed money lifting you with fame
Pop singer pop song tell me what's wrong with the game

Pop singer she got a pop song
Pop singer she sings a pop song
In the dream of scream they sing along
Pop singer she got a pop song

Late Night Call

Hey baby maybe you got a secret or two
I'm dreaming in color of what we could do
Close the lights it don't count if you can't see
I'm winning you're losing but it ain't victory

You got that hunger late-night call
She's younger you want it all
Castles and kingdoms are bound to fall
Horses running wild late-night call

Down on the dance floor the rhythm sways in the heat
Empty and aching looking to be complete
Left right twisting like a snake being charmed
You might get wounded but surely you won't be harmed

You got that hunger late-night call
She's younger you want it all
Castles and kingdoms are bound to fall
Horses running wild late-night call

Always on the run but never a place to go
Hither thither raise the curtain for the show
Booze and cocaine the local currency
When it's my pain or desire it's an urgency

You got that hunger late-night call
She's younger you want it all
Castles and kingdoms are bound to fall
Horses running wild late-night call

Star light star bright take me to a height
Obey all I say become my delight
Love is a word of dreams poets write
Consumed the doom let me hold you tight

With the rising sun your hour of glory is done
Leave with style give a big smile I had my fun
If we pass walking down the avenue
By a friend and pretend that we're meeting anew

You got that hunger late-night call
She's younger you want it all
Castles and kingdoms are bound to fall
Horses running wild late-night call

On The Run (Mare's Song)

When home is hell and you're seventeen
You're one gloomy teenybopper queen
F the world girl just split the scene
When home is hell and you're seventeen

She's on the run wanting to be free
Looking for fun a different reality
She's on the run she's number one
She's on the run what's done is done

You ain't old but you think that you are
In your lover's arms playing star
On the road taking it too far
Yesterday's a song played on guitar

She's on the run wanting to be free
Looking for fun a different reality
She's on the run she's number one
She's on the run what's done is done

Sing of sorrow sing of glee
Speak the spell to set me free
Dance the jig with all your might
Think real big it still ain't right

Here's a message on the radio
You ain't the only one with sorrow
Listen well can you hear my voice
Love is staying when you got a choice

She's on the run wanting to be free
Looking for fun a different reality
She's on the run she's number one
She's on the run what's done is done

Sorry you burnt the bridge darling Mare
It's not the case that I don't care
Sometimes God says no to your prayer
Keep on running the futures out there

She's on the run wanting to be free
Looking for fun a different reality
She's on the run she's number one
She's on the run what's done is done

Fantasy

In the mind you find it all in the mind
See the smile on the face of the blind
The fetters of love still they bite and bind
In the mind you find it all in the mind

You me and fantasy that's three
Breaking the rules of reality
Chaos forming from anarchy
Remember you me and fantasy

Temptation's snare are you really out there?
Faith's the substance of a dreamer's prayer
Lobster and steak make it medium rare
Fantasy is a partner without care

You me and fantasy that's three
Breaking the rules of reality
Chaos forming from anarchy
Remember you me and fantasy

Weary in the hour searching for the power
Purple daises in a rain shower
Butterfly flutters muttering a curse
Sacred tonic spices even dull verse

You me and fantasy that's three
Breaking the rules of reality
Chaos forming from anarchy
Remember you me and fantasy

Lyrics of losing love help me Lord
I shall be healed just say the word
Mary Magdalene she's a raging ten
Down on her knees hallelujah amen

Body dead but fantasies inside the head
Hope meeting joy so blissfully wed
Girl kissing boy so begins all tales
Fantasy wins when reality fails

You me and fantasy that's three
Breaking the rules of reality
Chaos forming from anarchy
Remember you me and fantasy

She's The Poetry

She's got silver bells that jingle on her shoes
Happy chords on the guitar mock the blues
Life is a long song and she's the poetry
Come on baby won't you come dancing with me

She's the poetry life's so alive
She's the poetry it's how we survive
She's the poetry rhythm and jive
She's the poetry life's so alive

Take time to rhyme can you hear the church bells chime?
A heart full of love that's my only crime
Hand in hand answering a prophetic call
When something rises then something else must fall

She's the poetry life's so alive
She's the poetry it's how we survive
She's the poetry rhythm and jive
She's the poetry life's so alive

Angels and demons flying on the winds of peace
Armies stop marching warships come to a cease
Dream of tomorrow dream of a better day
Come and follow the youth let them lead the way

She's the poetry life's so alive
She's the poetry it's how we survive
She's the poetry rhythm and jive
She's the poetry life's so alive

Flowers in her hair San Francisco Bay
Hours in care on her knees to pray
See the sunrise before innocent eyes
Peace love and understanding our prize

Shaking on shake down street they got subtle moves
The chorus before us got great grand grooves
Joy to the world the moment is now at hand
Take out the music score and strike up the band

She's the poetry life's so alive
She's the poetry it's how we survive
She's the poetry rhythm and jive
She's the poetry life's so alive

Train To Tomorrow

Tears speak when words fail
All ships were built to sail
Tonight was live or die
Only one answer goodbye

She's riding on that train to tomorrow
Her ticket bought with bills of sorrow
A life is something you can't borrow
She's riding on that train to tomorrow

Small towns never change
Funny faces stay strange
Tired of her point of view
Heaven must be something new

She's riding on that train to tomorrow
Her ticket bought with bills of sorrow
A life is something you can't borrow
She's riding on that train to tomorrow

Love is her desire
Oh let it burn cruel fire
One chance to touch the flame
Better is never the same

She's riding on that train to tomorrow
Her ticket bought with bills of sorrow
A life is something you can't borrow
She's riding on that train to tomorrow

Heaven shines a billion lights in the sky
To succeed or fail oh she had to try
When life fails walls become jails
Seizing the pen she'll write her own tales

Tracks come to an end
A new day a new friend
Fools never take a chance
Final station sweet romance

She's riding on that train to tomorrow
Her ticket bought with bills of sorrow
A life is something you can't borrow
She's riding on that train to tomorrow

Lovely Ladies Bargain Price

Leopard pants but she ain't going to the dance
Making love but there ain't no romance
She's a beauty you'll never have to guess
Ask her for a date and she'll say yes

Lovely ladies bargain price
Spread the doors to paradise
Enter in always nice
Lovely ladies bargain price

Comfortably numb lost in a frosty glaze
Hear her story void of those glory days
Round and round the world twirling without sound
If you're not lost how can you be found

Lovely ladies bargain price
Spread the doors to paradise
Enter in always nice
Lovely ladies bargain price

Summer's heat in a back seat sometimes they cheat
Victory a trick surrender defeat
Oh God where are you in this insane pain?
Prayer after prayer are they words but vain?

Lovely ladies bargain price
Spread the doors to paradise
Enter in always nice
Lovely ladies bargain price

Good girls don't but she just might
Pride fails when the stomach is tight
Closing their eyes the world is blind
Would it hurt so much if we were kind?

See a billion stars shine in heaven above
Who can you call mine oh who can you love?
We all sell out that's my truthful advice
See those lovely ladies bargain price

Lovely ladies bargain price
Spread the doors to paradise
Enter in always nice
Lovely ladies bargain price

A Loose Girl

I remember before yesterday
When La Rue Avenue was a one way
She was a loose girl with loose change
And the whole world it seemed so strange

A loose girl in a world so tight
He loves you at least for the night
It don't matter wrong or right
A loose girl in a world so tight

And today the bathrooms are liberated
While endless war isn't even debated
Sexual freedom is the choice you make
All the strong men eventually break

A loose girl in a world so tight
He loves you at least for the night
It don't matter wrong or right
A loose girl in a world so tight

Starving for lust please donate
Lady Lace a vixen to celebrate
Down on her knees but she don't pray
We're consenting adults so it's okay

In the shadows of the poet's verse
Rhyming words in rhythmic curse
The entire universe is a metaphor
She's just a whore we knew before

A loose girl in a world so tight
He loves you at least for the night
It don't matter wrong or right
A loose girl in a world so tight

A Secret Place

Quiet moments pass on by
The sun shines in heaven high
There is no world save you and I
And the forest's soft sigh

Love is a treasure
A measure of grace
Let me touch the pleasure
Forbidden hidden
In a secret place

Kiss me let us embrace
Touching the lips on our face
I hear our hearts race
We are safe
In a secret place

Love is a treasure
A measure of grace
Let me touch the pleasure
Forbidden hidden
In a secret place

We are a happy melody
I for you and you for me
Let us sing knowing no shame
In the end we are the same

Love is a treasure
A measure of grace
Let me touch the pleasure
Forbidden hidden
In a secret place

A Song Inside Of Me

On the corner she's singing strumming her guitar
Brenda Bops never stops dreaming of being a star
She sings songs that define La Rue Avenue
Good and bad happy and sad all are blue

There's a song inside of me
Fighting to be free
Tomorrow be my destiny
There's a song inside of me
Fighting to be free

All the people stand to listen for a while
Captivating heart and soul young and old wear a smile
Into her cup they will toss nickels and dimes
Some of them sing along with her rhymes

There's a song inside of me
Fighting to be free
Tomorrow be my destiny
There's a song inside of me
Fighting to be free

And the world overflows with hateful lies
Pushing you down with every attempt made to rise
But songs are holy overflowing with power
And Brenda Bops she will claim her hour

There's a song inside of me
Fighting to be free
Tomorrow be my destiny
There's a song inside of me
Fighting to be free

A Very Good Day

The robins were chirping a melody
The squirrels so happy to be free
Big Boy was sitting in the sun
It seemed I dreamed life had begun

It was a very good day when you said hello
Innocence by chance we all must let go
Life changes fast but the world changes slow
It was a very good day when you said hello

When I found you I could tell you were lost
Naming your pennies counting the cost
I said life should be without money
Like the bees making sweet honey

It was a very good day when you said hello
Innocence by chance we all must let go
Life changes fast but the world changes slow
It was a very good day when you said hello

There are mysteries hid in bad advice
We are constantly paying the price
Give more make a greater sacrifice
And they come take the biggest slice

It was a very good day when you said hello
Innocence by chance we all must let go
Life changes fast but the world changes slow
It was a very good day when you said hello

When the guns thundered and the bombs began to fall
We wondered why they always wanted to take it all
Love is a shared ideal that very few pursue
Like a midnight lover whose time is overdue

You and I well we had some good romance
Heaven it comes when you take a chance
Here we are chasing the lonesome moon
Singing my song a lover's tune

It was a very good day when you said hello
Innocence by chance we all must let go
Life changes fast but the world changes slow
It was a very good day when you said hello

An Endless Melody

I said madam am I falling in love
Day and night your all I'm thinking of
I can't escape you star in my dreams
I see your smile shining in sunbeams

I can't believe what's happening to me
I'm singing an endless melody
Like a blue bird flying free
I'm singing an endless melody

I'm thinking about you all of the time
You are the reason why all my words rhyme
A subtle strumming on my guitar
Inside of my song there you are

I can't believe what's happening to me
I'm singing an endless melody
Like a blue bird flying free
I'm singing an endless melody

I ain't no king but you're a queen for sure
Pretty and nice but there's something more
I had the blues but your love's the cure
Heaven awaits darling you're the door

Down at the dance all the men are in awe
You're the loveliest creature they ever saw
When the music is slow we sway so tight
It's perfect paradise on a Saturday night

I can't believe what's happening to me
I'm singing an endless melody
Like a blue bird flying free
I'm singing an endless melody

Tomorrow is a promise mighty grand
Let's stroll through this life hand in hand
Stairway to heaven climbing so high
You're the reason that the poet's sigh

I can't believe what's happening to me
I'm singing an endless melody
Like a blue bird flying free
I'm singing an endless melody

Before The Rain

I was falling falling
When I heard the word
You were calling calling
Life was endless pain
Before the rain

We once had Eden
In our years without sin
Then came a desert dry
Until God began to cry
Life was insane
Before the rain

Love is the lesson of living
To be kind gentle giving
All I knew was vain
So much I didn't know
But that was so long ago
Before the rain

And so I look to the sky
As the poets wonder why
Hear my cry
I cannot refrain
Black clouds gather on high
Before the rain
He's coming again

Beyond The Sky

Mick is a product of the street
Hustle and bustle for something to eat
His daddy unknown his mother a whore
Life don't come with a magical cure

You never dream if you don't sleep
Still the questions are rivers deep
Life ain't fair equality a lie
Heavens a place beyond the sky

The bell rings so excited for the fight
Dance and sing make a score for the night
Selling bags of dope on the avenue
Laced and cut just like life so untrue

You never dream if you don't sleep
Still the questions are rivers deep
Life ain't fair equality a lie
Heavens a place beyond the sky

Here comes a frat boy pretending to be cool
Mick charges them double that is the rule
Pale face invaders deep down in the hood
They don't come here to do any good

Blood in his veins pulsating
Anger in his brains now hating
Ain't no truth inside a song
Ain't no truth when all is wrong

You never dream if you don't sleep
Still the questions are rivers deep
Life ain't fair equality a lie
Heavens a place beyond the sky

Mick has a woman and a kid or two
He wants to help them but he has no clue
Hard questions come tell me the reason why
Mick knows the answer but it's just a lie

You never dream if you don't sleep
Still the questions are rivers deep
Life ain't fair equality a lie
Heavens a place beyond the sky

Big Tiny

Big Tiny is the main man to see
Without a doubt he's the authority
He runs the numbers and the drug trade
If you like darkness Big Tiny got your shade

He drives a Caddy shocking pink
A contradiction to make you think
Big Tiny is the king for real
See Big Tiny to make your deal

Big Tiny got teeth of solid gold
Each one of them is a story to be told
You never give the man any jive
He'll kick the devil's ass only to survive

He drives a Caddy shocking pink
A contradiction to make you think
Big Tiny is the king for real
See Big Tiny to make your deal

The man's a fan of the working girl
Really likes to sock 'em knock 'em rock their world
Big Tiny's king he don't share his loot
On La Rue Avenue he's an institute

He drives a Caddy shocking pink
A contradiction to make you think
Big Tiny is the king for real
See Big Tiny to make your deal

Big Tiny pays off all the police
The gangster makes sure that we all keep the peace
Crime is bad for business you see
And Big Tiny got tenderness for his money

He drives a Caddy shocking pink
A contradiction to make you think
Big Tiny is the king for real
See Big Tiny to make your deal

Broken Man

My guitar is missing a string
The blues is all that I sing
I never met any kings
And I know what tomorrow brings

I'm a broken man with a broken song
I wanna do right but I do some wrong
I wish I could be brave and strong
I'm a broken man with a broken song

I have a wicked cheating heart
I play the fool that's my part
I once had you in my life
I should have made you my wife

I'm a broken man with a broken song
I wanna do right but I do some wrong
I wish I could be brave and strong
I'm a broken man with a broken song

Oh you were everything and then something more
A holy angel full of tender love so pure
But I'm a broken man and I let you slip on by
And every day when I wake up I stop to cry

When I sing I can't keep a tune
I wait for the sun to get the moon
On the day I that I die
I'll go to heaven on high
Cause the door to that place
Is opened by love and grace

I'm a broken man with a broken song
I wanna do right but I do some wrong
I wish I could be brave and strong
I'm a broken man with a broken song

Buzzy Buzzy Bee

Buzzy buzzy bee flying in the sky
Buzzy buzzy bee feeling so high
Down to the flower pretty and pink
Down to the flower pretty and pink
Buzzy buzzy bee makes you think

Buzzy buzzy bee helps the flower
Buzzy buzzy bee helps the flower
Spreading seeds every hour
Spreading seeds every hour
Mother Nature's delicate power

Buzzy buzzy bee he gets fed
Buzzy buzzy bee he gets fed
And the flower's pollen is spread
And the flower's pollen is spread
That's a lot to be said

Buzzy buzzy bee flying in the sky
Buzzy buzzy bee feeling so high
Down to the flower pretty and pink
Down to the flower pretty and pink
Buzzy buzzy bee makes you think

Buzzy buzzy bee he's our friend
Buzzy buzzy bee he's our friend
Mother Nature can never end
Mother Nature can never end
She won't break only bend

So be kind to the creatures that you see
So be kind to the creatures that you see
Mother Nature lives in harmony
Mother Nature lives in harmony
A blessing to both you and me

Buzzy buzzy bee flying in the sky
Buzzy buzzy bee feeling so high
Down to the flower pretty and pink
Down to the flower pretty and pink
Buzzy buzzy bee makes you think

Call Of The Forest

We are racing deep into a green sea
I am you and you are me
We have begun the quest the test
Of eternity

The light of the day is hidden far away
I still have the hope to pray
Wondering what tomorrow shall bring
You the queen I the king

Can You See

Early in the morning before I rise
With darkness resting in my eyes
I wonder what the day will bring
Joining the birds as they sing
The hammer starts to sing its song
The world belongs to the strong

All the things under the sun
Victory is to be lost or won
Someday we shall overcome
Can you see where I coming from?

Down the street to catch the train
All their work and it's all in vain
Dressed so fine in suit and tie
Living something that's a lie
While the carpenter cuts his wood
And life is greatly misunderstood

All the things under the sun
Victory is to be lost or won
Someday we shall overcome
Can you see where I coming from?

And I sit and dream of a better day
But I'm a dreamer so what's to say
Peace and love and understanding
But the privileged are so demanding
Never do they lend a hand
They just bark off their command

All the things under the sun
Victory is to be lost or won
Someday we shall overcome
Can you see where I coming from?

A lifetime passes by in a blink
While crumble mountains of ink
Looking back when the end is near
Nothing to show for a career
But the house of wood and steel
That my friends is what is real

Chasing Shadows

I saw you standing by the apple tree
Under the sky wild and free
I cried to you in a desperate plea
Will you give your love to me?

I was chasing shadows chasing shadows
That's the way life goes
Chasing shadows chasing shadows
Where it ends nobody knows
Chasing shadows chasing shadows

You smiled and took me by the hand
Not a word said do you understand?
We started walking to the Promised Land
Love itself was at our command

I was chasing shadows chasing shadows
That's the way life goes
Chasing shadows chasing shadows
Where it ends nobody knows
Chasing shadows chasing shadows

Somewhere somehow we had lost our way
For every dream a price to pay
I sought the words I could not say
Forever I long for yesterday

I was chasing shadows chasing shadows
That's the way life goes
Chasing shadows chasing shadows
Where it ends nobody knows
Chasing shadows chasing shadows

Chief Joseph Is On The Run

Manifest Destiny is Satan's lie
Too much pride to say genocide is why
All the children believe in the sacred book
Unless of course they take a second look

Chief Joseph is on the run
Can't you understand?
He didn't want to sell the land
What evil has he done?
Chief Joseph is on the run

These are the fields where our ancestors lie
Mother Earth of great worth you cannot buy
Let us live here that is our only desire
With shame the white man came with guns of fire

Chief Joseph is on the run
Can't you understand?
He didn't want to sell the land
What evil has he done?
Chief Joseph is on the run

Tragedy my friend in the end what an evil story
Hunting women and children in a sin void of glory
But to the youth far from the truth we tell the fable
Thanksgiving meal is so real with turkey on the table

Chief Joseph is on the run
Can't you understand?
He didn't want to sell the land
What evil has he done?
Chief Joseph is on the run

Canada was only a day away
The tale is a tragedy sad to say
But the pen is still writing what is to come
As a spirit Chief Joseph is on the run

Chief Joseph is on the run
Can't you understand?
He didn't want to sell the land
What evil has he done?
Chief Joseph is on the run

Dark Things

The boat ain't sinking the ocean's rising
God is the devil you find it surprising?
Pedophilia is rampant in the church
Ring the bell, you rang says Lurch

Dark things like a starless night
Dark things like a nuclear fight
Dark things dark things
Crucify the king of kings
Dark things

Sonic Youth speaks the truth let it pass
You wanna rise up learn to kiss some ass
Eventually you're gonna ejaculate
Is the glass half empty let's have a debate

Dark things like a starless night
Dark things like a nuclear fight
Dark things dark things
Crucify the king of kings
Dark things

Hey pretty girl with the blue dress on
Is your mother home is your daddy gone?
I'd like to tie you to the bed and have some fun
It's easy to say yes when I hold a gun

I shattered the mirror
The glass is broken
Is the mystery clearer?
Can I visit Hoboken?
Down in the institute
Satan gives his salute
Down in the institute
They tried to recruit
Meeeeeeeeeeeeeeeeeeeeeeeeeeeeeeeeeeeeeeeeeeeee!!!!

Dark things like a starless night
Dark things like a nuclear fight
Dark things dark things
Crucify the king of kings
Dark things

Daybreak

Woke up this life is mine
A gift from the divine
Happy just to have a song
In a world where I belong

Daybreak the light shines bright
Daybreak all will work out right
Daybreak tomorrow is in sight
Daybreak the light shines bright

I wander in the forest deep
I have yearned I have learned
The secrets that they keep
I have learned I have turned
From my hazy sleep

Daybreak the light shines bright
Daybreak all will work out right
Daybreak tomorrow is in sight
Daybreak the light shines bright

I shout a cry of glory
No doubt this is my story
Forever lies before me
Forever lies before me

Daybreak the light shines bright
Daybreak all will work out right
Daybreak tomorrow is in sight
Daybreak the light shines bright

Days Are Slow

Grenada is an island of paradise
When life is good everyone wants a slice
Love will come please listen to my advice
The best things they don't have any price

Hey Mareze the days are slow
Secrets come and mysteries go
The more you learn the less you know
Hey Mareze the days are slow

Poets dream and starving is part of the art
Words beam like magic coming from the heart
But words they come and the price is real cheap
Promises are vows that all should keep

The ways of woman and man
God eternal has a plan
None were meant to walk alone
Love is something none can own
For everything a season
For everything a reason

Hey Mareze the days are slow
Secrets come and mysteries go
The more you learn the less you know
Hey Mareze the days are slow

If he offers you love put him to the test
Romance is no dance but an endless quest
In the give and take the good times will rhyme
And moving slowly is not a crime

Hey Mareze the days are slow
Secrets come and mysteries go
The more you learn the less you know
Hey Mareze the days are slow

Down On La Rue Avenue

Lady Lace she sheds her grace
Brightening up the whole place
No she ain't our queen
She's just our ace

This sky is not all that's blue
Down on La Rue Avenue
If you've never been
Well then you ain't got a clue
Down on La Rue Avenue

Big Tiny he rules the street
Sweet Alvin he walks the beat
They're connected to the CIA
That's what they all say

This sky is not all that's blue
Down on La Rue Avenue
If you've never been
Well then you ain't got a clue
Down on La Rue Avenue

Crack and smack they flow like wine
A church on every corner so divine
Say brother got a dollar to spare
Ain't got a dollar but I got a prayer

Brenda Bops she sings her song
Saying all is right and all is wrong
The lesson here is very strong
If you're down then you belong

This sky is not all that's blue
Down on La Rue Avenue
If you've never been
Well then you ain't got a clue
Down on La Rue Avenue

Dream The Day Away

In America dreams come true when you sleep
The devil makes promises never to keep
And cleaning ladies work late into the night
While their ship slowly sinks out of sight

The Spanish woman at the café
Never have a word to say
They just sip on their ice latte
And dream the day away
They just dream the day away

Scrubbing floors doing chores for an executive
The senoritas see they life that they want to live
But it's in and out they got a job to do
Paradise is for the chosen few

The Spanish woman at the café
Never have a word to say
They just sip on their ice latte
And dream the day away
They just dream the day away

Down at the library they tutor the rich girl
Learning the lying lessons of some other world
Two realities side by side in the same place
One a world of hardship the other grace

The Spanish woman at the café
Never have a word to say
They just sip on their ice latte
And dream the day away
They just dream the day away

Earth Dance

I offer you love take my hand
I have wisdom please understand
There is a calling to every land
We are tuning up the sacred band

Children of the sun not by chance
We celebrate today in this Earth dance
Sweetly so completely we romance
We celebrate today in this Earth dance

The rhythm of our dancing feet
Tomorrow we shall be complete
I have tasted your soul it was sweet
The rhythm of our dancing feet

Children of the sun not by chance
We celebrate today in this Earth dance
Sweetly so completely we romance
We celebrate today in this Earth dance

Don't be shy we welcome young and old
The music is our master do as you're told
Harvest is the season harvest is the reason
Earth dance the solution in every circumstance

Children of the sun not by chance
We celebrate today in this Earth dance
Sweetly so completely we romance
We celebrate today in this Earth dance

Forget All The Poor

The coffee is hot on this August day
Happy to be alive glad to get away
My insurance money is past overdue
While mercy is only for the chosen few

Billions for death and destruction
Greed indeed is how we function
We'd rather decimate in war
And forget all the poor

Sylvia's ill dementia her disease
I cannot live my life the way that I please
Twenty-four seven my beloved needs care
So day after day I am always there

Billions for death and destruction
Greed indeed is how we function
We'd rather decimate in war
And forget all the poor

Society tells me the purpose it holds
To protect the rich and keep safe all their gold
While the man on the street has naught to eat
The war on the poor brings a constant defeat

Billions for death and destruction
Greed indeed is how we function
We'd rather decimate in war
And forget all the poor

Someday we'll get wise
Come together and organize
See the truth past the lies
Wake up wake up open your eyes

We're all hustling just for some spare change
Selling souls for some pennies you find it strange?
When the leaders emerge the bullets fly
I hold Sylvia's hand while I softly cry

Billions for death and destruction
Greed indeed is how we function
We'd rather decimate in war
And forget all the poor

Hope Around Every Bend

Folded birds hanging by a string
What good thing will tomorrow bring?
Sunshine sharing warmth and grace
Golden kisses on your face

You have every reason to smile
Take a break and laugh a while
The story never comes to an end
There is hope around every bend

I leave these words a gift to you
So much struggle great works to do
See the meaning in each line
I promise it will work out fine

You have every reason to smile
Take a break and laugh a while
The story never comes to an end
There is hope around every bend

The farmer plows his precious seed
Mother Earth she provides our need
Stop trying to count the cost
Learn from the past or all is lost

You have every reason to smile
Take a break and laugh a while
The story never comes to an end
There is hope around every bend

I Am A Fool

There is not a song that I could sing
To tell you the truth about everything
I want to kiss you under the eternal sky
To make love with you until we die

I am a fool and you are my vice
I offer my all for the price
I'd surrender heaven for paradise
I am a fool and you are my vice

Life and death they are just passing time
I want to live the life of the deeper rhyme
I am a spirit a pilgrim of all the ages
My story is etched into the sacred pages

I am a fool and you are my vice
I offer my all for the price
I'd surrender heaven for paradise
I am a fool and you are my vice

I have lived many lives in years before
Each time for my ill you were the cure
But I need you for the forever dance
The bliss of kiss in perfect romance

I am a fool and you are my vice
I offer my all for the price
I'd surrender heaven for paradise
I am a fool and you are my vice

Daisies flowing growing
Even the fool knowing
You are the blessed cure
And then something more
Spread your wings to fly
We will soar to never die
Love is the highest high
Love is the reason why
So please don't be cruel
To you adoring fool

From the east the sun glows in glory
There are more than words to the story
Revelation is both the way and destination
Together as one is our sweet salvation

I am a fool and you are my vice
I offer my all for the price
I'd surrender heaven for paradise
I am a fool and you are my vice

I Am The Pilot

I am the tin man with the golden dream
Got no voice only a dismal scream
Our guitar solo is far from complete
I gladly lay my demo at your feet

I am the pilot that's our name
We are children in a man's game
Searching for fortune and fame
I am the pilot that's our name

Our groupies only come for the beer
Empty seats are our constant fear
But we won't let truth get in our way
We are only happy when we play

I am the pilot that's our name
We are children in a man's game
Searching for fortune and fame
I am the pilot that's our name

Welcome to the digital age
Maybe we'll be the next rage
We can record on our I phone
Oh my how we have grown

Walking down the yellow brick road
Our bomb is ready to explode
A fire cracker or nuclear holocaust
A dull drizzle and it's all lost

I am the pilot that's our name
We are children in a man's game
Searching for fortune and fame
I am the pilot that's our name

I Face The Wind

In the gentle breeze the chime rhymes
I am a sinner immense are my crimes

I climb the mountain
The mountain is high
I climb the mountain
But I can't reach the sky

Here I stand in the end
Here I stand without a friend
I face the wind
I face the wind

I heard love's call
I gave it my all
I heard love's call
Only to crash and fall

Here I stand in the end
Here I stand without a friend
I face the wind
I face the wind

I can never surrender
I the fool the pretender
Hope is around the bend
I face the wind

Here I stand in the end
Here I stand without a friend
I face the wind
I face the wind

I'll Be Okay

When dreams are lost at the end of the night
Sometimes I can't tell between wrong and right
I remember your kisses tender and sweet
I lay a dozen red roses at your feet

Gray days floating my way
In the end friend I'll be okay
For every blessing a price to pay
In the end friend I'll be okay

God spoke but I can't recall what He said
The rich are starving the poor overfed
Houses of prayer all registered with the state
They preach love divine to practice hate

Gray days floating my way
In the end friend I'll be okay
For every blessing a price to pay
In the end friend I'll be okay

The folk singers became digitalized
And all our best leaders compromised
Left or right money's always the bottom line
A perfect ten amen but I'll take a nine

Gray days floating my way
In the end friend I'll be okay
For every blessing a price to pay
In the end friend I'll be okay

The illusion was only sleight of hand
They applaud God but none do understand
The highway to hell the blind leading the blind
You can shackle the body but not the mind

Gray days floating my way
In the end friend I'll be okay
For every blessing a price to pay
In the end friend I'll be okay

I've Seen You Often

Beauty is the only word
A blessing of the good Lord
Perfection halleluiah amen
From one to ten an eleven

I've seen you often from afar
Wondering who you are
A beauty queen or movie star
I've seen you often from afar

Castles of glory a gold throne
I'll never leave you alone
But alas all is fantasy
A girl like you loving me

I've seen you often from afar
Wondering who you are
A beauty queen or movie star
I've seen you often from afar

On day I'll come say hello
Miracles happen you never know
Perhaps I will boldly confess
My undying love and tenderness

A face of amazing grace
Heaven forever in your face
A body of perfect form
The thunder of the final storm

I've seen you often from afar
Wondering who you are
A beauty queen or movie star
I've seen you often from afar

James

I was lost in a story of fame and glory
A million temptations hung on the cross before me
I said Jesus there's one thing I don't understand
Why is it a sin to use a violin in a rock and roll band

The women sing harmony in glee
Birds were meant to be wild and free
Silly children playing silly games
I point the finger of blame
I point the finger of shame
On you James

There comes a time when it's a crime to support the state
Our heroes in green are simply a machine of hate
But jumping Jimmy Z he is doing mighty fine
He conformed donned the uniform and marches right in line

The women sing harmony in glee
Birds were meant to be wild and free
Silly children playing silly games
I point the finger of blame
I point the finger of shame
On you James

Maybe you became a Methodist
Upward mobility is hard to resist
I'm losing paper writing letters big
In the end I'm your friend dig

You always lose the game if you play by the rules
Wise in your own eyes you became the jester of fools
You gave the salute in the institute by the river
And sweet Katie had grown and she alone can deliver

The women sing harmony in glee
Birds were meant to be wild and free
Silly children playing silly games
I point the finger of blame
I point the finger of shame
On you James

Jordan's Shore

Through the years past the tears
Together we faced all those fears
You and me my precious bride
Standing strong at my side

Walking to Jordan's shore
I can go no more
You're all I live for
Walking to Jordan's shore

For sickness and health
Whether poverty or wealth
For better or for worse
In blessing and the curse

Walking to Jordan's shore
I can go no more
You're all I live for
Walking to Jordan's shore

You lie there lost in the long goodbye
And when I think about it I cry
You've gone to heaven and left me behind
All I can do is treat you kind

So I write silly songs
And dream of a world with no wrongs
A place where all belong
And I am brave and strong

Walking to Jordan's shore
I can go no more
You're all I live for
Walking to Jordan's shore

Lady Isabella

Lady Isabella and your golden hair
Laughing with clowns at the fair
Life must be simple when you don't have a care
Hope comes easy so does secret prayer

Lady Isabella beauty of a queen
A vision of loveliness thin and lean
Lady Isabella beauty of a queen
By your mere presence you make a scene

Lady Isabella singing with the band
All the drunkards could understand
You give and take life never works as you planned
All the fools await your command

Lady Isabella beauty of a queen
A vision of loveliness thin and lean
Lady Isabella beauty of a queen
By your mere presence you make a scene

Lady Isabella awakening from your dream
Sounds of silence stifle your scream
Trust is an illusion or so does it seem
Morning breaks with a lone golden beam

Lady Isabella beauty of a queen
A vision of loveliness thin and lean
Lady Isabella beauty of a queen
By your mere presence you make a scene

Lady Isabella I give you my all
Angels fly high only to fall
They whispered dark secrets they told you it all
But not one can you even recall

Lady Isabella beauty of a queen
A vision of loveliness thin and lean
Lady Isabella beauty of a queen
By your mere presence you make a scene

Look Out Lolly Is About

Lolly is a jolly one searching for fun
If it weren't for the priests he'd hit on the nun
Driving his Caddy a slick quick machine
Lolly always keeps his motor clean

Look out look out Lolly is about
He pays extra if you scream and shout
He's a regular without a doubt
Look out look out Lolly is about

Lolly has a career he's an engineer
He eases his pain with cocaine shifting his gear
Lolly is looking for a big-time score
Something kinky and then something more

Look out look out Lolly is about
He pays extra if you scream and shout
He's a regular without a doubt
Look out look out Lolly is about

Some men do it for the thrill
Some men do it for the kill
But Lolly is quite insane
With an ego sadly vain
Lolly likes to inflict pain
But all the girls come again
Cause Lolly pays twice the rate
And all the girls think Lolly's great

Lolly fears getting busted by the police
A toke of coke makes the anxiety increase
So Lolly likes to take his sweet time
After all he's spending his own dime

Look out look out Lolly is about
He pays extra if you scream and shout
He's a regular without a doubt
Look out look out Lolly is about

Lolly's eyes lust away as the light is red
He imagines the fun done in a king size bed
Lolly smiles see him flash a wad of cash
He's got a cross for luck on his dash

Lost Souls

I am wondering who you are
Distant like a wandering star
You who I have taken as my wife
You who I share my very life

Lost souls living in a world of despair
Lost souls needing somebody to care
Lost souls our only hope is prayer
Lost souls is there anyone out there?

We are just intimate strangers
I long to touch I fear the dangers
I have sown my secrets in you
I have told you all that I knew

Lost souls living a world of despair
Lost souls needing somebody to care
Lost souls our only hope is prayer
Lost souls is there anyone out there?

To awaken knowing nothing at all
I've bitten the apple is this the fall?
God's hand in both great and small
To the powers that be hear my call

Lost souls living a world of despair
Lost souls needing somebody to care
Lost souls our only hope is prayer
Lost souls is there anyone out there?

Love And Lust

Your bio says you are made of stars
Cosmic wonders of electric guitars
But I'd settle for anything high
Like a mountain fading in the sky

Love and lust
Fear and trust
It's a must
Love and lust

Words are words truth and lies
I see you clear through the disguise
Red hair, a silly grin all over your face
A virgin whore seeking love and grace

Love and lust
Fear and trust
It's a must
Love and lust

Lay it down baby tonight we run
The song of Armageddon has begun
All the fools looking out for number one
Kiss me, embrace me lets touch the sun

Love and lust
Fear and trust
It's a must
Love and lust

You whisper hold me
You kiss me boldly
Between woman and man
Doing the best you can

Waking up to a reality of black
Youth has fled and you want it back
But life sweetheart is a one-way ride
In the end friend Love can't be denied

Love and lust
Fear and trust
It's a must
Love and lust

Love Is The Answer I Say

In that rare moment that none can steal
When you allow your heart to feel
And the tear drops fall like rain
Inside and outside all is pain

We can find a better way
Love is the answer I say
Starting with today
Love is the answer I say

Bombs are falling killing many
Bankers are making a pretty penny
Our soldiers shooting the innocent
From a nation refusing to repent

We can find a better way
Love is the answer I say
Starting with today
Love is the answer I say

Another massacre on the news
Hatred is a path that we chose
Red, white and blue the flag waves
At half-mast over the graves

We can find a better way
Love is the answer I say
Starting with today
Love is the answer I say

Pop singers sing about sex and glitz
Never knowing enough even for regrets
Shaking their thing for everybody to see
One step away from pornography

Hey lover let's take the walk
We need to talk the talk
The kingdom knocks on the door
Let's let the white dove soar

We can find a better way
Love is the answer I say
Starting with today
Love is the answer I say

March In Line

Save the world from toxic waste
Get rid of fluoride in tooth paste
Nothing as obscene as a vaccine
Worship the military machine
Slogans from the left
Slogans from the right
Pretty soon they're gonna fight

March in line march in line
Your world we will define
In the end all will be fine
March in line march in line

Robert E Lee is but history
Truth is shrouded in mystery
They want to take the statue down
The president wears a golden crown
Slogans from the left
Slogans from the right
Teeth were meant to give a bite

March in line march in line
Your world we will define
In the end all will be fine
March in line march in line

Make America great again
On your knees and scream amen
Greed is our nation's sacred creed
While millions suffer in need
Slogans from the left
Slogans from the right
Day has faded into night

Watch out or you'll go to Facebook jail
The side with the best meme shall prevail
I could tell you the truth but I would fail
Pride in genocide is a wicked tale

Well the ship may be sinking
But I've done some thinking
I know that Jesus won't fail me
So I carry my cross daily
Slogans with a smile
Slogans with style
Love is essential for survival

March in line march in line
Your world we will define
In the end all will be fine
March in line march in line

Nothing To Do On La Rue Avenue

Sunset comes and the day says goodbye
Welcome the stars up in heaven high
Under a street lamp glaring full of delight
There stands Lady Lace feeling alright

Ain't nothing to do
On La Rue Avenue
The boys are feeling blue
On La Rue Avenue
Things go on as they always do
On La Rue Avenue

A picture of grace is Lady Lace
Silver sparkle on her shining face
She can make you take you to a higher place
Her kiss of bliss is from outer space

Ain't nothing to do
On La Rue Avenue
The boys are feeling blue
On La Rue Avenue
Things go on as they always do
On La Rue Avenue

But its pay pay pay for a good time
It ain't by accident the words rhyme
Nothing is illegal but still it's a crime
For the right price you can say she's all mine

Ain't nothing to do
On La Rue Avenue
The boys are feeling blue
On La Rue Avenue
Things go on as they always do
On La Rue Avenue

And all the boys try to look so tough
Somehow it's always never enough
They save their money but still they can't pay the price
Can one ever afford paradise?

Old Man Oak

I am the strongest of the trees
My limbs my whims
They do not obey the breeze
I always do as I please
I am the strongest of the trees

Life is a hard journey tenuous at best
Around every bend we find yet another test
We scheme for the dream of eternal rest
All glory to the meek
Turn the other cheek to be blessed

I am the strongest of the trees
My limbs my whims
They do not obey the breeze
I always do as I please
I am the strongest of the trees

I have used many a name
To each one I brought shame
I threw the dice I played the game
To this place of fortune and fame
I was once a lowly seed
Now I am no longer the same

I am the strongest of the trees
My limbs my whims
They do not obey the breeze
I always do as I please
I am the strongest of the trees

Overgrown

The trees of the forest have grown tall
Clumsy clowns in the wind they fall

Overgrown, overgrown the seeds have been sown
Overgrown, overgrown tomorrow is yet unknown

The hart races through the tangled brush
The wind blows with a delicate hush

Overgrown, overgrown the seeds have been sown
Overgrown, overgrown tomorrow it yet unknown

Rhonda

Rhonda never was the talk of the town
Not a raving beauty only a clown
Her proportions fall all in the wrong place
But hey everybody needs a touch of grace

Rhonda keep your motor clean
A well-oiled slick machine
You can touch another's dream
Rhonda keep your motor clean

You see her walk down La Rue Avenue
Life is a puzzle and she ain't got a clue
For a little love it's the world to give
The rise and fall they take all so they live

Rhonda keep your motor clean
A well-oiled slick machine
You can touch another's dream
Rhonda keep your motor clean

And the acid offers no liberation
While God sells sweet salvation
Either way I say there's a price to pay
You and me Rhonda what you say
You and me Rhonda give it a try
A night of delight and then goodbye

Youth has fled and the living dead remains
No story of glory she sadly explains
Rhonda mourns but nobody counts her tears
Age is the only thing to show for her years

Rhonda keep your motor clean
A well-oiled slick machine
You can touch another's dream
Rhonda keep your motor clean

Running Just To Stand Still

There was a book of philosophy
I took a look at the real me
The light shined so bright I could not see
Turn the page to a new reality

And I'm running just to stand still
Over the mountain one day I will
You can't get happy from a pill
And I'm running just to stand still

The singer strummed his guitar
In the lyrics it's who you are
Since the beginning God He spoke
All was born and Love awoke

And I'm running just to stand still
Over the mountain one day I will
You can't get happy from a pill
And I'm running just to stand still

Life is sometimes an endless maze
You get lost in some wicked craze
The cheese is the prize to take
Never knowing its fake

And I'm running just to stand still
Over the mountain one day I will
You can't get happy from a pill
And I'm running just to stand still

At the library contemplating eternity
Wisdom dictates nothing is a certainty
You fall in love only for the world to change
You become your parents and find life strange

So here I go to square one
Thinking over all I've done
Seems my dreams have just begun
Déjà Vous we shall overcome

And I'm running just to stand still
Over the mountain one day I will
You can't get happy from a pill
And I'm running just to stand still

Scarecrow

The scarecrow was looking mighty thin
When into the barroom he walked in
He said give me double gin
I'm a playing this game to win

Jesus, Jesus, you're the boss
So sorry about the cross
But hey it wasn't a total loss
Jesus, Jesus, you're the boss

Well the scarecrow walked from the bar
And he grabbed my electric guitar
There He was the great I am
Wailing on my axe in one heavenly jam

Jesus, Jesus, you're the boss
So sorry about the cross
But hey it wasn't a total loss
Jesus, Jesus, you're the boss

Well he was playing mighty fine
It was a melody simply divine
The bassist laid down the beat
And the singer sung real sweet
Soon we were all dancing on our feet
Even Satan was humming in defeat

Well the scarecrow bid us goodbye
All the barmaids began to cry
I'll be coming again I'm no liar
Except the next time I'll bring the fire

Jesus, Jesus, you're the boss
So sorry about the cross
But hey it wasn't a total loss
Jesus, Jesus, you're the boss

So Much In The World That Ain't Right

Tommy got his money a giant slice
With a silver tongue oh he's so nice
But a rich man looks out for number one
While the poor man labors in the sun

See the well-dressed parasite
Shoe polished shiny and bright
His mansion of glory cold at night
So much in the world that ain't right
So much in the world that ain't right

Down to the Wellmont theatre to see the band
Front row tickets they cost him a grand
Material riches they can't buy grace
Tommy don't care about the human race

See the well-dressed parasite
Shoe polished shiny and bright
His mansion of glory cold at night
So much in the world that ain't right
So much in the world that ain't right

A friendly face a subtle smile
He utters lies in grandest style
An executive on Wall Street
At the finest restaurants to eat

And Tommy sold his soul for the dollar
All his life clean and white collar
When Syl needed him he wasn't there
When you hear this don't pretend you care

See the well-dressed parasite
Shoe polished shiny and bright
His mansion of glory cold at night
So much in the world that ain't right
So much in the world that ain't right

Songs Of Freedom

I only know Odetta as being old
And I don't care for silver and gold
But that road is a calling my name
And I'll be playing the rambling game

Songs of freedom
Sing them loud
Songs of freedom
Sing them proud

I am a preacher of the gospel of love
Heaven should be here not above
But the rich man don't wanna share
And the rich man he just don't care

Songs of freedom
Sing them loud
Songs of freedom
Sing them proud

Well t.v. preachers are real slick
And t.v. preachers make me sick
With a mansion and fancy jet plane
I tell you sister the world is insane

Songs of freedom
Sing them loud
Songs of freedom
Sing them proud

Woodie Guthrie well he ain't no saint
But what a masterpiece he did paint
Songs that should be sung by the youth
A man who cared enough to tell the truth

Songs of freedom
Sing them loud
Songs of freedom
Sing them proud

You can laugh at this simple melody
The caged bird don't know he's not free
I'll be blowing along with the breeze now
The worlds a farm I'm working the plow

Songs of freedom
Sing them loud
Songs of freedom
Sing them proud

Seeds of compassion planted deep
Watered by tears that the people weep
One day the plants they will grow
Hold on brother there is a tomorrow

Songs of freedom
Sing them loud
Songs of freedom
Sing them proud

Sylvia

So glad that you were mine
For a moment in time
You were simply divine
Impossible words that rhyme

Sylvia my beloved wife
Sylvia who shared my life
I say goodbye with this song
I'll try to stay strong

You were my inspiration grand
Teaching lessons to understand
I am here holding your frail hand
As you enter the Promised Land

Sylvia my beloved wife
Sylvia who shared my life
I say goodbye with this song
I'll try to stay strong

Heaven is on the other side
Wading through Jordan's tide
Death has yet to be denied
Heaven is on the other side

Sylvia my beloved wife
Sylvia who shared my life
I say goodbye with this song
I'll try to stay strong
In heaven fair surely you belong
I say goodbye with this song

The Cross Seems Heavy

We were walking the road to heaven
When the twelve became eleven
Thirty silver was the low price
For the one who brings paradise

The cross seems heavy at night
When darkness conquers light
And all that there is is the fight
The cross seems heavy tonight

Its straight and narrow they say
This long and winding way
I stumble, I fall and then I cry
Sorrow is the only reason why

The cross seems heavy at night
When darkness conquers light
And all that there is is the fight
The cross seems heavy tonight

I lost the love of the task
My smile was only a mask
But when I was brought down low
Truth was what I came to know

The cross seems heavy at night
When darkness conquers light
And all that there is is the fight
The cross seems heavy tonight

I can't count those who left me alone
All the good good people that I'd known
When you're riding high you have friends
When you lose well all that ends

Forgive and climb the hill
It is after all God's will
You and me at Calvary
The last stop before eternity

The cross seems heavy at night
When darkness conquers light
And all that there is is the fight
The cross seems heavy tonight

The Forest

I hear a whimsical laughter
It is the morning after
I feel your warmth by my side
I am naked nowhere to hide

The forest is green
With treasures unseen
In the East of Eden
Lies a land without sin

The glory of the new morning
All the birds are singing
Love eternal must have a start
I feel the beating of your heart

The forest is green
With treasures unseen
In the East of Eden
Lies a land without sin

The leaves are rustling like spirits they dance
I am leaving mankind on a chance
I am a seeker of knowledge what shall I learn
The fire is our light and the fire will burn

The forest is green
With treasures unseen
In the East of Eden
Lies a land without sin

What has been gained what has been lost?
For every dream there is a cost
In the end we are what we want to be
I hear the forest calling ever so softly

The Hollow Men

They sleep but never do they dream
Angry men afraid of their own scream
What little they have they gladly share
With all their hearts so do they care

These are the broken men the hollow men
The thought after the prayer the soft amen
These are the broken men the hollow men
The huddled masses you have forgotten

Hopeless they are full of desire
Kindle awaiting a sacred fire
Ignored deplored the victims of hate
Soon is their moment just wait

Lies and truth we mix them so well
They offer heaven and deliver hell
It's not the words but how they are uttered
It's not the meal but that the bread is buttered
Come salute the flag and don the uniform
The streets are cold the barracks are warm

These are the broken men the hollow men
The thought after the prayer the soft amen
These are the broken men the hollow men
The huddled masses you have forgotten

Minds molded shaped as if they're clay
For glory there is a price to pay
For the homeland we shall fight and kill
To our master we bend our will

These are the broken men the hollow men
The thought after the prayer the soft amen
These are the broken men the hollow men
The huddled masses you have forgotten

The Music Can Never Die (The Queen Of Soul)

You were never one for the choir
Too much voice a child of fire
Fame was the game of desire
And you my love took it higher
Heaven was your humble goal
And you were the queen of soul

The world got a little bluer today
Sad to say you went far away
Over the rainbow gone goodbye
But the music it can never die
No the music it can never die

You made it look easy with style
Singing bringing us all a smile
Reaching down with a brute force
And love was the happy source
You unleashed the spirit of the angel
And you were the queen of soul

The world got a little bluer today
Sad to say you went far away
Over the rainbow gone goodbye
But the music it can never die
No the music it can never die

Up and down and in and out
Hitting the road going about
The changes of life flow
And everybody gotta grow
But no matter what the toll
You were still the queen of soul

The world got a little bluer today
Sad to say you went far away
Over the rainbow gone goodbye
But the music it can never die
No the music it can never die

The Star Faded Away

Hugging pillows dreaming of tomorrow
All the hope I had I had to borrow
One day you'd walk into my life
Give me a kiss and be my wife

You came and gone
A star to wish upon
But the star faded away
So sad to say
The star faded away

School with its rules is for fools
Teaching us to be serious tools
Somewhere between here and there
I forgot the reason why I care

You came and gone
A star to wish upon
But the star faded away
So sad to say
The star faded away

With every twist I came to found
That nightmares and scares abound
Still there was that distant memory
Of the good things that were yet to be

You came and gone
A star to wish upon
But the star faded away
So sad to say
The star faded away

Well one day you entered in
A sultry soul more tempting than sin
We shared the precious hour
Our love bloomed as a flower

You came and gone
A star to wish upon
But the star faded away
So sad to say
The star faded away

Well seasons they come and go
And in came winter full of snow
You departed for warmer ground
And I lost everything I found

You came and gone
A star to wish upon
But the star faded away
So sad to say
The star faded away

The Wild Heart

She is leaning on my shoulder
My love is growing bolder
With infinite possibility
Hope is becoming real to me

Oh who can tame the wild heart?
Life is living a work of art
Promise me we'll never part
Oh who can tame the wild heart?

Life is endless metaphor
Peace and love will conquer war
What are we fighting for?
The forest, the forest
Let us explore

Oh who can tame the wild heart?
Life is living a work of art
Promise me we'll never part
Oh who can tame the wild heart?

My voice rises to the sky
To live and to never die
To know the answer of why
Me and you and you and I

Oh who can tame the wild heart?
Life is living a work of art
Promise me we'll never part
Oh who can tame the wild heart?

We Are What We Create

I was looking for a Cherokee woman
Who wasn't singing a sad song
I was looking for a happy pilgrim
Who could say he'd done no wrong

There are lies in history
We live in a mystery
Between love and hate
Rages endless debate
We are what we create
We are what we create

Walking in Manhattan down Broadway
With dreams and limousines for pay
The elite stepping over the man on the grate
I wonder why we think we're great

War machine sells a rocket
More money in the pocket
Fancy lies explain why
The rich prosper the poor die
We are what we create
We are what we create

A long time ago I was the breeze
I blew around wherever I please
Now the world has become insane
Smog in the sky acid in the rain

They're getting ready for the big war
Placing bets they all wanna score
The soldier sharpens his bayonet
World War three we'll all regret

Nuclear missile holocaust
Start counting the cost
Build your bunker on mars
We can't reach the stars
We are what we create
We are what we create

When The Bombs Blew

War is a whore with bankers pimping for more
Loans for weapons you can figure out the score
Digits rise while the poor man dies
After all we go to defend all of them lies

When the bombs blew
Genocide was nothing new
Nothing you could do
When the bombs blew

Babylon has gone into overdrive
It is a mad scramble just to survive
Bombs fall as I recall songs of hope
Gotta secure the oil and steal the dope

When the bombs blew
Genocide was nothing new
Nothing you could do
When the bombs blew

I want you screams good old Uncle Sam
When vets return wounded who gives a dam?
Don't you know that it was just a scam?
Better watch out says the Great I Am

When the bombs blew
Genocide was nothing new
Nothing you could do
When the bombs blew

Stormin' Norman stands showing off his scars
All day they do as he says cause of four stars
The insane jet plane of pain soars in the sky
You can't even stop to ask the question why

When the bombs blew
Genocide was nothing new
Nothing you could do
When the bombs blew

You Hold On

When you lose the hope to sing the blues
And Jesus Christ is only bad news
When the wordsmith changes his song
And everything right becomes wrong

You hold on, hold on real tight
Your rise to the challenge of the fight
You give a yell with all your might
You hold on, hold on real tight

When the sun fails to rise in the east
You open your eyes to see the beast
When pity is the popular tune
And the prophets predict dismal doom

You hold on, hold on real tight
Your rise to the challenge of the fight
You give a yell with all your might
You hold on, hold on real tight

Night is a season and it will pass by
Doing right is the reason truth is not a lie
For every seed planted there's a crop to grow
There's endless hope in the dream of tomorrow

Take my hand lean on my shoulder
We're getting wiser we're growing older
There is power in the heart that cares
Action is the greatest of prayers

You hold on, hold on real tight
Your rise to the challenge of the fight
You give a yell with all your might
You hold on, hold on real tight

A Better Day

I was seeking the rhyme in the song
For some place of grace I could belong
A beauty queen with flowers in her hair
There had to be somebody out there

Here we go running fast as we can
If only I could know the plan
Around to corner is a better day
That's what they all say
Around the corner a better day

Life was confusion and I was blind
Didn't know what I wanted to find
The glory of the story and some more
When I found it then I would be sure

Preachers and prophets wizards and fools
Life is a game without any rules
Go ahead throw the dice they are loaded
The past is gone the future exploded

Here we go running fast as we can
If only I could know the plan
Around to corner is a better day
That's what they all say
Around the corner a better day

How I am still running the race
Salvation is a smile on a face
One day I say I'll find the perfect prize
All I gotta do is open my eyes

Here we go running fast as we can
If only I could know the plan
Around to corner is a better day
That's what they all say
Around the corner a better day

A Love Song

Miracles they come true
I knew that when I met you
Heaven ain't a starry sky
Heaven is you and I

I can't write a love song
To say what I want to
I can't write a love song
I tell you how I love you

Storms came with thunder and rain
Life is full of trials and pain
But you remained my best friend
We walked the road to the end

I can't write a love song
To say what I want to
I can't write a love song
To tell you how I love you

You lay there halfway through the final door
We were soldiers fighting war after war
I gave you my all and you gave me more
I was sick of being lonely but you were the cure

Take the words straight from my heart
Love is eternal though we part
I just wish I could reveal
The exact way you make me feel

I can't write a love song
To say what I want to
I can't write a love song
I tell you how I love you

Barroom Brawl

Brass knuckle brawl
Beat you till ya crawl
I hate you all
You're bound to fall

Brother you don't know insanity
Brother you're full of vanity
Answering the highest call
We got us a barroom brawl

Your girl walked past
And I grabbed her ass
She gave a smile
Yeah I got style

Brother you don't know insanity
Brother you're full of vanity
Answering the highest call
We got us a barroom brawl

Motor Head is playing on the radio
Checking engines all systems go
Let me give you a welcome to my place
Come here I'll spit in your face

I can take a punch
I got me a hunch
Your blood is red
Soon you'll be dead

Brother you don't know insanity
Brother you're full of vanity
Answering the highest call
We got us a barroom brawl

Blues Lady

Juan slipped Don Quixote some L.S.D.
A minor victory for the forces of anarchy
The evening news gives clues about reality
And you my dear I truly fear mean nothing to me

Blues Lady dancing in a daze
You the sunshine of my days
Blues Lady through the night
Blues Lady you make me feel alright

The face of the clown melted into a permanent frown
In Manhattan at night the trains don't run downtown
Freaks and sheiks mingle debating minor affairs
The poor pay the lion's share of corporate welfare

Blues Lady dancing in a daze
You the sunshine of my days
Blues Lady through the night
Blues Lady you make me feel alright

She's a victim of technology
A lost soul in a murky mystery
Trying crying to be free
If she had the cash she'd pay the fee
But when the toll is your soul
You just gotta keep control

The psychotic soldier is now older and gray
He is lost in the holocaust of his yesterday
After the artillery they marched into the city
Sad to say mangled bodies are not too pretty

Blues Lady dancing in a daze
You the sunshine of my days
Blues Lady through the night
Blues Lady you make me feel alright

Carolyn

She was never tight for a Saturday night
But that was alright she was out of sight
In tender surrender such a slender delight
She gave it her all with all of her might

Carolyn so deep within
A sultry siren of sin
Carolyn give me a grin
Please please come again
Oh my darling Carolyn

Calling us names while playing drinking games
Carolyn wants to win she has no shames
The star of the party laughing with Marty
Carolyn gets good grades what a smarty

Carolyn so deep within
A sultry siren of sin
Carolyn give me a grin
Please please come again
Oh my darling Carolyn

Well girls are girls and boys are boys
Come on Carolyn lets go make some noise
At the institute we cherish forbidden fruit
There's a long line to give her a salute

The wheel was in spin and so was Carolyn
In bed with Ted and then Mikey did win
A happy couple until the fire began to burn
Off went Carolyn to give another a turn

Carolyn so deep within
A sultry siren of sin
Carolyn give me a grin
Please please come again
Oh my darling Carolyn

Celestial Lady

Somewhere there's a song nobody wrote
With a funky rhythm I can quote
Cause music is the medicine of life
Melody is kin closer than a wife

Strum that acoustic guitar
Drum your fingers quick on a star
Celestial Lady take a dance
Celestial Lady now's your chance

I'm dreaming trying to capture words
Listening to the songs of bluebirds
I stretch my wings getting ready to soar
I got me a hit I know that for sure

Strum that acoustic guitar
Drum your fingers quick on a star
Celestial Lady take a dance
Celestial Lady now's your chance

I've been searching the edges of the galaxy
Meditating inside trying to get free
I saw a supernova inside a black whole
Ain't nothing more precious than your own soul

A cosmic kid who never did junk
With spiked red hair a functioning punk
You could have been the answer to my prayer
As long as you knew how much I did care

Strum that acoustic guitar
Drum your fingers quick on a star
Celestial Lady take a dance
Celestial Lady now's your chance

So here we are so far doing fine
I am yours and baby you are mine
Hand in hand taking one step at a time
Gotta make sure all the words still rhyme

Strum that acoustic guitar
Drum your fingers quick on a star
Celestial Lady take a dance
Celestial Lady now's your chance

Cosmic Crusader

I want to write my name in the sky with a blazing fire
I'll kiss the night and die before I give up my desire
Without any fear I sore beyond the stratosphere
The past will never last but the future is always near

I'm a cosmic crusader
A spiritual space invader
So proud I laid her
I'm a cosmic crusader

They're tuning up guitars on mars for all of the stars
The juice is flowing loose in the topless bars
The opening band is really grand rocking away
We sit on the side bursting with pride ready to play

I'm a cosmic crusader
A spiritual space invader
So proud I laid her
I'm a cosmic crusader

Anticipating letting go
Seconds before the show
Cranking up to the max
There is no turning back
Walking out on the stage
Feeling the reeling rage

The groupies scream like a dream becoming real
Teenyboppers dance making romance in the deal
The instruments present the rock and roll story
Stay hungry cause you got one shot at glory

I'm a cosmic crusader
A spiritual space invader
So proud I laid her
I'm a cosmic crusader

Could I Borrow A Prayer

They got that far away look in their eyes
Because they can see the truth past the lies
A silly grin of sin is the perfect disguise
And heaven is a nice place beyond the skies

This is the world we share
Does anybody care?
Is anybody out there?
Could I borrow a prayer?

The weather is turning cold fall is here
Frigid breath and freezing to death is the fear
In mansions grand those in command turn up the heat
Some grow fat while others have nothing to eat

This is the world we share
Does anybody care?
Is anybody out there?
Could I borrow a prayer?

We're all equal so says the ideal
We're all equal and nothing is real
The biggest thieves stole the land
While raw flesh is in demand
The whore's on her knees to pray
Just to make it one more day
Don't worry it'll be okay
Though I have no words to pray

At eight o'clock they crowd the block downtown
There may be a fragile smile lost in the frown
Don't give me no jive I got to survive somehow
Our future awaits but no one debates the moment is now

This is the world we share
Does anybody care?
Is anybody out there?
Could I borrow a prayer?

Crazy

I'm searching in places high and low
Seeing faces that I did not know
A masked man said welcome to the show
The race began but I forgot to go

Crazy I've been there
Holy I've said a prayer
Music I wrote a song
History I got it wrong

The hoochie coochie woman waved her hand
Her luscious lips said please understand
God is merciful and God has a plan
I'm a woman and you're a man

Crazy I'm returning
Holy I'm still learning
Music the lyrics roll
History stole my soul

Some roll with the punches but not me
I go with my hunches then I see
I always despise the liquor and lies
Truth is the pill that Satan denies

Crazy there is a cure
Holy shining so pure
Music a gift to give
History a life to live

Delusion Song

I was looking for something I couldn't define
A little piece of heaven that I could call mine
I was a book filled with pages pure and white
Some wicked men with the devil's pen began to write

Confusion illusion delusion
A temporary solution
Lost in the institution
Confusion illusion delusion

God was a myth I need something that was real
If I couldn't beg or borrow then I would steal
Wise in my own eyes I made a little deal
I took wonderful chemicals that helped me to feel

Confusion illusion delusion
A temporary solution
Lost in the institution
Confusion illusion delusion

Hoping coping in this ordeal
Money never had any appeal
I needed a spiritual way
Something to get me through the day
Darkness became our light
And ain't nothing was right

Down the road ready to explode fragile to touch
With Hypo and Psycho I was smoking too much
Sweet Michelle she could tell what was on my heart
The clock struck twelve and I ran forever to depart

Confusion illusion delusion
A temporary solution
Lost in the institution
Confusion illusion delusion

Dream That You Can Fly

Life is what you make of it so take it for all you can
When you reach it will teach you how to be a man
Don't listen to those who shout doubt to bring you down
Persevere past the fear and the sin to win you crown

Dream that you can fly
Heaven may be high
But if you give it a try
You'll live till you die

Above full of love there awaits the endless blue
With all her charms and open arms she's waiting for you
Clouds are proud they shroud heaven's glory
All you do good and bad happy and sad tell the story

Dream that you can fly
If you ask them why
They'll answer with a lie
Dream that you can fly

I took a chance at romance holding you in the slow dance
You were an eleven from heaven in perfect circumstance
For a moment in the light all was right full of delight
I give you a kiss full of bliss and I held you tight

Dream that you can fly
They may hate and deny
But you'll get by
Dream that you can fly

Dreaming

Roller skating debating espresso or latte
The wind in my hair I had no care you came my way
You smiled like creation had burst into rapturous song
I look into your brown eyes and knew where you belong

I was dreaming of me and you
I was dreaming of the perfect two
I was dreaming of your pretty face
I was dreaming of love and grace
I was dreaming of me and you
I was dreaming that dreams came true

We walked on the beach the waves rolled gently onto the sand
With a listening ear trying hard to understand
Life was a long ordeal I surrendered I could not feel
But you opened my mind so I could find what was real

I was dreaming of me and you
I was dreaming of the perfect two
I was dreaming of your pretty face
I was dreaming of love and grace
I was dreaming of me and you
I was dreaming that dreams came true

We talked of poetry and the pleasure of the rhyme
You were generous giving your money and your time
I would have sacrificed all to answer the higher call
When we made love I touched heaven above so spiritual

I was dreaming of me and you
I was dreaming of the perfect two
I was dreaming of your pretty face
I was dreaming of love and grace
I was dreaming of me and you
I was dreaming that dreams came true

Easy Street

White picket fences and rose bushes galore
It's the American dream who could want more?
But behind the disguise lurks a host of lies
Late at night they fight you can hear their cries

Ain't nothing easy on Easy Street
Where luxury and getting ahead meet
Climbing the corporate ladder gotta compete
Ain't nothing easy on Easy Street

Working late the stress is great coming home tired
Job's insane the boss is vain you're feeling wired
Bottle of wine looks so fine pills on the side
The truth is a monster no place to hide

Ain't nothing easy on Easy Street
Where luxury and getting ahead meet
Climbing the corporate ladder gotta compete
Ain't nothing easy on Easy Street

Keeping up with the Jones' next door
And endless quest for more more more
Rig the economy and start a war
Searching for the perfect score

The pay is big but the expense bigger
Money high but you're in debt so go figure
A corvette and S.U.V, on credit
Materialism rules you let it

Ain't nothing easy on Easy Street
Where luxury and getting ahead meet
Climbing the corporate ladder gotta compete
Ain't nothing easy on Easy Street

Find A Way

Going in ten directions at the same time
Always dying trying to make the words rhyme
Love songs are always so personal
But the chords of the heart play universal

And if I could go back to yesterday
I would find a way--- somehow
And if could go back to yesterday
I would find a way ---but it's now

Here I am writing this sad song
My mind wondering what went wrong
I reach into the emptiness of the void
What was precious is now destroyed

And if I could go back to yesterday
I would find a way--- somehow
And if could go back to yesterday
I would find a way ---but it's now

Second guessing the blessing that was you
Nailed to the cross nothing I could do
You were gone I moved on to someone new
Left wishing upon a star in the sky deep blue

Sometimes in the dismal rain
Under the thunder I feel the pain
In life you only get one chance
And we never even had a dance

And if I could go back to yesterday
I would find a way--- somehow
And if could go back to yesterday
I would find a way ---but it's now

For Bruce

When you're small and life hits you wrong
Surrender all make it into a song
Drive your car down that Thunder Road
Play your guitar make it explode

I know where you've been Bruce Springsteen
The awkward age between man and teen
Past the lies and your disguise lurks your cross
You got it right event the boss has his cross

A blue-collar millionaire
The jewel of Jersey if I dare
Karen would give you her praise
You're her savior in many ways

I know where you've been Bruce Springsteen
The awkward age between man and teen
Past the lies and your disguise lurks your cross
You got it right event the boss has his cross

The heart is the part that rules the art
No doubt not selling out was really smart
Life is a journey it's a long way from Asbury Park
Tonight the light shines bright as we dance in the dark

What do you say about your sin?
Past the fame a regular man
Take it from me I understand
I too seek out the Promised Land

I know where you've been Bruce Springsteen
The awkward age between man and teen
Past the lies and your disguise lurks your cross
You got it right event the boss has his cross

I Need You

One day I woke up to a dream
Life bursting through in a brilliant beam
We laughed we cried we grew
We shared a love known to few

Angels are beyond the blue
Mysteries I don't have a clue
But one thing I know is true
Darling I need you
I want you in all I do
Darling I need you

Life is a gamble so I took a chance
I held your hand in sweet romance
Six months later with a grand smile
We were walking down the wedding aisle

Angels are beyond the blue
Mysteries I don't have a clue
But one thing I know is true
Darling I need you
I want you in all I do
Darling I need you

Be wise and understand
Nothing works as planned
You learn when you're older
Fate is a strong soldier
Who is beyond your command
You give it your best try
And don't question why

So here we are finishing the years
I can't turn to you without the tears
You embrace heaven I live hell
In the church yard they ring the bell

Angels are beyond the blue
Mysteries I don't have a clue
But one thing I know is true
Darling I need you
I want you in all I do
Darling I need you

It's All In The Song

Drinking juice listening to Bruce
Frustrating debating what's the use?
Want to hit the road forever
Want my words to be clever

It's all in the song
All that's right all that's wrong
Crying trying to be strong
It's all in the song

Love feels like fleeting fantasy
Darling you're everything to me
What do we have me and you
Is it something eternally true?

It's all in the song
All that's right all that's wrong
Crying trying to be strong
It's all in the song

I'm strumming my Stratocaster
Fingers linger I go faster
Playing magical chords
All I need are the right words

It's all in the song
All that's right all that's wrong
Crying trying to be strong
It's all in the song

In a kiss I made a promise
I was never expecting this
To get heaven you gotta risk hell
In life you really can never tell

It's all in the song
All that's right all that's wrong
Crying trying to be strong
It's all in the song

Joni

Harvest moons in endless Junes
Releasing balloons singing tunes
Blonde lady strumming her guitar
I wonder now just where you are?

Are you lonely Joni
If only if only
I could touch you with grace
And teach the human race
Songs of love from above
Are you lonely Joni

Night is a time full of glowing stars
Playing in small theatres and smoky bars
Yesterday has passed with a smile
But please allow me a little while

Are you lonely Joni
If only if only
I could touch you with grace
And teach the human race
Songs of love from above
Are you lonely Joni

Buffy was cool as a general rule
In the fall the weather turns cool
I am seeking what is beyond this
Say hello to the snow with a tender kiss

Are you lonely Joni
If only if only
I could touch you with grace
And teach the human race
Songs of love from above
Are you lonely Joni

Lady G

I'm sitting in the front row
Starring in the freak show
Daddy's money paid the price
All is wonderful and nice

Oh we snorted some cocaine
Took dope to ease the pain
Soaring high a flying kite
Feeling, feeling, feeling alright

Here we are wild and free
Are you listening Lady G?
You're who we want to be
Does that make you happy
Lady G?

To touch the greater whole
Long ago I lost my soul
But I can't get off the ride
I got my money and pride

We seek the greater thrill
Always looking for the kill
Quicker here comes the climax
There ain't no turning back

Here we are wild and free
Are you listening Lady G?
You're who we want to be
Does that make you happy
Lady G?

We don't know if you're a woman or a man
And frankly Lady G we don't give a damn
You a freak messiah with a synthetic cross
Understand we are the damned totally lost

You're a witch we're the spell
You're heaven and we're hell
You are our infinity
Have some mercy Lady G

Here we are wild and free
Are you listening Lady G?
You're who we want to be
Does that make you happy
Lady G?

Let Love Have Its Part

Life was once a list of endless rules
Get a degree from the better schools
Find a job work your way to the top
Not a moment to think or to stop

What about your heart?
When does the living start?
Let love have its part
Let love have its part

Bank account grew and my spirits fell
They promised heaven and I got hell
A rat in the maze seeking the cheese
Before my ideals down on my knees

What about your heart?
When does the living start?
Let love have its part
Let love have its part

Had a woman it was sexual
A constant battle for control
Living a lie with a painted face
With all I had not a drop of grace

What about your heart?
When does the living start?
Let love have its part
Let love have its part

Birds fly in the sky wild and free
Feeling rage in my golden cage of misery
The promises are lies that nobody denies
Such smart men then again none are wise

Drove my car with no destination
Money can't buy you salvation
I was living life both dead and blind
In my mind I needed something kind

What about your heart?
When does the living start?
Let love have its part
Let love have its part

Listen To The Tale

One man said to another comrade you're my brother
The world is wide open life is there to discover
So he put down the plow and walked the dusty road
It was good to be free without that load

And history fails to tell the mystery of hell
Words in time will rhyme oh so well
Top of the chart the poet's heart there on sale
If you refuse to choose you can never prevail
Open up drink the cup and listen to the tale

From the farm to the city with pockets empty
When you're young you have the hunger plenty
Exploited oppressed all decisions second guessed
The priest at the feast said boy you sure are blessed

And history fails to tell the mystery of hell
Words in time will rhyme oh so well
Top of the chart the poet's heart there on sale
If you refuse to choose you can never prevail
Open up drink the cup and listen to the tale

Chasing the wild searching for the woman child
He could not recall at all when he last smiled
His soul was sold for gold and whiskey cold
When you begin life's worst sin is getting old

And history fails to tell the mystery of hell
Words in time will rhyme oh so well
Top of the chart the poet's heart there on sale
If you refuse to choose you can never prevail
Open up drink the cup and listen to the tale

The moral of the story is please don't bore me
Enter in there awaits heaven in endless glory
The man cried as he died lavishing in pain
You can chase the dragon but it's all in vain

And history fails to tell the mystery of hell
Words in time will rhyme oh so well
Top of the chart the poet's heart there on sale
If you refuse to choose you can never prevail
Open up drink the cup and listen to the tale

Living Big At Tech

Running from the gloom and the doom
Forsaking the greedy who consume
Looking for a brand-new start
Kissed my girl Karen a last goodbye
I'll speak the truth I won't tell you a lie
Losing her broke my heart

A wobbly wreck
Living big at tech
Don't mean no disrespect
Living big at tech

I traveled to engineering school
With a brilliant mind I was a fool
I never suspected what was in store
Manipulated to make weapons of war
But I made myself many a friend
And we celebrated on the weekend

A wobbly wreck
Living big at tech
Don't mean no disrespect
Living big at tech

Reality slowly crumbled away
As monotony ruled each day
I learned equations to define all
And somewhere Love gave a call
But I couldn't even hear
As I sought refuge in a beer

A wobbly wreck
Living big at tech
Don't mean no disrespect
Living big at tech

Love Is A Mighty Force

Once I lived in a world alone
Hatred was all I had known
But years came and I've grown
I was all alone

Love is a mighty force
Like a river on its course
With an eternal source
Love is a mighty force

I was a lonely desert land
Life I didn't understand
But heaven came with the rain
I was born again

Love is a mighty force
Like a river on its course
With an eternal source
Love is a mighty force

Some days I stop to look behind
And I don't like what I find
That's the glory of grace
You can change your place

Love is a mighty force
Like a river on its course
With an eternal source
Love is a mighty force

I can hear you laughing at me
Misery of mockery
Love it turned the key
Love it set me free

Love is a mighty force
Like a river on its course
With an eternal source
Love is a mighty force

My Song To Share

Library bathroom a makeshift shower
A foul stench with potent power
Ragged wretches with no place to go
I wonder what secrets they know

Good or bad happy or sad life goes on
The clocks ticks quick until you're gone
Live the dream a life without care
An empty belly tells me it's a nightmare
This is my prayer my song to share

He came from the west on a sacred quest
The cruelty of man was a test
A folk singer a bringer of peace
Heroin brought him sweet release

Good or bad happy or sad life goes on
The clocks ticks quick until you're gone
Live the dream a life without care
An empty belly tells me it's a nightmare
This is my prayer my song to share

It's hard to play with ice on your strings
They crucified the King of Kings
Fantasy fails as hardship prevails
Life abounds with wicked details

Good or bad happy or sad life goes on
The clocks ticks quick until you're gone
Live the dream a life without care
An empty belly tells me it's a nightmare
This is my prayer my song to share

Manhattan Island do you understand
Satan is in command of the big brass band
They are playing nobody knows the troubles I've seen
While backstage awaits the underage queen

Pride will not let our great hero return
Besides he let his bridges burn
He pawned the guitar for one last hit
Life my friend is what you make of it

Good or bad happy or sad life goes on
The clocks ticks quick until you're gone
Live the dream a life without care
An empty belly tells me it's a nightmare
This is my prayer my song to share

Never Been To Nashville

Don't mess with my country I let it go
I came back with still don't know
Ridiculed schooled in the finer art
I thought you had a Christian heart

I've never been to Nashville and I never will
Guitar junkies are circling for the kill
It's only a sin when you know God's will
I've never been to Nashville and I never will

So easy to tear down with a frown
See the king sing without any crown
Where are you finding the perfect sound?
Nashville is now burning to the ground

I've never been to Nashville and I never will
Guitar junkies are circling for the kill
It's only a sin when you know God's will
I've never been to Nashville and I never will

It takes an ego to give it a go
And when you finally have a show
Some joker tells you no
Some joker tells you no
Yeah maybe I'll have a cry
But I won't let my dream die

Without the music Accapella style
Through the trial I had the strength to smile
Now take a look at the book mister star
You're so obscure and I've gone real far

I've never been to Nashville and I never will
Guitar junkies are circling for the kill
It's only a sin when you know God's will
I've never been to Nashville and I never will

New Rock And Roll

The guitar screeches
The singer preaches
The drum teaches
The bass reaches

The world of music is still evolving
Got more problems nobody is solving
Pop singer singing a pop song
Don't nobody tell me that ain't wrong

Ain't any new rock and roll on the radio
Just the old songs that we all know
Sometimes I wish the world would just explode
Ain't any new rock and roll on the radio

And its verse chorus and then another verse
If you ain't clever well you can always curse
Ain't got a dime for the time to rehearse
So we make it one take for better or worse

Ain't any new rock and roll on the radio
Just the old songs that we all know
Sometimes I wish the world would just explode
Ain't any new rock and roll on the radio

And here we go resurrection day
We deliver a double dose to play
Our mission is an ambition to save your soul
With new rock and roll taking control

Ain't any new rock and roll on the radio
Just the old songs that we all know
Sometimes I wish the world would just explode
Ain't any new rock and roll on the radio

On A Psychedelic Twist

A typo got me vexed instead of sexed
I was wondering just what was coming next
If I was seventeen I'd fall for Poly Styrene
If you ain't punk this junk is just obscene

On a psychedelic twist
It is futile to resist
I will be kind
I will hardwire your mind
Oh yes I must insist
On a psychedelic twist

I never saw Jimi play but still he is the way
I took a slip on the trip to a new golden day
In searches through churches I found endless crime
When you write a song it's wrong not to rhyme

On a psychedelic twist
It is futile to resist
I will be kind
I will hardwire your mind
Oh yes I must insist
On a psychedelic twist

I was chillin' with Bob Dylan doing the American thing
I said your half past dead soon you'll meet the king
Folk music was assassinated by electrical urge
I have a dollar in my pocket and I want to splurge

On a psychedelic twist
It is futile to resist
I will be kind
I will hardwire your mind
Oh yes I must insist
On a psychedelic twist

I gave a look in the holy book searching for hope
I roamed around and I found in Rome the pope
I tried on his hat and we had a hearty laugh
With vile hate we divided the collection plate in half

On a psychedelic twist
It is futile to resist
I will be kind

I will hardwire your mind
Oh yes I must insist
On a psychedelic twist

Paul Is Dead Part 2

Wouldn't it be a groovy thing
If I could dance if I could sing
I could be a Beatle playing bass guitar
I could be a Beatle and be a big star

Fifty years of singing the blues
Figuring out the secret clues
Have you heard the latest news
Paul is dead and paying his dues

I wrote a book it was but a disguise
Can you discern the truth and the lies
Never mind about a pretty motor maid
When you're famous you need to get paid

Fifty years of singing the blues
Figuring out the secret clues
Have you heard the latest news
Paul is dead and paying his dues

Playing records in reverse
Guessing is a grand curse
Walking barefoot on the road
Band about to explode
Where the undertaker sighs
And life overloads with lies

Teeny boppers couldn't handle truth
So we had to hide it from the youth
Imagine all of the things we never knew
Paul is dead so sorry it is true

Fifty years of singing the blues
Figuring out the secret clues
Have you heard the latest news
Paul is dead and paying his dues

Paul Is Dead

I tried to fly but my wings were weak
So I followed turning the other cheek
And Paul said I ain't dead but it's bleak
They say you'll find what you seek

You know what they said
Paul is dead Paul is dead
Get it inside your head
Paul is dead Paul is dead

I was walking barefoot on Galilee
With the internet we can't know reality
All day long I'll Google Paul
Right there on the screen it says all

You know what they said
Paul is dead Paul is dead
Get it inside your head
Paul is dead Paul is dead

I was walking the Damascus Road
When heaven in fire did explode
We had to cut it down to three o five
I was happy to get out of it alive

The Beatles and the Crickets
I got front row tickets
Money naturally brings crimes
The changing of the times
All the wrong words rhyme
Welcome to the sublime

Well you faithful don't have any fears
I'm glad to present to you Billy Shears
Remember me and remember Jack
In cinematic colors all white and black

You know what they said
Paul is dead Paul is dead
Get it inside your head
Paul is dead Paul is dead

Sad Day In Montclair

Front page rage of the Montclair times
A sinister story the foulest of crimes
James R Ray blew away Angela Bledsoe
Two elite I did not meet nor did I know

A sad day in Montclair
I offer you my thoughts and prayer
Hey I really do care
It's a sad day in Montclair

At the library the homeless congregate
Poverty is a poison infested with hate
James lived in a mansion made of dreams
So big you dig you could hear no screams

A sad day in Montclair
I offer you my thoughts and prayer
Hey I really do care
It's a sad day in Montclair

Money honey it's a bitch
Never enough even if you're rich
Open your blind eyes to see
Only the poor man is free
But so few chose poverty
And Jesus died at Calvary

Be careful crossing Bloomfield Avenue
The next statistic it could be you
We are the shadow of New York City
High in hope full of dope plenty of pity

A sad day in Montclair
I offer you my thoughts and prayer
Hey I really do care
It's a sad day in Montclair

Sipping Away

Where's a folk singer when you need a song
With truth and justice and a voice so strong
What happened to the acoustic guitar
Hay baby I'm wondering where you are

Sipping away Sunday at the café
Hoping for love to come my way
But if it don't that's okay
I still got my latte
Sipping away all of my day

I saw you back in nineteen eighty-three
You were the magic key that set me free
Down the road two divorces later
In my mind I find that you're even greater

Sipping away Sunday at the café
Hoping for love to come my way
But if it don't that's okay
I still got my latte
Sipping away all of my day

Pushing Monday morning out of my mind
Just looking for somebody to treat me kind
Who knows tomorrow just what I'll find
Life came in a storm and left me behind

Sipping away Sunday at the café
Hoping for love to come my way
But if it don't that's okay
I still got my latte
Sipping away all of my day

I can help you sing and I can help you write
I can hold you in the freezing cold of the night
I can kiss your lips and embrace you fire
I could be anything at all you desire

Sipping away Sunday at the café
Hoping for love to come my way
But if it don't that's okay
I still got my latte
Sipping away all of my day

Starving Artists

He's a genius and he'll tell you so
Hanging his pictures for a show
Presently obscure hoping for more
In the end we all enter death's door

Van Gogh died a failure sad to say
Picasso prospered procuring potent pay
Tomorrow well the wheel is in spin
And a million starving artists enter in

He's a little man with giant dreams
Life is never painted as it seems
Cubes and twisted angles dominate
Say what you will he'll still create

Van Gogh died a failure sad to say
Picasso prospered procuring potent pay
Tomorrow well the wheel is in spin
And a million starving artists enter in

And the angry man he curses foul
In a pleasant mood hear him growl
Violating the calm serene
Words can never tell the total scene
So with brush in hand he does persist
He's the wild joker the starving artist

On the wall I can see them all
I give him credit heeding his call
Dreams die if you never take chance
Art is a mistress go make romance

Van Gogh died a failure sad to say
Picasso prospered procuring potent pay
Tomorrow well the wheel is in spin
And a million starving artists enter in

Tell Me The Words I Want To Hear

I was searching for something you can't find
For a love that will thrill you till you're blind
A cosmic explosion to echo through the mind
The tears of a billion years that I left behind

Lady Lace whisper in my ear
Tell me the words I want to hear
Take away all that I fear
Tell me the words I want to hear

Cute in my silver suit space helmet in my hand
I played guitar on a star in a celestial band
Riding the rockets to places yet unknown
My heart is full of courage my mind is blown

Lady Lace whisper in my ear
Tell me the words I want to hear
Take away all that I fear
Tell me the words I want to hear

When the cameras are turned off I cry
It's a lonely place in outer space past the sky
Is it a crime to sometimes wish you could die?
I ain't a hero but I got something you can't deny

We all wear a face
We all need some grace
Science is not true
What can we do?
I'll just sing this song
Loud and strong
Read between the lines
Tell me what you find

I'm feeling cold feeling old doing as I'm told
When the price gets real high you'll be sold
A supernova merged with the black hole
I went a trillion light years looking for my soul

Lady Lace whisper in my ear
Tell me the words I want to hear
Take away all that I fear
Tell me the words I want to hear

The Bassman

Some people live the blues

My last card of the deck
You know it's the ace man
She's a heavenly speck
From outer space man
Levert gonna lay a hurt
Cause he's the Bassman

Slide into the room
Let me lay down the boom
Don't have no gloom
Let me lay down the boom

My last card of the deck
You know it's the ace man
She's a heavenly speck
From outer space man
Levert gonna lay a hurt
Cause he's the Bassman

The Old Man And Me

The old man I've never seen him smile
I say hello every once in a while
He's not well his life is living hell
As for tomorrow who can tell?

The old man once was young
Will these words ever be sung?
Life is a fantasy so does is seem
The man and me a passing dream

Sometimes he talks happy as can be
Then he slips back into black misery
The winds blows west and the wind blows east
We're all looking for a world of peace

The old man once was young
Will these words ever be sung?
Life is a fantasy so does is seem
The man and me a passing dream

Down at the library I do write
I'm counting the syllable making it tight
The old man he's sleeping in his chair
For the moment he ain't got a care

The old man once was young
Will these words ever be sung?
Life is a fantasy so does is seem
The man and me a passing dream

The old man drifts by caught in a haze
I dream of tomorrow and better days
Our two worlds with this moment to share
I don't think the old man is aware

The old man once was young
Will these words ever be sung?
Life is a fantasy so does is seem
The man and me a passing dream

The Wheels Turn

It was a day in the ordinary way
With men at work and the children at play
In the hustle of the bustle came a pop
In tragic magic life came to a stop

The wheels turn see them spinning
We never learn the devil's grinning
Life's a game who is winning
Feel the shame of all the sinning
The wheels turn see them spinning

The priest is a beast dressed in a black disguise
The minister of truth only speaks lies
Love is a word translated into lust
Climb ladder of success yes you must

The wheels turn see them spinning
We never learn the devil's grinning
Life's a game who is winning
Feel the shame of all the sinning
The wheels turn see them spinning

I want an hour to smell a flower
And politicians who don't abuse power
May endless war finally end
And my enemies become my friend

Traffic jam gives a slam downtown tonight
God damn a permanent frown just ain't right
Rats in a cage running on the wheel in rage
Up in age will we ever turn the page?

The wheels turn see them spinning
We never learn the devil's grinning
Life's a game who is winning
Feel the shame of all the sinning
The wheels turn see them spinning

There's A Price To Pay

On the evening news they major in the blues
Lies disguised in truth as cryptic clues
The big breasted blonde forecasts the weather
After they show you know they get together

You can go anyway – there's a price to pay
Day after day – there's a price to pay
Listen to what I say – there's a price to pay
Even if I pray – there's a price to pay

Down on the corner under the neon sign
The whore wants to score any John is fine
To slip into a trip to the twilight zone
If you pay extra she'll groan and moan

You can go anyway – there's a price to pay
Day after day – there's a price to pay
Listen to what I say – there's a price to pay
Even if I pray – there's a price to pay

In congress the cocaine is always pure
The best of the best but they long for more
Egos on the rise they compromise for cash
In an hour of power fame fades in a flash

You can go anyway – there's a price to pay
Day after day – there's a price to pay
Listen to what I say – there's a price to pay
Even if I pray – there's a price to pay

The Ancient Mariner is immortal in verse
It matters not he is synonymous with a curse
Will you remember me as time fades to sorrow?
My future now past was once distant tomorrow

You can go anyway – there's a price to pay
Day after day – there's a price to pay
Listen to what I say – there's a price to pay
Even if I pray – there's a price to pay

They Chase The Bull (Julio's Song)

Julio was a refugee from the Castro regime
Plenty to tempt me the American dream
Striving for control they sold their soul
Profits and more profits the solitary goal

Down on Wall Street they chase the bull
Money is a mistress wicked and cruel
It's the Earth to conquer the world to rule
Don on Wall Street they chase the bull

And Julio lives the life of the lie
If the Feds inquire he'll blame some other guy
While Judgment Day is a distant tomorrow
Cocaine and whores secure freedom from sorrow

Down on Wall Street they chase the bull
Money is a mistress wicked and cruel
It's the Earth to conquer the world to rule
Don on Wall Street they chase the bull

Gold plated cigarette case
Permanent smile on his face
Italian suits finest design
More more more make it mine
On the dragon's back see him fly
Soaring in the atmosphere high

Julio never dreams life is a fantasy
Chained to his portfolio far from free
In his mind he will find the question why
If he knew the answer he would die

Down on Wall Street they chase the bull
Money is a mistress wicked and cruel
It's the Earth to conquer the world to rule
Don on Wall Street they chase the bull

Tomorrow's Coming Fast

Cruel kids with a mocking tongue
Wicked songs the melody sung
And I never did belong
But the pain made me strong

Heaven is not a destination
Life is not an endless celebration
Yesterday is in the past
And tomorrow's coming fast

Well Joe went the American way
He salutes the flag every day
He was a stoner back in school
Graduating to the ranks of a fool

Heaven is not a destination
Life is not an endless celebration
Yesterday is in the past
And tomorrow's coming fast

Well here come the fascists with marching uniform
The commander demanding that everybody conform
The winds of wickedness are blowing a woeful storm
But in the eye of the evil this is simply the norm

Joe scares me as he tells his tale
God guts and guns will prevail
But America was never for sale
And Love it can never fail

Heaven is not a destination
Life is not an endless celebration
Yesterday is in the past
And tomorrow's coming fast

We're On Our Way

I awoke with the birds singing at sunrise
The glory of heaven flooded my eyes
A new day so I can give it one more try
To find the truth to find the reason why

There are songs we have yet to create
And love hasn't conquered hate
But allow me to take the time to say
We're on our way
We're on our way
For a better day
We're on our way

There some of us who have kept our ideals
Who wonder how the stranger really feels
I extend my hand won't you please take it
Understand together we can make it

There are songs we have yet to create
And love hasn't conquered hate
But allow me to take the time to say
We're on our way
We're on our way
For a better day
We're on our way

I took my lover on an endless walk
We kissed and cried and had a talk
We shared the secrets we could not say
Together for better we're on our way

Tomorrow ain't here let's fix it today
Get off of your knees and do more than pray
Love is an action word you gotta do your part
Follow the love that lurks deep in your heart

There are songs we have yet to create
And love hasn't conquered hate
But allow me to take the time to say
We're on our way
We're on our way
For a better day
We're on our way

Where Are You Paul?

I made up this song with Theodore
Peace and love will defeat all war
LSD was free and I took my share
Down on your knees in pleas of prayer

Where are you Paul?
You took the fall
For a higher call
Where are you Paul?

I was smoking bones with Rolling Stones
Rock and roll is full of guttural groans
Good band bad band do you understand?
Ground control is taking command

Where are you Paul?
You took the fall
For a higher call
Where are you Paul?

FIREWIND well that's something new
The sky is changing to a better view
In the lyrics is the answer you seek
Tell me who said to turn the cheek

In Laurel Canyon I laid me down to sleep
And Charlie Manson is a creepy creep
The real criminals feast on caviar
And nothing is as fake as a rock star

Where are you Paul?
You took the fall
For a higher call
Where are you Paul?

These words well yes they're meant to scare
There are really eight sides in a square
And Paul was left handed just like me
I am John now how clear can I be?

Where are you Paul?
You took the fall
For a higher call
Where are you Paul?

Why Don't We Play In A Band

You don't hear protest songs on the radio
While all the best belongs on the TV show
Take a picture of life we can photo shop
Make pleasure with your wife don't you ever stop

Why don't we play in a band?
With cryptic lyrics none can understand
Truth for the youth is in high demand
So why don't we play in a band?

The freak speaks about turning the other cheek
Pacifism is wisdom so unique
Read the news sing the blues you know it's a lie
Greed indeed is the single reason for why

Why don't we play in a band?
With cryptic lyrics none can understand
Truth for the youth is in high demand
So why don't we play in a band?

I'd like to meet a television evangelist
The Love of God is something none can resist
I'll donate a dollar and sing Kumbaya
And take a moment to say hi to my Ma

Lovely simply lovely she says with a smile
If we had evidence we would have a trial
As it is in show biz you're quickly forgotten
At least that's the story of Johnny Rotten

Why don't we play in a band?
With cryptic lyrics none can understand
Truth for the youth is in high demand
So why don't we play in a band?

Wild Jill

I was out searching for some sin
She was far from a beauty queen
But I was new to the scene
In fact I had never been

We all called her Wild Jill
A lonely lady seeking a thrill
Don't you worry she's on the pill
We all called her Wild Jill

Stumbling drunk we took a walk
In the deep night we had a talk
I was desperate looking for touch
But Wild Jill she was too much

We all called her Wild Jill
A lonely lady seeking a thrill
Don't you worry she's on the pill
We all called her Wild Jill

Philosophy is the study of how thoughts are made
I was dancing to the song the piper played
But the devil is someone who wants to get paid
And Wild Jill she was hoping to get laid

In innocence lying on the grass
I let eternity pass
She rolled on me looking to score
Wild Jill she was such a whore

We all called her Wild Jill
A lonely lady seeking a thrill
Don't you worry she's on the pill
We all called her Wild Jill

Thirty years later still I smile
This life is an endless trial
I pushed Wild Jill far away
And she got lost in yesterday

We all called her Wild Jill
A lonely lady seeking a thrill
Don't you worry she's on the pill
We all called her Wild Jill

Witchy Woman

Books of magic she casts her spell
She's water deep from the well
Beauty outside and inside more
A precious treasure you want for sure

Witchy woman from a dream
At midnight hour hear love's scream
Lose the world to gain her hand
If you knew her you'd understand

Eyes of longing pierce your soul
You give in surrender control
To take the ride it costs you all
Eagerly you answer the call

Witchy woman from a dream
At midnight hour hear love's scream
Lose the world to gain her hand
If you knew her you'd understand

Carnal pleasure is her treasure
Perfect paradise in double measure
Feel her touch both flesh and mind
You plead to her that she'll be kind

Many men they never cease
The fire cannot offer peace
Touch the flame it's no game
See the burns you're not the same

Witchy woman from a dream
At midnight hour hear love's scream
Lose the world to gain her hand
If you knew her you'd understand

Yesterday It Faded Away

He was a hippie with long hair
Raised on the promise of prayer
He had the courage to care
When others weren't aware

Yesterday it faded away
To a new rambling day
What did Woody say?
Yesterday it faded away

Smoking weed was just fine
And the music simply divine
If only he could stop the war
As if Love could be the cure

Well peace love and understanding
They turn out to be quite demanding
Living free is quite the thrill
But living free don't pay the bill

Yesterday it faded away
To a new rambling day
What did Woody say?
Yesterday it faded away

He got lost in the computer age
Couldn't manage to turn the page
He dreams and he always will
Of a cross on a forgotten hill

Yesterday it faded away
To a new rambling day
What did Woody say?
Yesterday it faded away

He can find the strength to smile
And life it has been worth while
It isn't how far that you go
It's the way which the winds blow

Yesterday it faded away
To a new rambling day
What did Woody say?
Yesterday it faded away

Young And Free

Walking across God's kingdom
Getting some rides by thumb
West Virginia was paradise
Everybody so kind and nice

Young and free
That was me
Walking through eternity
Young and free
May it always be
Young and free

Sleeping in the bus station
Preaching about salvation
The people just keep giving
I'm just happy to be living

Young and free
That was me
Walking through eternity
Young and free
May it always be
Young and free

Clearwater River in Idaho
Stars in the heavens glow
I am blessed under God's sky
Memories they never die

I was searching without to find within
I learned that surrender was the greatest sin
We can always try we can always begin

Young and free
That was me
Walking through eternity
Young and free
May it always be
Young and free

I write down words on the page
A fragment from another age
I am there walking each bend
The journey it never does end

Young and free
That was me
Walking through eternity
Young and free
May it always be
Young and free

All Halo Eve 18

Murder is rolling off her tongue
She is fantasy for the young
A killer thriller from a dream
She'll make you moan she'll make you scream

I'll help you believe
As you give so shall you receive
I'll help you believe
On all Halo Eve

The spider lurks looking for the fly
She's a question the wicked 'Why?'
Zombie soldiers marching in line
Never mind your mind all is fine

I'll help you believe
As you give so shall you receive
I'll help you believe
On all Halo Eve

Win, win, win with a Satanic grin
Let me pour some juice into your gin
Soon you will have some wings to fly
We only live until we die

I'll help you believe
As you give so shall you receive
I'll help you believe
On all Halo Eve

Under heaven nothing is right
The blade flashes in the moon light
I cut your heart I cut your soul
It's all about complete control

I'll help you believe
As you give so shall you receive
I'll help you believe
On all Halo Eve

Alumina

Woke up with a grin
Like I was born again
Got dressed and showered
My joy overpowered

I was early to my work
Said hello to the clerk
The boss gave me praise
It was one of those days

Alumina a shiny tin can
Love and love is the plan
Alumina a woman and a man
Alumina playing in the band

I went to local bar
Hendrix was playing guitar
The blonde beauty said hi
Excuse me as I kiss the sky

We danced real tight
It was Friday night
The music was just right
No doubt out of sight

Alumina a shiny tin can
Love and love is the plan
Alumina a woman and a man
Alumina playing in the band

We walked under the stars
Not too near not too far
I was wondering about life
I needed me a wife

Well the world's a dream
But grace it will redeem
Forever begins to start
When love enters the heart

Alumina a shiny tin can
Love and love is the plan
Alumina a woman and a man
Alumina playing in the band

Ambient 001

Here there everywhere
God hears your prayer
Cause He's there
Here there everywhere

Ambient light shining bright
Laying the beat oh so tight
Finally got the magic right
Ambient light shining bright

Love is the great unknown
Plant a seed leave it alone
Soon it will have grown
Love is the great unknown

Ambient light shining bright
Laying the beat oh so tight
Finally got the magic right
Ambient light shining bright

Henry hustles to the puzzle one last piece
He can't make it fit there's no release
Sometimes you gotta rock outside the box
The door may be closed but there are no locks

There is music in the sky
Angels singing on high
Heaven can never die
There is music in the sky

Ambient light shining bright
Laying the beat oh so tight
Finally got the magic right
Ambient light shining bright

Blighted The World

You spent days in the maze going all ways
Hyped you typed the words to the latest craze
What a pretender you can never surrender
Through the door the Minotaur the game ender

Scorned by your girl
So you blighted the world
The whore of the Minotaur
So you blighted the world

The rat runs from the cat chases the cheese
When you are homeless you do as you please
You served your time and you did no crime
Except for obeying orders and marching in line

Scorned by your girl
So you blighted the world
The whore of the Minotaur
So you blighted the world

They are gentrifying Harlem way uptown
The orders are given from the banks on down
While the disheveled veteran sleeps on grate
Mass production it's hard to function with hate

LSD slips in his juice
He is free fabulously loose
He chases the dragon today
Tomorrow is the time to pay
Tomorrow and what more
Enter the Minotaur

Scorned by your girl
So you blighted the world
The whore of the Minotaur
So you blighted the world

In that fatal moment when insanity becomes real
You cannot repent or even see the total deal
And with open eyes you realize Babylon
With trembling lips time slips and all is gone

Scorned by your girl / So you blighted the world
The whore of the Minotaur / So you blighted the world

Crunch Time

Out on the street they like the beat
Everybody hustles in the heat
That's because they want to eat
Surviving not giving in to defeat

If you don't get caught it ain't a crime
Swaying playing we're all saying crunch time
It's like making the wrong words rhyme
Swaying playing we're all saying crunch time

Lady Lace she paints up her face
On her knees but she ain't giving grace
Sweet Alvin packs a knife and a gun
He'll slit your throat just for fun

If you don't get caught it ain't a crime
Swaying playing we're all saying crunch time
It's like making the wrong words rhyme
Swaying playing we're all saying crunch time

The undercover cop dresses like a blind man
With a cane tin cup and a sinister plan
He sees the mayor show up at the whore house
The undercover cop leaves quiet as a mouse

Don't you know we all sin?
Says the devil with a grin
Pick a card pick any card
This game really ain't hard
Take my very best advice
Drugs, liquor, stealing and vice

If you don't get caught it ain't a crime
Swaying playing we're all saying crunch time
It's like making the wrong words rhyme
Swaying playing we're all saying crunch time

Reverend Wanna Be preaches about being free
They pass the plates he waits for the currency
God's man is divine he gotta dress so fine
At the end of the day we all pay at crunch time

If you don't get caught it ain't a crime/ Swaying playing we're all saying crunch time
It's like making the wrong words rhyme / Swaying playing we're all saying crunch time

Darkness Surrounds You 3

Welcome to the void
You will be destroyed
Run baby try to run
I'm going to have some fun

Goodbye to the azure blue
Darkness surrounds you
All the lies are true
Darkness surrounds you

You scream but there in nobody near
I consume your intoxicating fear
Midnight with no light in sight
A ferocious feast of fatal fright

Goodbye to the azure blue
Darkness surrounds you
All the lies are true
Darkness surrounds you

Welcome to my humble lair
In vain is your prayer
Meet your new friend death
Breath your final breath

Goodbye to the azure blue
Darkness surrounds you
All the lies are true
Darkness surrounds you

A spiritual rape none can escape
Choked by endless cords of red tape
Enter in through sin to hell
In pain you shall remain to dwell

Goodbye to the azure blue
Darkness surrounds you
All the lies are true
Darkness surrounds you

Dig It Up

Thanksgiving dinner it's a winner
At the table the saint and sinner
Everything is just fine and then
You open your big fat mouth again

Like a stinking corpse
You dig it up, dig it up
The past was painful enough
But you gotta dig it dig up

Remember when the words they slice
Why didn't listen to my advice
You should never have married you wife
The tongue slicing dicing like a knife

Like a stinking corpse
You dig it up, dig it up
The past was painful enough
But you gotta dig it dig up

Angry over things forty years past
The love fades the pain will last
The details are fuzzy and gray
Stuck in the muck of yesterday

Like a stinking corpse
You dig it up, dig it up
The past was painful enough
But you gotta dig it dig up

So upset you get up and leave
I am right both sides believe
At Christmas we'll try once more
On and on goes the silly war

Like a stinking corpse
You dig it up, dig it up
The past was painful enough
But you gotta dig it dig up

Eany Meany

Little ones it's time to play
Run run run away
Hide and seek it's just a game
If Father Rollie Polly gets you
You'll never be the same

Eany meany eany meany
God is heaven
Watching the good children
Eany meany eany meany
Only the devil can see me

The basement is dark as a dream
Nobody can hear you scream
Come closer sit right next to me
Can you help make me happy?

Eany meany eany meany
God is heaven
Watching the good children
Eany meany eany meany
Only the devil can see me

Scary nightmares infest her mind
The rapture came she was left behind
All of the sins weren't written in stone
There's a reason she stays all alone

Eany meany eany meany
God is heaven
Watching the good children
Eany meany eany meany
Only the devil can see me

Electric Knife

If you want to get your blessing
There is no second guessing
Keep on playing keep on pressing
Do what you do all that messing

They'll kill you in the prime of your life
Slice you down with that electric knife
They'll slaughter your children and your wife
Slice you down with that electric knife

Only room for one on top of the chart
You gotta have courage you gotta have heart
Cause the critics will tear you apart
They don't care or aware that it's art

They'll kill you in the prime of your life
Slice you down with that electric knife
They'll slaughter your children and your wife
Slice you down with that electric knife

The team at the magazine is all obscene
They play dirty not even close the clean
But there is purity in the soul of the teen
You lay it down they'll know what you mean

They'll kill you in the prime of your life
Slice you down with that electric knife
They'll slaughter your children and your wife
Slice you down with that electric knife

When you arrive I'll give you a big smile
Cause despite our flaws it's all worth while
It ain't about the money it's all survival
No jerk its back to work with one more trial

They'll kill you in the prime of your life
Slice you down with that electric knife
They'll slaughter your children and your wife
Slice you down with that electric knife

Ellsworth

The road goes on forever
Riding till the fifth of never
Looking for my city of gold
Just another lie you told

Ellsworth you're out there
Somewhere somewhere
Ellsworth you're out there
You're why I still believe in prayer
Ellsworth you're out there
Somewhere somewhere

I believe that dreams came true
I say the day I met you
Now the sky doesn't look so blue
What's a poor boy to do
Except to bear all his hurt
And cry out for Ellsworth

Ellsworth you're out there
Somewhere somewhere
Ellsworth you're out there
You're why I still believe in prayer
Ellsworth you're out there
Somewhere somewhere

I ain't got a treasure map to use
Only a handful of clever clues
In the seeking one is created
Your Love Ellsworth can't be debated
You gave even when you were hated
You gave and the world celebrated

Ellsworth you're out there
Somewhere somewhere
Ellsworth you're out there
You're why I still believe in prayer
Ellsworth you're out there
Somewhere somewhere

END ROADS

What's a pretty girl like you
Doing with a man like me
What's a pretty girl like you
Doing in a place like this?
What's a pretty girl like you?
Giving me a kiss

This is where the road ends
But say can't we be friends
I love you so she pretends
This is where the road ends

What's a pretty girl like you
Doing laying in my bed
Didn't you believe it's true
All the things your momma said

This is where the road ends
But say can't we be friends
I love you so she pretends
This is where the road ends

What's a pretty girl like you?
Standing on the corner of the avenue
What's a pretty girl like you?
Asking me to go for a ride

This is where the road ends
But say can't we be friends
I love you so she pretends
This is where the road ends

The sin of heroin addiction
Just gotta get it again
Just gotta get it again
When will this hell end?
Just gotta get it again

Growler

Greased hair strong cologne
All alone Yeah he's alone
Slinking at the end of the bar
Wondering just who you are

Worse than the prowler
He's the one and only growler
You couldn't get any fouler
Cause he's the gruesome growler

See his beady little eyes
Fake mustache he's in disguise
He's got a little surprise
Something more potent than his lies

Worse than the prowler
He's the one and only growler
You couldn't get any fouler
Cause he's the gruesome growler

White powder knock drug
Just in case you don't budge
You're tipsy girl but think
He's gonna spike your drink

Worse than the prowler
He's the one and only growler
You couldn't get any fouler
Cause he's the gruesome growler

Is This The Way Its Supposed To Be?

Be a good citizen march in line
Dream of heaven mighty fine
Do as mommy and daddy say
You'll understand one distant day
One day oh yes one day

Is this the way it's supposed to be?
Is this hell or is it just me?
A slave in the land of the free
Is this the way it's supposed to be?

High schools full of rules
Get good grades avoid the fools
Go to college get a degree
Major in the art of agony

Is this the way it's supposed to be?
Is this hell or is it just me?
A slave in the land of the free
Is this the way it's supposed to be?

There is a chemical imbalance inside your brain
Clinically practically you have gone insane
Never mind about the illogical disconnect
The lying hate of the state we must protect

Jesus Christ He is the Son of God
Crucified and slandered a fraud
Never mind the words that He said
We'll tell you what to think instead

Is this the way it's supposed to be?
Is this hell or is it just me?
A slave in the land of the free
Is this the way it's supposed to be?

Lassie Come Home

Sorry is a hard word to say
When we do wrong we pay
Wish I could change that day
Go back to yesterday

Lassie come home Lassie come home
I'll give you my steak bone
I'm here all alone
You the best dog I've ever known
Lassie come home Lassie come home

You went running in the rain
My heart broke with pain
I searched near and far
Wonder where you are

Lassie come home Lassie come home
I'll give you my steak bone
I'm here all alone
You the best dog I've ever known
Lassie come home Lassie come home

I'm sorry about the feline
I know I crossed the line
You were always number one
My God what have I done!!??!!

Lassie come home Lassie come home
I'll give you my steak bone
I'm here all alone
You the best dog I've ever known
Lassie come home Lassie come home

Left Handed

Went down to a Spanish café
Where for a peso they'll play
A song with a swinging beat
And just for a special treat

Senorita will dance with you
She knows how to move
She knows how to grove
But you gotta understand it
She's left-handed left-handed

Well all the guys got their eyes
Watching as everyone tries
To win her with sweet little lies
But she will never compromise

Senorita will dance with you
She knows how to move
She knows how to grove
But you gotta understand it
She's left-handed left-handed

Oh we go late into the night
Everyone's feeling alright
The men are hoping that they might
Be Senorita's special delight

Senorita will dance with you
She knows how to move
She knows how to grove
But you gotta understand it
She's left-handed left-handed

When they close down the place
Surprise is on all the men's face
Arm in arm they walk to the car
Senorita with the maid of the bar

Senorita will dance with you
She knows how to move
She knows how to grove
But you gotta understand it
She's left-handed left-handed

Legacy Bass 16

Friday night everybody's hanging around
The band at the bar got a new sound
Electric rhythm he's jamming the bass
A divine mainline to amazing grace

If you're here for fun don't you dare draw the ace
Pick a queen with a hot body and a pretty face
Don't frown the beat is laid down with a legacy bass
I wonder in the thunder if we won't tear down the place
Snapping slapping it's what's happening
The legacy bass

He's a mean machine slick and lean
Served as a marine he curses obscene
He's on the prowl like wolf in heat
Rock and roll makes the scene complete

If you're here for fun don't you dare draw the ace
Pick a queen with a hot body and a pretty face
Don't frown the beat is laid down with a legacy bass
I wonder in the thunder if we won't tear down the place
Snapping slapping it's what's happening
The legacy bass

In truth the soldier never dies
But with whiskey and gin he tries
Love is this life's elusive goal
Win the world and you lose your soul

If you're here for fun don't you dare draw the ace
Pick a queen with a hot body and a pretty face
Don't frown the beat is laid down with a legacy bass
I wonder in the thunder if we won't tear down the place
Snapping slapping it's what's happening
The legacy bass

New Blues Groove 6

You know what I wanna do
I wanna make love to you
And never ever get through
I wanna make love to you

We'll take it slow
We'll take it fast
But you know damn sure
We'll make it last

You know what I wanna do
I wanna make love to you
And never ever get through
I want make love to you

Baby it's never too soon
All morning all afternoon
We'll be feeling alright
Making love into the night

You know what I wanna do
I wanna make love to you
And never ever get through
I wanna make love to you

We'll take it slow
We'll take it fast
But you know damn sure
We'll make it last

You know what I wanna do
I wanna make love to you
And never ever get through
I wanna make love to you

New Song

The trumpet blew
A melody brand new
The words nobody knew
Except the chosen few

A new song for a new year
A new song sing it loud and clear
And new song dismiss all fear
A new song the time is here

And here we are with hope in hand
Talking in tongues none understand
A billion bursting superstars
Angles jamming on electric guitars

A new song for a new year
A new song sing it loud and clear
And new song dismiss all fear
A new song the time is here

The sky on fire
Reaching ever higher
Embrace the living flame
You are pure without shame

In a flash the dead came to life
The groom had returned for his wife
Raising up our voice to rejoice
Singing our new song maddening noise

A new song for a new year
A new song sing it loud and clear
And new song dismiss all fear
A new song the time is here

Northern Lights

Endless snow heaven is white
Can't tell if it's day or night
It's freezing fifty below
Mother nature puts on a show

Northern lights see them glow
Teaching secrets none can know
Ready aim and go
Northern lights see them glow

Aurora Borealis singing her chorus
Living life can be so glorious
High in the sky is the reason why
Truth testifies and none can deny

Northern lights see them glow
Teaching secrets none can know
Ready aim and go
Northern lights see them glow

I see the wisdom shine above
The key is life is learning to love
Give and take that is how to be
When you surrender all you are free

Northern lights see them glow
Teaching secrets none can know
Ready aim and go
Northern lights see them glow

One Man Union

This is the story of Joe Hill
Hated assassinated
His case widely debated
Did he or didn't he kill?

No!
Joe was innocent of the crime
A victim of the evil time
Don't listen to the lies
With songs Joe would organize

He was a one-man union
That was the illusion
For the lesson I recall
Is one big union for us all

Rich men lust in greed
They take from those in need
They will murder and kill
So their coffers fill

But Joe stood up to say no
And power began to flow
To the common man
That was the worker's plan

He was a one-man union
That was the illusion
For the lesson I recall
Is one big union for us all

With sad news I report
The verdict of the kangaroo court
Guilty said the judge of course
And then all the transcripts were lost

Well Joe could never die
He's home in the worker's cry
His soul haunts this land
And still he makes his demand
Power to the people
An injury to one is an injury to all

He was a one-man union
That was the illusion
For the lesson I recall
Is one big union for us all

Pendulum

Swinging singing a song
Lip synching the lyrics wrong
What do I care what do I care
I'm already there already there

The pendulum click clock
The pendulum tick tock
Long live the god of rock
The pendulum click clock
The pendulum tick tock

Times Square New Year's Eve
Hard to believe hard to believe
The whole world watching on
I was totally gone totally gone

The pendulum click clock
The pendulum tick tock
Long live the god of rock
The pendulum click clock
The pendulum tick tock

Oversexed and over paid
Haven't slept but the bed is made
Searching deep inside my soul
Fortune and fame takes its toll

I have the life of the young girl's fantasy
I have everything but you know I ain't free
Learn this wisdom from the pendulum
For a little peace of mind I'd sell my kingdom

The pendulum click clock
The pendulum tick tock
Long live the god of rock
The pendulum click clock
The pendulum tick tock

<u>Picknada</u>

In them hills there's gold
That's the story I was told
I'm gonna ride out west
They tell me that's best

Me my horse and a six gun
There's a wilderness to be won
With a little sin and a little fun
Picknada time to get it done

I met me an Indian squaw
Loveliest thing I ever saw
She said 'Can I ride your horse?"
I said "Well yes, of course"

Me my horse and a six gun
There's a wilderness to be won
With a little sin and a little fun
Picknada time to get it done

Have you ever seen Mother Nature dressed in green?
It's like going to heaven maybe half way in between
I'd play the banjo as my woman hummed along
When you make it up as you go you can't be wrong

Me my horse and a six gun
There's a wilderness to be won
With a little sin and a little fun
Picknada time to get it done

The stars have a story
War has no glory
What is civilization?
Love is my destination

Me my horse and a six gun
There's a wilderness to be won
With a little sin and a little fun
Picknada time to get it done

Right Next To Me

Hey baby let me lick your soul
Give me a smile get wild lose control
Stay right here where you gotta be
Right next to me right next to me

The rhythm rules the dance floor
We're all looking for something more
The perfect person the perfect score
Love is the bug there is no cure

Hey did you paint those pants on?
Let's hurry soon the night will be gone
Drink up from the cup pure ecstasy
Stay right here where you gotta be
Right next to me right next to me

Moving swaying my way of saying
I'm for real this ain't no game I'm playing
I offer you my heart on a silver platter
Nothing else in the universe does matter

Hand in hand we leave a happy two
It's late at night and the sky is blue
Let my love be the thing to set your free
Stay right here where you gotta be
Right next to me right next to me

After the act so matter of fact
Heaven has faded into eternal black
I have one request a final plea
Stay right here where you gotta be
Right next to me right next to me
If you are near I'll always be happy
Stay right here where you gotta be
Right next to me right next to me

Sea Of Uncertainty

Do I love her?
Does she love me?
Will it be a sin?
If I let her in

Waves are rolling high and free
On the sea of uncertainty
My sails fail as the wind roars
I long for the safety of the shores
O woe woe is me
On the sea of uncertainty

Look twice before you cross the street
Wash your hands if you're about to eat
Never talk to a stranger it's deadly danger
Don't go to the temple for a money changer

Waves are rolling high and free
On the sea of uncertainty
My sails fail AS the wind roars
I long for the safety of the shores
O woe woe is me
On the sea of uncertainty

Well she say yes?
Will she say no
If I never ask
I'll never know

Waves are rolling high and free
On the sea of uncertainty
My sails fail as the wind roars
I long for the safety of the shores
O woe woe is me
On the sea of uncertainty

Sideways

The blue pill takes you high
The red one brings you low
If you give them both a try
Well then I really don't know

I smoked a toke went in a daze
The world spun it was sideways
I cried crucified in a craze
A wonder to amaze sideways

Madame Essex with her crystal ball
Summoned Jimi as best I can recall
The Ancient of days in a purple haze
He held his Stratocaster sideways

I smoked a toke went in a daze
The world spun it was sideways
I cried crucified in a craze
A wonder to amaze sideways

Head was spinning I was beginning
To ask God to spare me one more time
I promised to give up all my sinning
I would surrender with no crime

I smoked a toke went in a daze
The world spun it was sideways
I cried crucified in a craze
A wonder to amaze sideways

The lavender giraffe had good laugh
She said you should see my better half
I cried hallelujah in a fit of praise
Life is more holy if seen sideways

I smoked a toke went in a daze
The world spun it was sideways
I cried crucified in a craze
A wonder to amaze sideways

Soft Drill

And the hummingbirds arose in the rosy skies
With the fluttering nothingness of butterflies
Creation began to whistle life's melody
Adam ate the apple and man was set free

I saw the lion lay down with the lamb
Satan played backgammon with the great I Am
The bankers rejoiced and burned all their money
Now I've really said something funny

Engraved on the stone
Four words all alone
Though shall not kill
Yellow alert it's a soft drill

Gravity took a vacation on a three-week holiday
We wanted a longer stay but he couldn't pay
The rocks floated happily as he was away
The reason for the treason none dare to say

Engraved on the stone
Four words all alone
Though shall not kill
Yellow alert it's a soft drill

I kissed her lips with the passion of a hurricane
The calm eye is why the world is totally insane
The universe was reduced to a finite point
We made love then exhausted we shared a joint

Engraved on the stone
Four words all alone
Though shall not kill
Yellow alert it's a soft drill

I found if the Earth is round the sun always sets
Whether a winner or a sinner we all have regrets
Will I be a person that nobody ever forgets?
The bookie liked the rookie go place your bets

Engraved on the stone
Four words all alone
Though shall not kill
Yellow alert it's a soft drill

Staring At The Water

The wind whispers in my ear like you used to
But you're nowhere near now are you?
You can leave a woman but not a memory
Is this what it is being free?

Sitting staring at the water
Will it be a son or a daughter?
Or an abortion to slaughter?
Sitting staring at the water

Guilt flows nobody knows the sadness of sin
Except people like me who entered in
Thinking it over wondering what went wrong
Maybe I'll write me a song

Sitting staring at the water
Will it be a son or a daughter?
Or an abortion to slaughter?
Sitting staring at the water

When you throw the dice sometimes you pay the price
Love is a two-edged sword it can really slice
Strange how the world can change in a flash
Out of work and you need some cash

Sitting staring at the water
Will it be a son or a daughter?
Or an abortion to slaughter?
Sitting staring at the water

Lost in the blue thinking of you and the child unborn
Sun will rise to shine in your eyes every morn
I could jump and end it all but I'll never quit
Somehow baby we'll make it

Sitting staring at the water
Will it be a son or a daughter?
Or an abortion to slaughter?
Sitting staring at the water

The Cats Whisper

She's strolling just like she's the queen
The solitary star of the movie screen
She's a perfect ten just short heaven's high
Everybody notices her as she walks on by

The cat's whisper is soft and meek
Say mister turn the other cheek
Everybody listen's when you speak
The cat's whisper is soft and meek

Her man owns the banks and much more
He's the rude dude who creates war
Some say she's nothing but a high-class whore
But they can't pay the fee that's for sure

The cat's whisper is soft and meek
Say mister turn the other cheek
Everybody listen's when you speak
The cat's whisper is soft and meek

Her furs have pearls see the diamonds shine
Of all the girls I wish that she was mine
Sexual wonderful I'd die just for one try
Fantasy may be glorious but it's a lie

The cat's whisper is soft and meek
Say mister turn the other cheek
Everybody listen's when you speak
The cat's whisper is soft and meek

Her head don't turn to check out the scene
She just slips into her black limousine
A puff of smoke and the tires they squeal
All the men wonder if what they saw was real

The cat's whisper is soft and meek
Say mister turn the other cheek
Everybody listen's when you speak
The cat's whisper is soft and meek

The Folds

Heaven's door opens to something more
It seems in a dream I've been here before
White clouds and those proud streets of gold
Eternal glory a story for me to behold

Mother is mad mother scolds
He has the winning had but he folds
Be a good boy do as you're told
If you can't pay ain't no way you'll grow old
Four aces with smiling faces he folds

Win the battle and you lose the war
Pain in the cocaine still she wants more
For the high she'll try the part of the whore
It's a common story we heard before

Mother is mad mother scolds
He has the winning had but he folds
Be a good boy do as you're told
If you can't pay ain't no way you'll grow old
Four aces with smiling faces he folds

Strip poker the joker hung a cross
For your garments the dice they toss
Beaten and bloody this ain't funny
But they'll do it again for the money

Mother is mad mother scolds
He has the winning had but he folds
Be a good boy do as you're told
If you can't pay ain't no way you'll grow old
Four aces with smiling faces he folds

Manic Nirvana outer space
Everybody down here needs some grace
She sleeps I cry tomorrow we all die
I ask questions and the worst one is 'Why?'

Mother is mad mother scolds
He has the winning had but he folds
Be a good boy do as you're told
If you can't pay ain't no way you'll grow old
Four aces with smiling faces he folds

The Jubilee Of Life 6

On top of the Ferris wheel I steal a kiss
Round and round on the merry go round of bliss
Cotton candy life is dandy hand me your heart
Together forever I promise I'll never part

Me and my merry wife
Living the Jubilee of life
Sailing through the strife
Living the Jubilee of life

The waves roll in on the sea of eternity
Heaven is any place my true love is with me
There is a boat for two sailing through the sky blue
In delight past the stars bright just me and you

Me and my merry wife
Living the Jubilee of life
Sailing through the strife
Living the Jubilee of life

Hand in hand beginning to understand love
All in all the Earth looks so small from above
Peace is the way I say let's do it today
If we try we can create the perfect day

Me and my merry wife
Living the Jubilee of life
Sailing through the strife
Living the Jubilee of life

Spin your partner to the right
Hold her with all of your might
The song it really never does end

The Terrier

She was a shy girl with a pretty face
Don't know why she always felt out of place
At the dance she wouldn't take a chance
Though she dreams day and night of romance

Some dogs they bite and growl
Others they whine and howl
But none are more merrier
Then our beloved terrier

She studies hard and always keeps her guard
Sometimes she was bullied on the school yard
Tomorrow was a golden day so she thought
Well worth the battle that was being fought

Some dogs they bite and growl
Others they whine and howl
But none are more merrier
Then our beloved terrier

Let's comb your hair nice and straight
With a pretty yellow bow you look so great
You can run cause the leash is long
We will define your right and wrong

Inside there is a fantasy dark and naughty
But for now she'll do as mommy taught me
A proper girl will go far oh yes she might
Watch out you never know when she'll bite

Some dogs they bite and growl
Others they whine and howl
But none are more merrier
Then our beloved terrier

Traveling Advertisements

Ghost town with the hotel full
Life can be mean downright cruel
Billboard said five miles on the right
Been a hundred nothing in sight

On the road nobody repents
Traveling advertisements
Never a message heaven sent
Traveling advertisements

Buy one and you get two free
All you can eat makes me happy
But take this subtle hint
Be sure to read the fine print

On the road nobody repents
Traveling advertisements
Never a message heaven sent
Traveling advertisements

I paid the whore but don't you know
She left out the bathroom window
Down at the bar was happy hour
Somebody sure needed a shower

On the road nobody repents
Traveling advertisements
Never a message heaven sent
Traveling advertisements

Traveling salesmen with lonely hearts
There's real money in the fine arts
Wasting time spinning my wheels
A handshake seals the deals

On the road nobody repents
Traveling advertisements
Never a message heaven sent
Traveling advertisements

Unity Gain

Kisses sickly sweet
Pleasures plenty to eat
Running in the rain
Laughing at the pain

Living life in vain
Unity gain unity gain
I cannot refrain
Unity gain unity gain
Sensually insane
Unity gain unity gain

You don't gotta guess about her red dress
I never knew almost nothing could impress
Celestial angel I can tell that all ain't well
Feel the fire of my desire give me your hell

Living life in vain
Unity gain unity gain
I cannot refrain
Unity gain unity gain
Sensually insane
Unity gain unity gain

Lipstick rocking red
Quickly shocking me dead
Higher take me higher
Give all I require

Living life in vain
Unity gain unity gain
I cannot refrain
Unity gain unity gain
Sensually insane
Unity gain unity gain

Every stranger is a danger to you
Dreaming of you screaming until they're through
Fantasy they find in your fertile perverted mind
I've seen the face of the goddess I am blind

Living life in vain
Unity gain unity gain
I cannot refrain

Unity gain unity gain
Sensually insane
Unity gain unity gain

You're a memory
Never more to be free
Will we meet again?
Will we meet again?

Living life in vain
Unity gain unity gain
I cannot refrain
Unity gain unity gain
Sensually insane
Unity gain unity gain

What's Wrong With Us?

We fell in love like a fantasy come to life
We kissed in bliss and became man and wife
No it seems the screams cut like a knife
My heart is torn apart in all the strife

Can you tell me what's wrong with us
Always a fight always a fuss
Sweet Lord Jesus can you help us?
Can you tell me what's wrong with us

Every issue with you brings about endless debate
Coming home tired after working late
Your asleep you ate dinner and couldn't wait
Once we only had love know there is hate

Can you tell me what's wrong with us
Always a fight always a fuss
Sweet Lord Jesus can you help us?
Can you tell me what's wrong with us

We fought for days over about the holidays
Maybe it's time we went our separate ways
I punched my fist right through the wall
When we last made love I can't recall

Can you tell me what's wrong with us
Always a fight always a fuss
Sweet Lord Jesus can you help us?
Can you tell me what's wrong with us

Zen Surf

Janny skips on the winter beach
Perfect harmony within reach
Summer is in restful slumber
Want a try well go take a number

All the surfers have gone away
They went to college but not for knowledge
All the surfers have gone away
Buddha moved into their cottage

Janny likes him but he's just too fat
He's like Dylan but no Siamese cat
Still she will sit at his feet for a while
It's rare that a prayer can make you smile

All the surfers have gone away
They went to college but not for knowledge
All the surfers have gone away
Buddha moved into their cottage

Janny has come to understand
There is a lesson a meaning
In every twinkling star
In every grain of sand
If you seek so shall you find
It's already there in your mind
Above all recall to be kind
Love may be a mystery
But it is the most potent force in history

Janny she no longer plays the game
The surfers returned but it's not the same
There is something in her sparkling eye
A subtle hint for the reason 'Why?'

All the surfers have gone away
They went to college but not for knowledge
All the surfers have gone away
Buddha moved into their cottage

All the surfers have earned their degree
A horrible lesson in agony
Middle management ain't what is cut up to be
And Janny, well she's free

All the surfers have gone away
They went to college but not for knowledge
All the surfers have gone away
Buddha moved into their cottage

A Child Of Promise

The white witch dabbled in voodoo
She knows your future now do you?
And Mother Mary she don't come down here
Some say she's too good but it's really fear

And I was a child of promise
Born in the summer bliss
Precious as Judas' kiss
I was a child of promise

Hey Jesus would you like a trick
Hanging on a cross I'll make it quick
Son of God, Son of Man, What do I care
God never listens to my prayer

And I was a child of promise
Born in the summer bliss
Precious as Judas' kiss
I was a child of promise

Father's name I heard it was John
Long before I was born he was gone
Mother was a virgin so I am told
I'll be the Queen Of Hell when I get old

Well the white witch bitched at the priest
Who are we to starve while you feast?
Go to your church hide behind your walls of stone
Pray to God on his throne and leave us alone

And I was a child of promise
Born in the summer bliss
Precious as Judas' kiss
I was a child of promise

Scarecrow

I was as thin as the wind
My dirty long hair was a sin
The holes in my jeans weren't style
Still I did my best to smile

Mother was always pushing me out
Another uncle visiting no doubt
An x rated deflated reality
Best to flee to a happy fantasy

I was always on the go
Went by the name scarecrow
I have secrets you don't know
Please call me scarecrow

It's a terrible thing to want to die
When like rain endless tears I cry
I would like to ask the Good Lord why
But I hear loud and clear he's but a lie

I was always on the go
Went by the name scarecrow
I have secrets you don't know
Please call me scarecrow

Seven years old and the world is black
I'm going to run never coming back
But I know the dangers of the street
What children will do for a bite to eat

I was always on the go
Went by the name scarecrow
I have secrets you don't know
Please call me scarecrow

I am hollow with a brain of straw
Believing in love was my tragic flaw
I wish I went blind seeing what I saw
You can never leave once you enter the door

I was always on the go
Went by the name scarecrow
I have secrets you don't know
Please call me scarecrow

Dusty Old Guitar

Hustling bustling trying to survive
Never a fool for school and all that jive
Smoking cigarettes trying to be cool
Looking out for me was my only rule

It seems my dreams died in screams
Hope to cope slipped through the seams
Without a word he captured my heart
A gentle song from top of the chart

He had a dusty old guitar
And he didn't care who you are
He would play the melody
He would play for free
He was a cosmic superstar
Him and his dusty old guitar

Music was the web and I was the fly
He made me laugh he made me cry
Hours fled as smoke into the sky
I had the answer to the question 'Why?'

It was like a miracle from the Good Book
Conquered I surrendered at one look
I was shy but he insisted that I'd sing
You never know what tomorrow will bring

He had a dusty old guitar
And he didn't care who you are
He would play the melody
He would play for free
He was a cosmic superstar
Him and his dusty old guitar

We were a team singing out on the street
I was an angel with voice divinely sweet
For once I thought life could be more
Then being the runt child of a whore

He had a dusty old guitar
And he didn't care who you are
He would play the melody
He would play for free
He was a cosmic superstar / Him and his dusty old guitar

I Ain't Going Momma's Way

They kiss and say things so sweet
Always hungry looking to eat
Watch out once they get their treat
You'll be back out on the street

And I'd always say
I ain't going momma's way
I would live a better day
I ain't going momma's way

Oh they're handsome and fine
Watch out for some tingling line
Oh baby I'd swim the deepest sea
Oh baby I'll give you eternity

And I'd always say
I ain't going momma's way
I would live a better day
I ain't going momma's way

I've had friends who played with the fire
Nobody pretends that they ain't got the desire
But every man has the lustful heart of a liar
And I won't settle for being just one of the choir

And my music is my dream
I won't surrender for a lover's scream
My music it has the power to redeem
I won't surrender for a lover's scream

And I'd always say
I ain't going momma's way
I would live a better day
I ain't going momma's way

From the gutter to the stage
The urchin with the wild rage
Singing in the club and the bar
The destiny of a rising star

And I'd always say
I ain't going momma's way
I would live a better day
I ain't going momma's way

There She Goes

Walking down Chancellor Avenue
Nothing better for me to do
Suddenly just like the winds blows
Somebody shouts 'there she goes'

I ain't somebody steeped in fame
I ain't a diva the good Lord knows
All the same they know my name
There she goes, oh there she goes

Sun glasses when the sky is gray
Reluctant to leave in the light of day
Most of all is the constant fear
That somebody is lurking near

I ain't somebody steeped in fame
I ain't a diva the good Lord knows
All the same they know my name
There she goes, oh there she goes

Starting to feel like playing a game
My life it will never be the same
Dreams and nightmares so they share
Kiss goodbye life without a care

I ain't somebody steeped in fame
I ain't a diva the good Lord knows
All the same they know my name
There she goes, oh there she goes

Once I was running down the way
Never thought about the price to pay
It get more intense after the shows
There she goes, oh there she goes

I ain't somebody steeped in fame
I ain't a diva the good Lord knows
All the same they know my name
There she goes, oh there she goes

Round And Round

My muse is singing the blues
Late at night paying my dues
I am a star shining in the sky
On a cloudy night asking why

On the circle round and round
Wondering what I have found
Wondering where I am bound
On the circle round and round

In my mind I philosophize
Trying to find truth past lies
So much suffering in vain
So much anguish so much pain

On the circle round and round
Wondering what I have found
Wondering where I am bound
On the circle round and round

Here I am trying to catch a shooting star
Strumming the chords on an acoustic guitar
Searching for something high above
A quest for the ambiguous love

I hear the preacher give a cry
I wonder am I living a lie
Over the hill at eighteen
If you only knew where I've been

On the circle round and round
Wondering what I have found
Wondering where I am bound
On the circle round and round

If I finish the song I can sleep
I never wished to go so deep
But life is a bottomless pit
And the best is counterfeit

On the circle round and round
Wondering what I have found
Wondering where I am bound
On the circle round and round

The Fire

Up on the stage in a rage
In a dingy bar underage
Doing my thing like the night before
Confident in victory so sure

I should have known
I should have learned
The fire burned
The fire burned

I was the queen glory my crown
Ruler of the shady side of town
Still there is always the dream
Always searching for the bigger scream

I should have known
I should have learned
The fire burned
The fire burned

After the show I saw his face
Fancy suit so out of place
I like your music oh so fine
Here are the papers come sign

And never make a deal with the devil
Take my hint
Never make a deal with the devil
Without reading the fine print

I should have known
I should have learned
The fire burned
The fire burned

I saw numbers I saw fame
I said finally I had won the game
Oh the big letters from my hand
Welcome to the world of the damned

I should have known
I should have learned
The fire burned
The fire burned

The Limousine

I never knew any royalty
Rich people didn't bother with me
Never desired the caviar scene
But oh how I love the limousine

Long and sleek black and proud
Standing number one in the crowd
Answer to the dreamer's dream
Going to the show in the limousine

All the jealous eyes looking on
A heap of my innocence now gone
One ride is a week's wages
All to get on time to the stage

Long and sleek black and proud
Standing number one in the crowd
Answer to the dreamer's dream
Going to the show in the limousine

Sipping on a glass of Champaign
Something just to kill the pain
Learning life is futile and vain
I just heard momma went insane
I just heard momma died
Of all things suicide

So I sung my saddest song
Momma she did me much wrong
But momma she did her best
And momma loved me more than the rest

Long and sleek black and proud
Standing number one in the crowd
Answer to the dreamer's dream
Going to the show in the limousine

So here I am dressed all in black
Momma is gone no coming back
We laid her six feet down under
The purpose of living I wonder

Long and sleek black and proud / Standing number one in the crowd
Answer to the dreamer's dream / Going to the show in the limousine

Sinister Smiles

Just between the two of us you can trust me like Jesus
There ain't no me ain't no you know it's us
So sign your name on the line and all will be fine
Oh yes sign your name on the line and all will be fine

They dress in the latest styles and wear sinister smiles
After a life full of trials finally finding things worthwhile
Love and greed the two ends that none could reconcile
They dress in the latest style and wear sinister smiles

My name is Big Ben pick up the pen and let's seal the deal
You see my golden teeth now make it real
You'll make millions now need I make a subtle hint
Never mind what it says and please ignore the fine print

They dress in the latest styles and wear sinister smiles
After a life full of trials finally finding things worthwhile
Love and greed the two ends that none could reconcile
They dress in the latest style and wear sinister smiles

In the haze of the days I signed away my very soul
Hard to see the light when you're in a hole
More money is the mantra making slaves the goal
Some seek money others covet power and control

They dress in the latest styles and wear sinister smiles
After a life full of trials finally finding things worthwhile
Love and greed the two ends that none could reconcile
They dress in the latest style and wear sinister smiles

Push and shove the blazing fire burns
Crush and love it's cruel how one learns
In a minute the past and future merge
In a second I signed on an urge

Heaven have mercy how it hurts me they're all just the same
Men for money honey they have no shame
Art is from the heart while business is from the mind
See their sick sinister smiles as they leave you behind

They dress in the latest styles and wear sinister smiles
After a life full of trials finally finding things worthwhile
Love and greed the two ends that none could reconcile
They dress in the latest style and wear sinister smiles

Hitting The High Note

Rage back stage waiting to turn the sacred page
Pacing racing like chasing a rat in a cage
Pumped up like a balloon inside a cloud
Quenching fear's thirst then comes a burst from the crowd

Ecstasy is a verse none can quote
Here I am hitting the high note
My song is the story life wrote
Here I am hitting the high note

Seconds are hours I feel the sweat on my brow
The past the future all a singularity of now
A quest for the best ascending the chart
Love is truly following what's in your heart

Ecstasy is a verse none can quote
Here I am hitting the high note
My song is the story life wrote
Here I am hitting the high note

Blinded by the light I'm deafened by the roar
I dance in my pants so tight I mimic a whore
First fast then slow letting everything go
I've traded my soul for the goal of the show

Record company accountants machines in motion
Bowing to Baal the Bull void of all emotion
Follow the money she is the wicked wanton queen
For a bonus they give the advice to sacrifice the dream

Ecstasy is a verse none can quote
Here I am hitting the high note
My song is the story life wrote
Here I am hitting the high note

The chorus girls swaying in a cosmic high
I've read my bio I'm nothing more than a lie
Still in the thrill I am now set free
I discover what it means to be me

Ecstasy is a verse none can quote
Here I am hitting the high note
My song is the story life wrote
Here I am hitting the high note

Children

I had to laugh at the golden calf
I looked in the mirror where's the better half
I'm caught hard between heaven and hell
Ask me how I'm doing I can't tell

Children they're gonna grow old
Still they want you to do as told
The saint was faint his soul was sold
Children they're gonna grow old

Sometimes it hurts and sometimes I forget
Tomorrow there's still always one more bet
I've got some years full of fears and sin
Look near or far we all are children

Children they're gonna grow old
Still they want you to do as told
The saint was faint his soul was sold
Children they're gonna grow old

I let it all out when I sing this song
You're old enough to know your right from wrong
I die every day on a cruel cross
Money's the only master of course

Children they're gonna grow old
Still they want you to do as told
The saint was faint his soul was sold
Children they're gonna grow old

Color inside the lines do as the teacher tells
War is fine for the preacher and sex sells
Prince of Peace never mind turning the cheek
Hear the word of God but now I speak

Would that these words be a balm of peace
Could the evil we know forever cease
If only we could be born again
To once more as before be children

Children they're gonna grow old
Still they want you to do as told
The saint was faint his soul was sold
Children they're gonna grow old

A Better Day

I awoke as the bombs fell
Tell me again why we need hell
Wondering if I am going to die
Wondering about the reason why

Jesus loves you so they say
And God hears when you pray
I keep hoping for a better day
Tomorrow will be a better day

Across the world the land of the free
What do they know about me?
On the tele the dirty infidel
Ratings go up and weapons sell

Jesus loves you so they say
And God hears when you pray
I keep hoping for a better day
Tomorrow will be a better day

Scavenging on the ruins of the street
If I'm lucky today I'll eat
They say God is in heaven above
I look up to see missiles not love

Jesus loves you so they say
And God hears when you pray
I keep hoping for a better day
Tomorrow will be a better day

Do I need to tell you something is wrong?
Do I need to sing you this song?
Alternative facts and double speak
The prize is to the violent screw the meek

It's a holy war divine
The mantra of make it all mine
Gain the world and lose the soul
I say the bankers in control

Jesus loves you so they say
And God hears when you pray
I keep hoping for a better day
Tomorrow will be a better day

A Dancing Bimbo

Who you fooling you didn't write the song
You even lip synch the lyrics wrong
When you strut you just show slut
Rock and roll was never this corrupt

She's just a dancing bimbo
Ready to ride to Limbo
She's just a dancing bimbo
A perfect fit for Jimbo
She's just a dancing bimbo

We're already on the fifty fourth take
And your breasts are silicone fake
I'm a man who searches for meaning deep
I'll bounce you once never to keep

She's just a dancing bimbo
Ready to ride to Limbo
She's just a dancing bimbo
A perfect fit for Jimbo
She's just a dancing bimbo

The devil he came and made you a deal
I'll give you everything that you can steal
All you gotta do is simply perform
All you gotta do is simply conform

She's just a dancing bimbo
Ready to ride to Limbo
She's just a dancing bimbo
A perfect fit for Jimbo
She's just a dancing bimbo

And nobody dreams of becoming a whore
Bankers masturbate thinking of war
Red lipstick thick like the night before
Rolling Stone defines the perfect score

And Jesus loves you but that's all
You're going up darling only to fall
Between the heroin and sin lies doom
But baby maybe consumers consume

She's just a dancing bimbo
Ready to ride to Limbo
She's just a dancing bimbo
A perfect fit for Jimbo
She's just a dancing bimbo

So the limousine is from a dream
While on the scene teeny boppers scream
You blasphemy ever tenet of God's will
But then again there is the dollar bill

She's just a dancing bimbo
Ready to ride to Limbo
She's just a dancing bimbo
A perfect fit for Jimbo
She's just a dancing bimbo

A Legend In His Own Mind

He was yesterday's hero
But now the score is zero
Between the pride and the booze
He learned how to lose

A legend in his own mind
Life has left him behind
He gave up on being kind
A legend in his own mind

Every Sunday afternoon
The games can't come too soon
Relishing in the sin
Thinking about what might have been

A legend in his own mind
Life has left him behind
He gave up on being kind
A legend in his own mind

His cheerleader is flabby fat
And his kid a number one brat
In his mind he knows every stat
Hear him say "Wow look at that"

A legend in his own mind
Life has left him behind
He gave up on being kind
A legend in his own mind

America the land of the free
Prisons galore endless military
A perpetual quest to be number one
Oh Lord we shall overcome

Late at night something wrong
A feeling like he don't belong
How could that be he's so strong?
Could it be that he's so wrong?

A legend in his own mind
Life has left him behind
He gave up on being kind
A legend in his own mind

A New Age Dream

You've been down this road a billion times or more
The only rule is there no rules in war
And you know Jesus loves you but you ain't to sure
On the table sits the magical mystical cure

Riding on the waves of a new age dream
Nothing is nothing know what I mean
Reality is illusion bursting through the seams
Riding on the waves of a new age dream

Tomorrow is calling with the promise of today
No matter which road you chose there's a toll to pay
Listen carefully to all the words that they say
Not that it matters because lying is the natural way

Riding on the waves of a new age dream
Nothing is nothing know what I mean
Reality is illusion bursting through the seams
Riding on the waves of a new age dream

Empires rise while empires fall
Through the chaos you hear the call
Don't get greedy just take it all
He who is lost is he who does stall

Love was the promise the seed sown in the heart
But the soil was ravaged as a bomb blew it apart
Water is scarce but blood is found all about
There's only one sin and that is your doubt

Riding on the waves of a new age dream
Nothing is nothing know what I mean
Reality is illusion bursting through the seams
Riding on the waves of a new age dream

A Pretty Song

I'm slipping into the blue of the sky
Wondering as thoughts are thundering why
Love is such a grand old-fashioned game
Everybody is guilty we're all to blame

Sitting with a pretty song
Swing in the jungle with King Kong
Everything that can will go wrong
Singing such a pretty song

Memories of times I never got to live
Sins of the crimes one could never forgive
The holocaust is coming in stereo sound
For all your searching just what have you found?

Sitting with a pretty song
Swing in the jungle with King Kong
Everything that can will go wrong
Singing such a pretty song

Truth is the only heresy
Hey watch what you say
Don't criticize the land of the free
Down on your knees try to pray
Never mind we bind agony
We'll tell you the holy way

Ave Maria love the virgin whore
Got my marching orders for the next war
Engineers without fears inventing hell
In the Middle East peace don't work well

Sitting with a pretty song
Swing in the jungle with King Kong
Everything that can will go wrong
Singing such a pretty song

All In All

She was the beauty queen of heaven's stars
The symphony of Venus touching mars
Down on Earth we walk hand in hand
Love the mystery none can understand

You are the song of the living
Your love is always giving
You are the secret I recall
You are the all in all
You are the all in all

Tomorrow seemed eternally away
Love was the only word I could say
Dreams come true I had one in you
But the morning came with the sky so blue

You are the song of the living
Your love is always giving
You are the secret I recall
You are the all in all
You are the all in all

College and careers carnal desires
Promises forsaken words spoken by liars
Soon the fires were ashes of memory
Did I ever tell you what you meant to me?

You are the song of the living
Your love is always giving
You are the secret I recall
You are the all in all
You are the all in all

True love by rumor never ends
With goodbye it's we'll still be friends
My shattered world of could have been
Losing love by far the greatest sin

You are the song of the living
Your love is always giving
You are the secret I recall
You are the all in all
You are the all in all

American Nightmare

Superstars jamming electric guitars
Losers boozers frequenting bars
The Prince of Peace holds his breath
Speak the Truth than welcome death

Welcome to the American nightmare
You only see if you're aware
If you well to do you don't care
Welcome to the American nightmare

The model is mostly silicone
It ain't her mind men want to bone
Half-naked in the magazine
Society simmers sickly obscene

Welcome to the American nightmare
You only see if you're aware
If you well to do you don't care
Welcome to the American nightmare

And money is the bottom line
God is fine but cash divine
While the poor fight an endless war
Wall Street junkies scream for more

Pilgrim pride founded on genocide
The slave system is Southern pride
Here comes Jesus don't be denied
Every day the Lord is crucified

Welcome to the American nightmare
You only see if you're aware
If you well to do you don't care
Welcome to the American nightmare

His finger rests on the red button
One second and all is nothing
United States standing so tall
Pride always comes before the fall

Welcome to the American nightmare
You only see if you're aware
If you well to do you don't care
Welcome to the American nightmare

An Endless Quest

Sing the blues you got good company
Ocean and sky we were all born free
Welcome to school learn to be the fool
They teach you all save the Golden Rule

Momma loves you you're the best
So strong and brave you passed the test
A folded flag forever you shall rest
Freedom of markets an endless quest

Staring poverty right in the face
God is good I proclaim His great grace
Love alone will save the human race
An empty heart who can take your place?

Momma loves you you're the best
So strong and brave you passed the test
A folded flag forever you shall rest
Freedom of markets an endless quest

They Love you best when you're riding high
To the desert sand sent to kill or die
We're all human each a kindred soul
But greedy men they lust for control

Momma loves you you're the best
So strong and brave you passed the test
A folded flag forever you shall rest
Freedom of markets an endless quest

Black and white the words on the page
A window is open to another age
Angry bombs preach a sermon of rage
Hatred is the world's cruelest cage

Flowers placed on the marble tombstone
Tears of torment she's always alone
He got a medal his child is grown
Every good dog is tossed a bone

Momma loves you you're the best
So strong and brave you passed the test
A folded flag forever you shall rest
Freedom of markets an endless quest

And I Cry

You sat quietly with that funny smile
In your poverty the definition of style
You sneaked past the locks of my heart
You were a genius living was your art

And I cry, and I cry, and I cry
I jump and I never fly
Asking the question why
To live, to love and to die
And I cry, and I cry, and I cry

We took a chance and became friends
Never knowing that love never ends
We were growing soaring in the sky
And I cry, and I cry, and I cry

And I cry, and I cry, and I cry
I jump and I never fly
Asking the question why
To live, to love and to die
And I cry, and I cry, and I cry

I took you and we shared infinity
I swear we touched pure divinity
I held you into the chill of the morn
Something fundamental had been born

And I cry, and I cry, and I cry
I jump and I never fly
Asking the question why
To live, to love and to die
And I cry, and I cry, and I cry

The philosophers invited the poets to a duel
The soldiers were trained in basics cruel
Dreams are not for sleeping dreams are for keeping
And I awoke to find the nightmare of weeping

You could only have died too young
A memory of a melody to be sung
A lesson to carry into tomorrow
A cross of eternal sorrow

Auction Block

Dreams are for those who can sleep
The sky is blue and the ocean deep
Hollywood is polyester gold
To the highest bidder you are sold

Auction block
Selling disco and rock
It'll all for the shock
Auction block

Trevor hangs with his good old dad
For a godless atheist he ain't so bad
While preachers lie about the holocaust
You can never find what was never lost

Auction block
Selling disco and rock
It'll all for the shock
Auction block

Punk singers perform only for the fun
Poly Styrene never reached number one
Pop charts broken hearts smoke a joint
This song is a needle get the point?

Forever pretending
Oh so condescending
You're such a pretty face
Singing Amazing Grace
Sell out your soul
On American Idol

Auction block
Selling disco and rock
It'll all for the shock
Auction block

Let me sell you a packaged protest
Meanwhile we'll tell you what's best
Some other has been as a special guest
Money honey is our endless quest

Auction block /Selling disco and rock
It'll all for the shock/ Auction block

My Broken Cross

We all got dreams it makes us
You and me and even Jesus
It ain't that bad being denied
You coulda been crucified

Carrying my broken cross
Getting ready for the loss
Giving the dice one more toss
Cursing my broken cross

So the money is running low
Syl is ill don't you know?
Flapping my broken wings
I know why the dead bird sings

Carrying my broken cross
Getting ready for the loss
Giving the dice one more toss
Cursing my broken cross

And Marsha plays it real sly
So pleasant in the bigger lie
I am here your distant savior
Oh and yes one last favor

Carrying my broken cross
Getting ready for the loss
Giving the dice one more toss
Cursing my broken cross

This is the part where I show my broken heart
The world is crashing all I got is my art
Looking at the streets in an intimate way
I love the Sioux so the cavalry won't save the day

And in Africa they cry
While in Syria they die
So who am I to complain?
But rain after all is rain

Carrying my broken cross
Getting ready for the loss
Giving the dice one more toss
Cursing my broken cross

By God's Grace

Fighting a war inside my mind
Less ahead and more behind
The maze twists and turns
Overtime everybody learns

Fifty is two weeks away
But it's okay yeah it's okay
Somehow by God's grace I pray
No work and the rent to pay
Somehow by God's grace I pray

So I sit and dream of success
As every move I second guess
One way out of this awful mess
The hand of God, He can bless

Fifty is two weeks away
But it's okay yeah it's okay
Somehow by God's grace I pray
No work and the rent to pay
Somehow by God's grace I pray

Martin's father was from sunny Sicily
A corvette at seventeen was his reality
I had a brilliant mind it ran too fast
I am struggling with the present and past

This ordeal was Martin's band
Gave it up to take Kate's hand
Life never goes how it's planned
Only the chosen few understand

Fifty is two weeks away
But it's okay yeah it's okay
Somehow by God's grace I pray
No work and the rent to pay
Somehow by God's grace I pray

Can't We Try Love For A While

What is wrong that we have sunk so low?
Where are the secrets that we don't know?
We split the atom and our neighbor's our foe
One day the whole thing's going to blow

Can't we try love for a while
It's necessary for survival
Can't we try love for a while
Can't we try love for a while

You hate me without any good reason
And all the puppets lead us to treason
Where brothers are torn apart in war
All so we can feed the insatiable whore

Can't we try love for a while
It's necessary for survival
Can't we try love for a while
Can't we try love for a while

There's a little bird whistling a blues song
Folk singers want to right every wrong
All we need is lyrics and a perfect melody
I'll sing this song until everybody is free

Can't we try love for a while
It's necessary for survival
Can't we try love for a while
Can't we try love for a while

Down in the Chesapeake Bay
They're on their knees but not to pray
As hearts of gold slowly decay
With the system leading the way

I'd put this gun down but I'm afraid
In the mirror I see the demon they made
Hollywood heroes never give up
And there goes the drunk to fill his cup

Can't we try love for a while
It's necessary for survival
Can't we try love for a while
Can't we try love for a while

Come And Join The Resistance

This world is polluted with lies
Where truth is always in disguise
From sea to polluted to sea
We're free to pursue agony

Come and join the resistance
We're trying to make a difference
To improve our existence
Come and join the resistance

Big business well they're number one
They pull the strings and hold the gun
Everybody has their free speech
Until you practice what they teach

Come and join the resistance
We're trying to make a difference
To improve our existence
Come and join the resistance

I see the skies perpetual gray
And no, everything's not okay
We weren't made to live this way
We need to fight for a better day

Come and join the resistance
We're trying to make a difference
To improve our existence
Come and join the resistance

In the wilderness the Baptist cries a righteous call
There is a time that you must give it your all
At the crossroads do you know which way to go?
Peace love and understanding are the lessons to know

They're gunning down our children
Soldiers on foreign shores sharing sin
The bankers they have a master plan
Stand up, stand up and be a man

Come and join the resistance
We're trying to make a difference
To improve our existence
Come and join the resistance

Dementia's Sleep

She was strong the rock of my life
A beautiful woman my lovely wife
Now she is a child with a silent tongue
Living in yesterday forever young

Sylvia lies in dementia's sleep
And I got a promise to keep
Sometimes the words run deep
Other times I can only weep

She used to run looking for her home
On the streets of Montclair she would roam
Calling me in panic on the cellular phone
Weeping and wailing she was all alone

Sylvia lies in dementia's sleep
And I got a promise to keep
Sometimes the words run deep
Other times I can only weep

I can't hold a job she needs constant care
So late in the night I write a sacred prayer
Lord have mercy make my dreams come true
Sylvia and I need a great blessing from you

Sylvia lies in dementia's sleep
And I got a promise to keep
Sometimes the words run deep
Other times I can only weep

Some say life is evil and God is cruel
I won't speak the words of a total fool
I have my faith and this is my test
I won't be perfect but I'll give it my best

Sylvia lies in dementia's sleep
And I got a promise to keep
Sometimes the words run deep
Other times I can only weep

Different Worlds

Saturday night dumpster diving
Teaching the art of surviving
Gray sky threatening rain
What words can I use to explain?

Too much salt on my caviar
Slick chicks hanging at the bar
For a dozen it'll cost a dime
Poverty ain't illegal but it's a crime

When we meet out on the street
Different worlds different worlds
We don't say hello we never greet
Different worlds different worlds
Your victory is my defeat
Different worlds different worlds

Kings in castles with crowns of gold
So goes the story I am told
Raising armies for endless more
Lies and cries we heard before

It's a free nation so the rumor goes
Tell the truth then we become foes
Pull yourself up by the boot strap
You will find that the mind will snap

When we meet out on the street
Different worlds different worlds
We don't say hello we never greet
Different worlds different worlds
Your victory is my defeat
Different worlds different worlds

In Manhattan there are towers that touch the sky
Executives they don't care if you live or die
They have sheets that their profits are shown
Rising numbers is the greatest joy ever known
And in the end it's all a game of pretend
Because by the power of the gun all will bend

I am the one serving the table
You reach my children your fable
To you God is but another tool
And I am but the perfect fool

When we meet out on the street
Different worlds different worlds
We don't say hello we never greet
Different worlds different worlds
Your victory is my defeat
Different worlds different worlds

Dirty Old Man

Wrestling with the dark of the night
Giving in to sin but I fight
Some they come to curse others bless
And my hand sneaks up her silk dress

Dirty old man with a dirty mind
Only pretending to be kind
Leering around to see what he can find
Dirty old man with a dirty mind

Saturday night cruising the avenue
Watch out ladies he's looking for you
Checking out the fresh meat with a drool
Behind the smile something so cruel

Dirty old man with a dirty mind
Only pretending to be kind
Leering around to see what he can find
Dirty old man with a dirty mind

Don't be tempted by papers green
It comes with a price know what I mean
Some things are worse than obscene
You'll be lucky if he's even clean

Dirty old man with a dirty mind
Only pretending to be kind
Leering around to see what he can find
Dirty old man with a dirty mind

What went wrong dirty old man what went wrong?
You call a filthy mind and I got me a filthy song
Sometimes in our weakness we find we are strong
What went wrong dirty old man what went wrong?

So I lay on my bed satisfied
Dreams my darling can't be denied
Come inside and let's take a ride
When I said I love you I lied

Dirty old man with a dirty mind
Only pretending to be kind
Leering around to see what he can find
Dirty old man with a dirty mind

Don't Tell Me

Stumbling fingers strum the guitar
In the back of a noisy bar
Her outfit is not by choice
It makes up for lack of voice

Don't tell me that I can't sing
Who knows what tomorrow will bring
If I wasn't the queen I'd be the king
Don't tell me that I can't sing

Daddy says find a good man
Momma says try another plan
In life you only get one turn
So into hell and let it burn

Don't tell me that I can't sing
Who knows what tomorrow will bring
If I wasn't the queen I'd be king
Don't tell me that I can't sing

Dreams are precious even if they are fantasy
I'm going to make it is my only reality
White lies from guys just trying to make it
I'm going to be a star even if I have to fake it

Tomorrow on the radio
Madison Square Garden show
Late at night out come fears
Truth rains sorrowful tears

Don't tell me that I can't sing
Who knows what tomorrow will bring
If I wasn't the queen I'd be king
Don't tell me that I can't sing

Words are thoughts on paper
Truth you cannot escape her
What is behind this song?
We all need a place to belong

Don't tell me that I can't sing
Who knows what tomorrow will bring
If I wasn't the queen I'd be king
Don't tell me that I can't sing

Dreaming Of What Is To Be

Late at night eyes heavy with sleep
Doing right I've a promise to keep
I made a vow for better or worse
To hold you until that black hearse

Dreaming of what is to be
Staring in the face of reality
The odds are one in infinity
Dreaming of what is to be

So here I am writing this simple song
In fear trying so hard to be strong
My chances are only pure fantasy
Let's dance to the end of the melody

Dreaming of what is to be
Staring in the face of reality
The odds are one in infinity
Dreaming of what is to be

I'll walk you to Jordan's peaceful shore
Till your time on Earth is no more
I will cry with tears bitter and sweet
Cause I'm losing what made me complete

Dreaming of what is to be
Staring in the face of reality
The odds are one in infinity
Dreaming of what is to be

I don't blame God cause he's our friend
You see every beginning it has an end
Still I have to ask the question why
And tears of sorrow tomorrow to cry

Now I'm closing these words down
I have a smile and not a frown
When you hear this on the radio
Everyone will know I loved you so

Dreaming of what is to be
Staring in the face of reality
The odds are one in infinity
Dreaming of what is to be

Dreams Come Real

Sylvia lies sleeping on her bed
With visions floating in her head
But life ain't never been the same
Since the dementia came

Writing is just better than surrender
Fighting I am the great pretender
Dreams come real, it is true
Dreams come real, yes they do
And baby I'm dreaming of you

I can barely see cause of the tears
But I am free to express my fears
There's a million people on the scam
And nobody seems to give a damn

Writing is just better than surrender
Fighting I am the great pretender
Dreams come real, it is true
Dreams come real, yes they do
And baby I'm dreaming of you

Horror stories are for children
And Kasey finds glory in her sin
While Jimmy is in the hospital
And we want life to be wonderful

Writing is just better than surrender
Fighting I am the great pretender
Dreams come real, it is true
Dreams come real, yes they do
And baby I'm dreaming of you

And when I said I love you
Tell me what did you do?
You hung up the telephone
You deserve to be all alone

Writing is just better than surrender
Fighting I am the great pretender
Dreams come real, it is true
Dreams come real, yes they do
And baby I'm dreaming of you

Electric Voodoo

Grunge singer rapping pop songs
In a world where nobody belongs
While the black moon sings the wrong tune
Summer solstice always comes in June

Electric voodoo
Burning from me to you
What did you do?
Electric voodoo

Say there's something about hanging loose
And there's something bout hanging by a noose
And in the end my friend what's the use
Another day just to face the abuse

Electric voodoo
Burning from me to you
What did you do?
Electric voodoo

And it's a dark day Chris Cornell
I'll be hanging with you in hell
We'll roast Henry Kissinger's heart
And discuss the subtleties of art

Electric voodoo
Burning from me to you
What did you do?
Electric voodoo

And damn it what the hell was going on in your brain?
And damn it why couldn't you simply confess the pain?
Now we got legions of losers laughing insane
Contemplating, debating that life is simply vain

Well at least we got what we got
Someday you will simply be forgot
But till then I hold a candle in the wind
As we learn the wages of sin

Electric voodoo
Burning from me to you
What did you do?
Electric voodoo

Every John Needs Their Paul

This is the call for Jerry Paul
You're only an angel until the fall
Brothers forever in room seven
What happened to our happy heaven?

Every John needs their Paul
Someone to give it their all
And Frank's friend he was fat
A merry day in our happy frat

Intoxicated by science and booze
I got an official license to lose
Now I write lyrics never to be sung
What a delight to be clever and young

Every John needs their Paul
Someone to give it their all
And Frank's friend he was fat
A merry day in our happy frat

I checked out of college in pursuit of truth
Manic depression was the lesson of my youth
Can you dig the locked doors and the Thorazine?
We heard it before in welcome to the machine

Well the devil is in the detail
Show your work or you will fail
I lost my mind just to find a heart
I am sorry that we had to part

Every John needs their Paul
Someone to give it their all
And Frank's friend he was fat
A merry day in our happy frat

Fantasy Island

Men will be men and boys will be boys
Pretty little girls bring endless joys
Billionaires can break any kind of law
But hey every system has its flaw

He whispers I love you all in a dream
She shudders wanting to give a scream
Fantasy Island everything is real
Fantasy Island just don't squeal
Fantasy Island you know the deal

Some sweetheart from a broken home
Left an agony to go on the roam
Here baby it's nice and warm inside
Oh come on in its one hell of a ride

He whispers I love you all in a dream
She shudders wanting to give a scream
Fantasy Island everything is real
Fantasy Island just don't squeal
Fantasy Island you know the deal

Do this, do that, just as I say
Smile more and I'll up the pay
When we're done you can shower
But give my money's worth for the hour

It's a laugh and one mighty good time
Only when you're caught is it a crime
But everybody's got madam's cell
God is in heaven Washington is Hell

He whispers I love you all in a dream
She shudders wanting to give a scream
Fantasy Island everything is real
Fantasy Island just don't squeal
Fantasy Island you know the deal

Horror Ball

She likes black as a general rule
Takes the wise makes them a fool
Down on her knees she will please
I really dig this kind of disease

She wants to dance at the Horror Ball
The night is black can you hear it call
She wants to dance at the Horror Ball
Offer what you will she takes it all

She's kinky licking your neck
All of a sudden a little peck
Blood trickles red and warm
She goes crazy as a summer storm

She wants to dance at the Horror Ball
The night is black can you hear it call
She wants to dance at the Horror Ball
Offer what you will she takes it all

Black candles burning in the room
Sweet smell but it's not perfume
She offers chains a kinky game
You'll never be quite the same

She is a demon an evil succubus
You're dreaming making it us
Carnal pleasures in an endless night
It feels so good but there's nothing right

She wants to dance at the Horror Ball
The night is black can you hear it call
She wants to dance at the Horror Ball
Offer what you will she takes it all

In the morning you are all alone
Your head echoes with her moan
A scar on your chest over your heart
She took it all when she did depart

She wants to dance at the Horror Ball
The night is black can you hear it call
She wants to dance at the Horror Ball
Offer what you will she takes it all

I Found Out Who You Are

A cosmic kid always on the run
Searching for some tricks of fun
Doors open with daddy's name
You know how to play the game

It was on Jupitar
In a seedy bar
I found out who you are
I found out who you are

In the mirror the devil does grin
I didn't hesitate to let you in
If you never deal how can you win?
All of the saints are guilty of sin

It was on Jupitar
In a seedy bar
I found out who you are
I found out who you are

I see the body beyond the face
Redefining amazing grace
I said let's get out of this place
And look around for Lady Lace

The affairs of the billionaires who cares
She's down on her knees with empty prayers
They say reality is mostly empty space
I am the high card I am the eternal ace

It was on Jupitar
In a seedy bar
I found out who you are
I found out who you are

In the mourning head aching
Cursing scorning no faking
I forgot what I did last night
Sure it was one hell of a fight

It was on Jupitar
In a seedy bar
I found out who you are
I found out who you are

I Love You

With every passing fraction of time
I contemplate the greater rhyme
I fantasize creating the divine
Some perfection I can call mine

I want to say I love you
Just to get it out
Just so there's no doubt
I want you to know
I love you

Don't you know that I'm frail and fragile
That something timid lurks behind the smile
It takes all I have just to rise in the morn
Conflicting voices offer no choices but scorn

I want to say I love you
Just to get it out
Just so there's no doubt
I want you to know
I love you

Life is not a continuous celebration
It's a lesson of love with a destination
To forget the bitterness and selfish greed
To live to give to others who are in need

I want to say I love you
Just to get it out
Just so there's no doubt
I want you to know
I love you

Fools from high school who liked to break the rules
Create an atmosphere of fear the cruelest of cruels
Live and let live forget the past always forgive
Here is the part when I depart and simply adlib

So here I offer you my very best
Let grace and mercy finish the rest
Life is an often-futile quest
In the end my friend I request
That you come down to the show
Because I have something to let go

I Never Did Graduate

A single jump to the story of glory
The whole world bows down before me
I have no wings but I am sure to fly
Lay down the cards for the answer why

Freud destroyed psychology
See the prostitute salute biology
In college I majored in hate
But I never did graduate

Lyrics are written not to make sense
A wandering whimsical defense
What are we to do Charlie is dead?
And Grace Slick is feeding her head

Freud destroyed psychology
See the prostitute salute biology
In college I majored in hate
But I never did graduate

Sylvia is sleeping happy in a dream
And I can't think beyond a scream
While Jesus is hanging on his cross
Makes it seem small my petty loss

Freud destroyed psychology
See the prostitute salute biology
In college I majored in hate
But I never did graduate

In engineering school they have a single rule
If you're to design bombs you need to be cruel
The bigger the blast well the longer you'll last
You can change tomorrow but never the past

God why is there so much pain
So much evil but yet you refrain
Am I on my knees praying in vain?
It hurts when the world is so insane

Freud destroyed psychology
See the prostitute salute biology
In college I majored in hate
But I never did graduate

In Vain

In the hood you can't shake the heat
Its money for rent or for food to eat
While pale face crosses the tracks
To by some weed from the blacks

These words are written in vain
They labeled me insane
Taking a ride on the crazy train
These words are written in vain

I came down to knock on your door
With a message of love so pure
Mainline the divine with grace
All the while with a smile on my face

These words are written in vain
They labeled me insane
Taking a ride on the crazy train
These words are written in vain

Well back in the land of middle class
They aren't willing to give you a pass
Lights in the mirror flashing red and blue
We got a suspect he's black like you

Politicians they're teaming up with Uncle Tom
For God country and don't forget good old mom
Go and kill the yellow man so we can safely steal
Sign on the line I will cheat on the deal

These words are written in vain
They labeled me insane
Taking a ride on the crazy train
These words are written in vain

Wall Street junkies with eyes of hate
Whatever the time the answer is wait
Instead all that is said is idle debate
White chalk talks on the black slate

These words are written in vain
They labeled me insane
Taking a ride on the crazy train
These words are written in vain

Jenny

She was pretty at least they said so
And she could sing but not let go
She knew the chords but couldn't pluck
While her hot body brought her luck

Jenny, Jenny, where have you gone?
Jenny, Jenny, what have you done?
Sacrificed your youth
For a hard lesson in the truth
Jenny, Jenny, your all alone
Jenny, Jenny, come on home

At seventeen she left to chase a dream
Early in the morning she split the scene
As the sun rose she was on the road
A backpack and guitar her only load

Jenny, Jenny, where have you gone?
Jenny, Jenny, what have you done?
Sacrificed your youth
For a hard lesson in the truth
Jenny, Jenny, your all alone
Jenny, Jenny, come on home

Up to New York City to become a star
Found a job waitressing in a bar
Bills came and the rent was overdue
Oh Jenny, Jenny what you gonna do?

Jenny, Jenny, where have you gone?
Jenny, Jenny, what have you done?
Sacrificed your youth
For a hard lesson in the truth
Jenny, Jenny, your all alone
Jenny, Jenny, come on home

And Jenny baby you're just a sad song
A sad lesson in everything that is wrong
And Jenny if you were real I'd say
Get out your guitar and play, play, play

Jenny, Jenny, where have you gone? / Jenny, Jenny, what have you done?
Sacrificed your youth / For a hard lesson in the truth
Jenny, Jenny, your all alone / Jenny, Jenny, come on home

J J

You always were a beautiful boy
Strumming your guitar with joy
Magical music in your hand
Jamming with your rock and roll band

J J won't you play for me
Outside is cloudy and gray
JJ won't you play for me
And make life a sunny day

You live life once so chase your dreams
Fame and fortune ain't what it seems
When you get lost in hurry and worry
A simple tune has the love to cure me

J J won't you play for me
Outside is cloudy and gray
JJ won't you play for me
And make life a sunny day

Wine woman and song
How can you go wrong?
You wake up some place far
Wondering who you are

Thousands of people swinging slow
You never lose the thrill of the show
Something to be said of on the go
But there more to life we all know

J J won't you play for me
Outside is cloudy and gray
JJ won't you play for me
And make life a sunny day

King Of The Hill

Hands of stone heart of gold
Now but a legend told
Heroes rise heroes fall
Can you answer the call?

One two three in God we trust
Fight and kill we always will
Love has been exchanged for lust
Trying to be king of the hill

To be a man you must fight
Even though it ain't right
Sing the song out of tune
Take a ride to the moon

One two three in God we trust
Fight and kill we always will
Love has been exchanged for lust
Trying to be king of the hill

The bookies let the green papers pass
The faithful bow their knees in mass
Take a dive but do it with some class
Whitman wrote a book Leaves of Grass

Number one be on top
The mad dance does not stop
The truth exchanged for lies
See sorrow as truth dies

One two three in God we trust
Fight and kill we always will
Love has been exchanged for lust
Trying to be king of the hill

Lady Butterfly

Smoking cigarettes whistling at the boys
She's a Fender guitar strumming noise
A virtuoso in the art of having fun
She's so old and life has just begun

They call her lady butterfly
Ask any guy who gave a try
We always ask her to stay
And gone she flutters away
Please don't cry, lady butterfly

School is a bore the teachers seek control
Life is the lyrics of old rock and roll
Taking a trip to the edge of the universe
If life ain't a blessing than life is a curse

They call her lady butterfly
Ask any guy who gave a try
We always ask her to stay
And gone she flutters away
Please don't cry, lady butterfly

Life is but a flower
Lust holds great power
Now is the only hour
Come and devour

A hunger for love in any form
Unique in God's eye she won't conform
Wise old men devour with their eyes
Preaching the truth while practicing lies

They call her lady butterfly
Ask any guy who gave a try
We always ask her to stay
And gone she flutters away
Please don't cry, lady butterfly

Life Is Only A Game

Here I go asking you for a dance
Romance the chance of circumstance
Let me tell the band what song to play
Ain't got no gold it's my soul to pay

They say life is only a game
Win or lose it's all the same
I cry and ask why the shame
They say life is only a game

Jet fighters flying by at mach three
Dealing doses of double agony
Sultans with gold plated toilet seats
Homeless veterans starve on our streets

They say life is only a game
Win or lose it's all the same
I cry and ask why the shame
They say life is only a game

So long ago my heart still broken
So many words will be unspoken
But I need some lyrics for the song
So I will reminisce on the wrong

They say life is only a game
Win or lose it's all the same
I cry and ask why the shame
They say life is only a game

Love and war always demanding more
See the beast hanging with Babylon the Whore
I always said that you looked your best in red
Armageddon is really gonna knock 'em dead

See the cardboard sign will work for food
He was our best but now he is no good
Thanks for your leg and arm good sir
These days empty praise is all we offer

They say life is only a game
Win or lose it's all the same
I cry and ask why the shame
They say life is only a game

Lost My Way

Bullies cruising down the hall
Girls smoke cigarettes by the wall
Not sure if my parents are gonna split
Really can't take much more of it

Back in the day
I had lost my way
Nothing left to say
I had lost my way

Teachers struggle to keep control
Christians got no love in their soul
Football heads boast and brag
They make me salute the flag

Back in the day
I had lost my way
Nothing left to say
I had lost my way

Learning facts to spit out on a test
Killing and hatred seems we're the best
Without a doubt number one
And me I never have any fun

Back in the day
I had lost my way
Nothing left to say
I had lost my way

Philosophy is the art of thinking things new
High school is for a fool with one point of view
They subjugate and teach you to bow to the state
The truth dear youth is you never graduate

And rock and roll was pure
Down at the old record store
Ten dollars for a plastic disc
Throw the dice and take a risk

Back in the day
I had lost my way
Nothing left to say
I had lost my way

Love Is The Way

Hand in hand walking in the park
Sneaking a kiss while in the dark
Long conversations on the phone
Thinking of him when all alone

Love is the way to live
You take and you give
Forever that is what I say
Day after day after day
Love is the way

Special moment dressed all in white
Smiling faces of endless delight
Rings swapped the vows are made
The memories they never fade

Love is the way to live
You take and you give
Forever that is what I say
Day after day after day
Love is the way

Life is a journey and sometimes we crash and burn
Always a lesson seek out what you must learn
Cancer like a demon rages a radical turn
Now the trial of survival is the sole concern

Holding hands saying goodbye
Being strong trying not to cry
The reality of two being one
And then a new journey begun

Love is the way to live
You take and you give
Forever that is what I say
Day after day after day
Love is the way

For the children you must be strong
Asking God, what went wrong?
Sometimes the silence is pain
Look for sunshine after rain
Allow me to fully explain
Love is never in vain

Love To Borrow (John Denver's Song)

First of all we shared our name
A man who lived in fables
And they said we looked the same
When I worked bussing tables

Sing me a song of tomorrow
I have some love to borrow
When you died I cried in sorrow
I have some love to borrow

And I remember Colorado
I cannot dare speak a lie
The time I came to know
A Rocky Mountain high

Sing me a song of tomorrow
I have some love to borrow
When you died I cried in sorrow
I have some love to borrow

And West Virginia was truth
Cause in heaven we're all kind
You touched me as a youth
So much to seek and find

Sing me a song of tomorrow
I have some love to borrow
When you died I cried in sorrow
I have some love to borrow

You died far too young
John Denver a man of vision
Your songs are still sung
In the end love will win

Sing me a song of tomorrow
I have some love to borrow
When you died I cried in sorrow
I have some love to borrow

Luck is a Lady

When dreams don't come true
What can you do?
When the song comes to an end
And you cannot pretend

Luck, they say is a lady
Cold hearted and cruel
Luck, they say is a lady
And I am the perfect fool

When you gave it your all
Only to fall
They're ringing the final bell
No more stories to tell

Luck, they say is a lady
Cold hearted and cruel
Luck, they say is a lady
And I am the perfect fool

Architects and engineers
Have mathematical fears
Cold hearted is the art of science
On logic is steadfast reliance
In the end it's all about the green
I think you know what I mean

Inside it's all wrong
My final song
Only one can win the prize
Though everybody tries

Luck, they say is a lady
Cold hearted and cruel
Luck, they say is a lady
And I am the perfect fool

Meltdown

The bass and the drum became one
She laughed I ain't having fun
I am one with the universe
But alas it's only for the worse

Meltdown
From smile to frown
Molten iron flows
Anger grows
Downtown uptown
Meltdown

A friend is somebody you can trust
You and I baby its true lust
In and out we're conquering doubt
I know you like it please don't shout

Meltdown
From smile to frown
Molten iron flows
Anger grows
Downtown uptown
Meltdown

Well we just passed for a night
And I asked to hold you tight
I was so tricky so clever
And made something forever

Meltdown
From smile to frown
Molten iron flows
Anger grows
Downtown uptown
Meltdown

I have a reputation that I need to maintain
Hey life is nothing without a little pain
Little bastard he's got his father's eyes
Take a rest the DNA test it never lies

Love is from a point of view
Patrick is the son you never knew
He had a one room apartment
And a life full of torment

Meltdown
From smile to frown
Molten iron flows
Anger grows
Downtown uptown
Meltdown

Money And More

Boy band hit Disney Land with dream in hand
Synthetic sounds do you understand?
Give me your confidence have no doubt
I build you into the perfect sell out

Money, money, and more
See pop idols in the store
A step above a whore
Money, money and more

I got a magic formula to give a try
If you can't make it alive just die
Sign your name on the bottom line
Sell me your soul I'll make you mine

Money, money, and more
See pop idols in the store
A step above a whore
Money, money and more

Stand like this walk like that
Eat some more don't get fat
Thirty minutes make it go
Mirrors make the perfect show

And poets search the depths of their heart
Words written that can never depart
A hundred years a flash in the pan
Boy band forever never a real man

Music Is What We Are

It's the same song only the lyrics change
I'm saying I'm wrong is that strange?
I think Pink signed the line with ink
Let's cut out of here when I wink

Singing underage in bars
Dreaming of being stars
You sing I play guitar
Music is what we are

Frat boys make noise but are empty air
Its thirty years and I really don't care
All you are is ten seconds on the radio
Why don't you come down to the show?

Singing underage in bars
Dreaming of being stars
You sing I play guitar
Music is what we are

Singing bringing a tingling back to my heart
I was so clever by why did we ever part?
I took the path the others shunned to take
I embraced love and it made my heart break

Songs in the institution
Lyrics longing for revolution
I offer you my very soul
On the altar of rock and roll

Singing underage in bars
Dreaming of being stars
You sing I play guitar
Music is what we are

My Lovecraft

From digital to analog
The ritual of the fog
She's praying to the demon
Smiling while she's dreamin'

I'm practicing my Lovecraft
Working on a wonderful spell
Several steps below hell
I'm practicing my Lovecraft

There's a mountain of doom
Full of the darkest gloom
Witches and ghosts cry
All of it in the mind's eye

I'm practicing my Lovecraft
Working on a wonderful spell
Several steps below hell
I'm practicing my Lovecraft

He sure was one creepy dude
Rather rough rather rude
But we love him all the same
A give him proper fame

So here I go running after salvation
A twisting turning road to damnation
The sun is red and the moon is dead
Can you remember the words I said?

I'm practicing my Lovecraft
Working on a wonderful spell
Several steps below hell
I'm practicing my Lovecraft

Now Is Not Your Time

There's a soul to save and a song to sing
We got love and that's everything
Now if only I could find food to eat
And get myself off of the street

Now is not your time
But I enjoyed your rhyme
Hey failing ain't a crime
Now is not your time

Damien came seeking some fame
Played the fool in the cheater's game
But the cold-hearted answer was the same
Losing earns you a ticket to shame

Now is not your time
But I enjoyed your rhyme
Hey failing ain't a crime
Now is not your time

Sleeping on the subway through the night
Hey somebody say this ain't right
Billion-dollar jet bombers to destroy
But don't ask me for a dime lazy boy

Now is not your time
But I enjoyed your rhyme
Hey failing ain't a crime
Now is not your time

Chasing dreams through midnight screams
Fame is a game life ain't what it seams
Down in India they bow to the sacred cow
Maybe tomorrow but today I say not now

What does it matter old and gray?
Everybody had some dues to pay
Except you couldn't afford the toll
All you did kid was sell your soul

Now is not your time
But I enjoyed your rhyme
Hey failing ain't a crime
Now is not your time

Olivia

Hi Olivia this is a song for you
I wish you skies forever blue
But I know, just know, one day
That they're going to turn gray
For in every life a little rain
For in every life a little pain

But don't you get mad
And don't you get sad
Try your best to be glad
There's only one life to be had

Hi Olivia you're going to grow old
Truth and lies you will be told
So from you to me this is a prayer
A little something to know I care
When your world is lost in confusion
See the love past the illusion

But don't you get mad
And don't you get sad
Try your best to be glad
There's only one life to be had

Hi Olivia the future is at hand
One day I'm sure you'll understand
You'll have children of your own
As you reap what you have sown
Allow me a moment to explain
Giving love is never in vain

But don't you get mad
And don't you get sad
Try your best to be glad
There's only one life to be had

Our Liberty

She sailed the high seas proud as could be
The good old U.S.S. liberty
She was a ship that was built for war
But now she sits on the Ocean's floor

Oh remember me remember me
Cries the good old Liberty
Our ally was our enemy
Cries the good old Liberty
Oh remember me remember me

Truth is something in high debate
We got leaders calling love hate
But we will fight all tyranny
And raise up the good old Liberty

Oh remember me remember me
Cries the good old Liberty
Our ally was our enemy
Cries the good old Liberty
Oh remember me remember me

Evil is the wickedest game
And Israel is clearly to blame
The American flag waved high
To be seen from miles in the sky

Oh remember me remember me
Cries the good old Liberty
Our ally was our enemy
Cries the good old Liberty
Oh remember me remember me

Well the pilot checked his command
It's American don't you understand
Orders came and there's no turning back
The Mirage fired in brutal attack

Oh remember me remember me
Cries the good old Liberty
Our ally was our enemy
Cries the good old Liberty
Oh remember me remember me

They tried to ignore the thirty-four
We will not be silent any more
We shall cry out so all can see
The truth of the gold old Liberty

Oh remember me remember me
Cries the good old Liberty
Our ally was our enemy
Cries the good old Liberty
Oh remember me remember me

Jan

Jan she sure can complain
She got the thunder she got the rain
Every day is just dark skies
Will be till the day she dies

Jan well she is Jan
Like God is the great I Am
She lies I don't give a damn
Jan well she is Jan

A sixties child with no flower
A sweet lemon now only sour
Every coin it has two sides
Behind the hatred Jan hides

Jan well she is Jan
Like God is the great I Am
She lies I don't give a damn
Jan well she is Jan

It ain't that Jan ain't nice
She's cut from a delicious slice
Time has come pay the price
They all hate me is her advice

And somewhere you just gotta free your mind
And sometime you just gotta leave the past behind
I know there's wrong there's some in this song
But life is for the beautiful and not the strong

Jan well she is Jan
Like God is the great I Am
She lies I don't give a damn
Jan well she is Jan

Race isn't something you run
And evil is a spell to be spun
And Jan can't be number one
Unless of course we shall overcome

Jan well she is Jan
Like God is the great I Am
She lies I don't give a damn
Jan well she is Jan

Razor's Blade

What can I use in the place of a bass?
How can I save the human race?
I remember when I couldn't tie my shoe
What in the world am I going to do?

Rock and roll is a razor's blade
Got good women to get laid
The executives are all overpaid
Rock and roll is a razor's blade

Major from Harlem is a friend of mine
He's mixing the Stones he's big time
Major how in the world do you stay sane?
Keeping myself away from the cocaine

Rock and roll is a razor's blade
Got good women to get laid
The executives are all overpaid
Rock and roll is a razor's blade

Please check your ego in at the door
Your groupie is nothing but a whore
I heard your story and it's a bore
But you can sing baby that's for sure

Rock and roll is a razor's blade
Got good women to get laid
The executives are all overpaid
Rock and roll is a razor's blade

I subscribe to the philosophy of Jesus Christ
Learn from Adam don't fuck up paradise
The snake is imagery Eve she was well fed
Grace Slick always told us to feed our head

The charts are cruel and the critics fierce
Don't bend over swords they pierce
Donovan lives in the shadow of Dylan
Pop stars that can't play guitars make a killin'

Rock and roll is a razor's blade
Got good women to get laid
The executives are all overpaid
Rock and roll is a razor's blade

Revelation Blues

I want you to know that they called me crazy
I want you to know that they called me lazy
While it didn't really phase me
Deep down it certainly did amaze me

Revelation blues
Preaching the good news
Paying my dues
Revelation blues

And you are reading this in some future time
While I write this I haven't done the crime
Instead in my head tomorrow is just this rhyme
If I wasn't cryptic they would call me sublime

Revelation blues
Preaching the good news
Paying my dues
Revelation blues

Hey Jesus they really like to mock your name
And can you really cast them any blame?
As evangelicals preach mammon and hate
And a nuclear attack is the common debate

Revelation blues
Preaching the good news
Paying my dues
Revelation blues

Come here I offer all to share
Cause words alone show no care
You are in my thoughts and prayer
The language of the nightmare

I am weary my eyes teary and my spirit broke
They are laughing but I didn't hear the joke
Wall Street executives keeping their hands clean
Making love into something pornographically obscene

Revelation blues
Preaching the good news
Paying my dues
Revelation blues

Rock And Roll Memory

I can't do those fancy moves no more
Ain't no sensation on the dance floor
But music is still rocking my core
Rock and roll opened up the door

Rock and roll memory
You still loved me
We were young and free
Rock and roll memory

In my youth truth was the radio
High as the sky we went to show
Lurking between heaven and hell
Was a paradise we knew so well

Rock and roll memory
You still loved me
We were young and free
Rock and roll memory

Years came and the world changed
Up and down it was rearranged
Now I can laugh in the mirror
Love is the lesson life can't get clearer

Rock and roll memory
You still loved me
We were young and free
Rock and roll memory

On the oldies station my favorite band
In surrender I look to lend a hand
Believe it or not I do understand
It's just that you're beyond my command

And the angels and the demons did double time
Missing in action is the world's greatest crime
Never forget that you are worthy of this place
And when you fall recall the power of grace

Rock and roll memory
You still loved me
We were young and free
Rock and roll memory

Sailing On

Hello I was just sailing on by
There is wind blowing on high
Maybe you'd like to take a ride
And feel the thrill of the tide

I'm sailing on, sailing on
Now that you are gone
Lady Ocean I lean upon
I'm sailing on, sailing on

We can sail to the ocean's end
You don't love me but I pretend
Still in the cold starry night
Could I hold you close and tight?

I'm sailing on, sailing on
Now that you are gone
Lady Ocean I lean upon
I'm sailing on, sailing on

There is a point of no return
In heartbreak a lesson to learn
Still the sun rises every day
While dolphins laugh and play

I'm sailing on, sailing on
Now that you are gone
Lady Ocean I lean upon
I'm sailing on, sailing on

One day I'll sail to tomorrow
Gone will be all my sorrow
I'll reach Heaven's golden shore
And won't have trouble any more

I'm sailing on, sailing on
Now that you are gone
Lady Ocean I lean upon
I'm sailing on, sailing on

Scarecrow

I was chasing the angels of the night
Cause dreaming is my great delight
Past the banker down the rabbit hole
I traded my heart for a simple soul

The scarecrow hangs on the cross
His gain well it was my loss
And Kasey insists she's the boss
The scarecrow hangs on the cross

I was meditating upon a lie
The unending saga of Anne Mc Fry
While holy men kill with a Holy book
And nobody bothers to take a look

The scarecrow hangs on the cross
His gain well it was my loss
And Kasey insists she's the boss
The scarecrow hangs on the cross

I made a deal with the devil
He said he was on the level
I looked at the papers with a squint
It's all great never mind the fine print

Casey joined motivated by a lie
And Cindy every day is a day to die
While the philosophers don't answer why
Listen and you can hear the scarecrow cry

The scarecrow hangs on the cross
His gain well it was my loss
And Kasey insists she's the boss
The scarecrow hangs on the cross

Searching

I remember when we would smoke the night away
We needed something to help us forget the day
In the institute bowing to the greater mind
Clearly in all those theories there was nothing to find

Michael and me confused
Feeling like we were being used
Sometimes reaching for the stars
You don't realize the bars
We were searching for who we are

When seeing Bruch Springsteen was just a dream
Revolution is the solution or so it does seem
Don't feel bad for me Michael at least I am free
Behind bars showing my scars writing poetry

Michael and me confused
Feeling like we were being used
Sometimes reaching for the stars
You don't realize the bars
We were searching for who we are

You see I never surrendered I kept hold of my heart
I learned that loving others is the greatest art
Take my advice sacrifice is the price of paradise
And when Bruce turns this song loose it will be nice

Michael and me confused
Feeling like we were being used
Sometimes reaching for the stars
You don't realize the bars
We were searching for who we are

I knew Michelle well she surrendered heaven for hell
Winners and losers stoners and boozers who can tell
I don't want to return but I will learn the lessons of youth
Cause despite my flaws I know unjust laws from the truth

Michael and me confused
Feeling like we were being used
Sometimes reaching for the stars
You don't realize the bars
We were searching for who we are

Since You Said Goodbye

I'm standing in a world without you
And crying is all I can do
But who can question God's hand
And Love's mystery understand

Since you said goodbye
The truth turned to a lie
And the only question is why
Since you said goodbye

Your ship sank in the deep blue sea
Leaving me on land so lonely
You must be singing in heaven's choir
And I shedding tears of fire

Since you said goodbye
The truth turned to a lie
And the only question is why
Since you said goodbye

I'll never forget your sweet smile
Your grace and elegant style
You were strong, strong as could be
Now Love's slave has been set free

Since you said goodbye
The truth turned to a lie
And the only question is why
Since you said goodbye

Time passes but nothing does change
And the entire world I would exchange
For an hour of holding you tight
And kissing you through the night

Since you said goodbye
The truth turned to a lie
And the only question is why
Since you said goodbye

I am a song without a melody
I am knight missing my lady
And when I walk through tomorrow's door
I'll be holding you on heaven's shore

Sing With Me

I'm looking for a voice for my song
Someone to rejoice to help me be strong
Do you like to stay up late in the night?
Do you pray for a world that is right?

So sing with me
Until we're all free
In perfect harmony
Sing with me

History is being written into lies
The truth is drowned out in angry cries
There is wisdom in the chords of the guitar
What we think makes us what we are

So sing with me
Until we're all free
In perfect harmony
Sing with me

It's simple idea, no more war
What are we even fighting for
Same old story as before
It's a simple idea, no more war

To escape the hood the recruiter smiles
Here's your ticket from all your trials
Just sign with your blood on the line
Trust me sucker all will be just fine

So sing with me
Until we're all free
In perfect harmony
Sing with me

There is strength in being in the right
There is pain in fleeing from a fight
But the Lord said turn the other cheek
But they mock me and rock me when I speak

So sing with me
Until we're all free
In perfect harmony
Sing with me

Song Of Bliss

I want to say I love you
I really do
I want to say I care
Like you're my prayer
On a cold lonely night
When nothing is right

This is a song of bliss
To celebrate our kiss
Saying more, more of this
This is a song of bliss

I want to say I love you
And my love is true
I want to draw you near
Just to feel you're here
To rest safe in your arms
Far from all life's harms

This is a song of bliss
To celebrate our kiss
Saying more, more of this
This is a song of bliss

I met you in another world we were much younger
I kissed you and missed you I had such a hunger
Time came and with great shame I lost my way
But don't depart my dear heart we'll have our day

I want to say I love you
Ain't nothing I wouldn't do
I want to say I love you
I really do
I want to say I love you
And my love is true

This is a song of bliss
To celebrate our kiss
Saying more, more of this
This is a song of bliss

So Sorry

Dream busters don't let the balloon fly
Let go and give love a try
Out comes the needle to bust
In the middle of the night only lust

Singers fighting down in Nashville
Sharpening guitar strings for the kill
You'll never make it declares Neal
So sorry for just being real

God in heaven He's got a plan
Boy meets girl woman loves man
In the end all that matters is why
For love I live and for love I die

Singers fighting down in Nashville
Sharpening guitar strings for the kill
You'll never make it declares Neal
So sorry for just being real

And little men with little minds what do they find
They sail into the ocean but can't leave the shore behind
And little men with little minds are truly blind
Once I was lost but I found comfort in words kind

I ain't on a quest of endless greed
Sylvia is calling out in need
Faith without deeds is death
And I'll fight to my last breath

Singers fighting down in Nashville
Sharpening guitar strings for the kill
You'll never make it declares Neal
So sorry for just being real

Sweetheart

For every dream for every fantasy
For everybody reaching for eternity
Fortune and fame is a hard game
But I love you all the same

I met you in the go-go bar
You said "I'm gonna be a star"
Sweetheart you already are
Sweet heart you already are

Well the bass player got real drunk
And the sound system just stunk
While we played rage on the stage
And between acts I turned a page

We fell in love out on the road
We shared the burdens of the load
Sweetheart we have just begun
Sweetheart you're number one

You are the life behind this song
You are the right that fixes the wrong
I love you is all that I can say
I love you through night and day

Playing the part of two old people
Don't search for God under the steeple
There's more truth in Woody's song
Then all the churches preaching wrong

Philosophy is thinking too hard
With you I can let down my guard
Sweetheart your closer than me
Sweetheart you make me free

And here we go; I just have to let you know
I'm taking you home after the show
Cause your just too fine to let go
I wanna hold you when the bombs blow

Looking forward to turning gray
When we say remember the day
Sweetheart you make me believe
Sweetheart please never leave

Sylvia's Song

I can't whisper words in your ear
You're here but you ain't here
The rock I used to lean upon
You're close but you're gone

This is Sylvia's song
Where life went wrong
Victory is for the strong
This is Sylvia's song

Well life it twists and turns
Through suffering one learns
We promised better or worse
Love was the eternal source

This is Sylvia's song
Where life went wrong
Victory is for the strong
This is Sylvia's song

Laughing in the Caribbean sun
Grenada was a life time of fun
Lurking in the shadows a disease
Cut you down right to your knees

Heaven now waits for you
Nothing left I can do
Except to pray and pray
Till God takes you away

This is Sylvia's song
Where life went wrong
Victory is for the strong
This is Sylvia's song

Alone writing with tears
Facing the worst of fears
Here's to a happy end
Here's to let's pretend

This is Sylvia's song
Where life went wrong
Victory is for the strong
This is Sylvia's song

The End Of The Fight

Trouble was the meal of your day
On your knees to work and pray
But your smile it never did fade
Though you were highly underpaid

I was a seeker of righteousness
Insane in the bosom of God's bliss
There must be more to life than this
And then I felt your loving kiss

I never let go of your sweet hand
Until the Lord took your light
I never let go of your sweet hand
Till the end of the fight

Survival is a common story
All to the Lord praise and glory
Love is a word meaning action
Love is the greatest satisfaction

The winds blew in the tempest
All the strong go through the test
And with you by my side near
I felt secure without a hint of fear

I never let go of your sweet hand
Until the Lord took your light
I never let go of your sweet hand
Till the end of the fight

Some sweet voice should sing this song
With a beauty grand and strong
To give you the honor and praise
For choosing the narrowest of ways

When I was down you held me tight
When I suffered you made it right
So this is my goodbye dear friend
This is the celebration of the end

I never let go of your sweet hand
Until the Lord took your light
I never let go of your sweet hand
Till the end of the fight

The Greatest Story Ever Told

Sing a song to fill the day
Show me the hidden way
Teach me how to be kind
Open the eyes of the blind

The greatest story ever told
More precious than silver and gold
A glory to behold
The greatest story ever told

I walked the Damascus Road
Carrying a heavy load
The sun burst through the skies
And I saw beyond the lies

The greatest story ever told
More precious than silver and gold
A glory to behold
The greatest story ever told

Love is the lesson to learn
To feel the fire and not burn
To surrender only to gain
To live a life that isn't vain

The greatest story ever told
More precious than silver and gold
A glory to behold
The greatest story ever told

The Love You've Never Known

Say sweetheart please don't depart
I've got an aching in my heart
Between the cocaine and the pain
I'd have to say life is in vain

Lady Lace take your place by my throne
I promise I won't leave you alone
I'll give you the love you've never known
I'll give you the love you've never known

You're beautiful in the morning light
And who can discern wrong from right
All I know is darkness comes from night
Hold me darling just hold me tight

Lady Lace take your place by my throne
I promise I won't leave you alone
I'll give you the love you've never known
I'll give you the love you've never known

Life is a battle life is a war
Rattle the cages that make you a whore
Fill the belly but you got the hunger
Hey Lady Lace we ain't getting younger

Lady Lace take your place by my throne
I promise I won't leave you alone
I'll give you the love you've never known
I'll give you the love you've never known

Let's pretend and fairy tales
In the end God fails
Let's pretend and fairy tales
In the end Love prevails

I believe we can leave and be free
You and I we'll make it happy we
I am certain this is our destiny
All you gotta do is just agree

Lady Lace take your place by my throne
I promise I won't leave you alone
I'll give you the love you've never known
I'll give you the love you've never known

The Perfect Plan

The way she moves excites my bone
Making love on the telephone
Hear me cry come hear me moan
At least I ain't all alone

Love isn't for losers
Only arrogant users
I got the perfect scam
I got the perfect plan

Lying is an art you explain
Come beautiful snort some cocaine
Never had sex when I was sober
Don't worry it's already over

Love isn't for losers
Only arrogant users
I got the perfect scam
I got the perfect plan

I think of room eight and a half
Jokers and smokers make me laugh
But hell look at where I ended up
On the street with a beggar's cup

Love isn't for losers
Only arrogant users
I got the perfect scam
I got the perfect plan

I remember when God came calling
I was so low but still I was falling
Torn between dream and fantasy
Love was only a word to me

Love is something divine
A gift so mighty fine
I got the Son of Man
I got the perfect plan

Tight Dress

Selling the songs on the internet
Place down the dollar for the bet
I'm the best above the rest
Peace and love an endless quest

See my tight dress tight dress
My lipstick red my hair a mess
Soon you won't have to guess
I'll be taking off this tight dress

Sex is snorted imported pure
In the mourning you'll want more
But watch out there ain't no cure
I'm a singer and a sweet whore

See my tight dress tight dress
My lipstick red my hair a mess
Soon you won't have to guess
I'll be taking off this tight dress

Shake it make it break it so cool
Folly is a dolly and I'm a fool
The melody is magic without end
Forever and a night my friend

See my tight dress tight dress
My lipstick red my hair a mess
Soon you won't have to guess
I'll be taking off this tight dress

See the perfect machine oiled and greased
All my thinking has finally been released
Up and down round and round chase the buck
One thing for sure I'll give a good luck

Close your eyes dream through the day
For every blessing a price to pay
Besides I don't want to be alone
You're the best stranger I've known

See my tight dress tight dress
My lipstick red my hair a mess
Soon you won't have to guess
I'll be taking off this tight dress

Toss The Dog A Bone

Workers walking home from the train
Sky is turning gray maybe rain
Child crying parents try to explain
What is the answer to endless pain?

Toss the dog a bone
Maybe with a morsel of meat
Isn't that a treat?
Who cares if they beg or moan?
Toss the dog a bone

He was a genius of the highest degree
Destroyed by the notion of superiority
Manipulated by what he hated
But it paid well that's not debated

Toss the dog a bone
Maybe with a morsel of meat
Isn't that a treat?
Who cares if they beg or moan?
Toss the dog a bone

All the best jobs are protected
And every letter is doubly inspected
While virgins try to write the wrong
That's why you'll never hear this song

Toss the dog a bone
Maybe with a morsel of meat
Isn't that a treat?
Who cares if they beg or moan?
Toss the dog a bone

Gentrification is mighty white
We got a volunteer army to fight
Poverty gives a taste of hunger
And God knows I ain't getting younger

Toss the dog a bone
Maybe with a morsel of meat
Isn't that a treat?
Who cares if they beg or moan?
Toss the dog a bone

True Desire

A third-rate band playing in a four-star bar
You were eyeing the man playing guitar
I bought you a drink vodka and rum
You were looking so good I had to have some

A lonely night on the town
Until you came around
An angel with a burning fire
My hearts true desire

Well when you got up and took my hand to dance
I thought to myself what a wonderful circumstance
Between the booze and the sweet melody
In your arms swayed by your charms I was free

A lonely night on the town
Until you came around
An angel with a burning fire
My hearts true desire

The room was turning and my soul burning
A lesson in love I needed some more learning
Lust is a bust a mocking replica of love
It ain't right day and night you're all I think of

A lonely night on the town
Until you came around
An angel with a burning fire
My hearts true desire

I can still smell you perfume
I can still see the room
But when all went black
I can never go back

The curtain descends but the drama never ends
We parted as lovers but we were never friends
Haunted taunted I was willing and able
Hollywood ain't no good just a fable

A lonely night on the town
Until you came around
An angel with a burning fire
My hearts true desire

Why

Love is something full of surprise
A fancy twinkle in your eyes
Takes control of your thought
Then you really know you're caught

I didn't want to make you cry
But I just couldn't lie
Birds they were meant to fly
Heaven is the highest high
And the hardest question is why

Life is always complicated
Blatant truth constantly debated
The rich they covet more and more
While the poor go and fight their war

I didn't want to make you cry
But I just couldn't lie
Birds they were meant to fly
Heaven is the highest high
And the hardest question is why

Riding in a horse drawn carriage in Central Park
Walking hand in hand down the avenue in the dark
Uptown, downtown, making love in a subway car
Ten million people and they all know who you are

Writing lyrics in grandest style
Ain't nothing on Earth worth the trial
Eight billion people all in denial
Sin can never win as long as you smile

I didn't want to make you cry
But I just couldn't lie
Birds they were meant to fly
Heaven is the highest high
And the hardest question is why

Why

You left me to bleed and die
Retreated as I gave out a cry
All so you could go and get high
I have to ask you why

Why do we fight war?
Why do the rich want more?
Why do they hate the poor?
And why don't God
Yes why don't God
Answer the knocking on His door

My cross was too heavy to bear
But you didn't care
I doubt you even said a prayer
But I gave my all to share
The truth you cannot deny
I have to ask you why

Why do we fight war?
Why do the rich want more?
Why do they hate the poor?
And why don't God
Yes why don't God
Answer the knocking on His door

I was an arrogant fool
Humbled to learn the golden rule
The kind hand can also be cruel
And wisdom isn't learned in school
No their truth is but a lie
I have to ask you why

Why do we fight war?
Why do the rich want more?
Why do they hate the poor?
And why don't God
Yes why don't God
Answer the knocking on His door

The is a time coming when I will harvest my seed
Hear the rhyme learn I won't return to bleed
Father of mercy when the fires explode into flame
Look to yourselves you have nobody left to blame

Every day I crawl another yard
I dig the soil the ground is hard
Money is green and obscene
A harlot posing as a beauty queen
Some days I find it hard to try
I have to ask you why

Why do we fight war?
Why do the rich want more?
Why do they hate the poor?
And why don't God
Yes why don't God
Answer the knocking on His door

Wild Bill's

Lady Lace spiked the juice at the freak dance
Nero the hero claimed to be a victim of circumstance
The pure whore didn't use any alcohol
Rather she poured in LSD to free the soul

Come on down to Wild Bill's
On the menu a list of thrills
Fatten the lamb for the kill
Come on down to Wild Bill's

And we boogied as one with the universe
Riding in a psychedelic pretty pink hearse
When playing one card stud you just can't bluff
And Nero the zero screamed I've had enough

Come on down to Wild Bill's
On the menu a list of thrills
Fatten the lamb for the kill
Come on down to Wild Bill's

Engineers make careers out of fears
Logical lies cutting through the tears
It's about the money sweet honey
But do you find cluster bombs funny?

I had finally reached an epiphany higher than heaven
I was counting my blessings but I stopped at eleven
When I opened my eyes and realized in surprise
That all of my life my never wife had hateful eyes

Come on down to Wild Bill's
On the menu a list of thrills
Fatten the lamb for the kill
Come on down to Wild Bill's

The story of the glory broke as the sun rising before me
The Thorazine cocktails were strong but couldn't cure me
Lady Lace ran off with Nero because he paid in gold
And grace has its place but only when you get old

Come on down to Wild Bill's
On the menu a list of thrills
Fatten the lamb for the kill
Come on down to Wild Bill's

Wild Domain of the Brain

Jerry Paul where did our dreams go?
Are there still secrets we don't know?
I heard in heaven it's one hell of a show
The beer is cold and pure is the blow

Have you heard I went insane?
Too much torment too much pain
I curse the sun and laugh at the rain
In the wild domain of the brain

Our favorite bands are old and gray
You know that wasn't so yesterday
And here I am in this scam called fame
With nobody but you to cast the blame

Have you heard I went insane?
Too much torment too much pain
I curse the sun and laugh at the rain
In the wild domain of the brain

They sold out for the dollar bill
They never cared about God's will
It was all a game of seeking a thrill
Meet me Paul in that mansion on the hill

Have you heard I went insane?
Too much torment too much pain
I curse the sun and laugh at the rain
In the wild domain of the brain

Porn stars dancing with a Playboy bunny
Third rate comedians trying to be funny
When you're old you call everyone honey
And the meaning of life is to make money

We're so happy we can hardly count
We're so horny we can hardly mount
Who cares about truth we'll just lie
We'll live it big till the day we die

Have you heard I went insane?
Too much torment too much pain
I curse the sun and laugh at the rain
In the wild domain of the brain

And Jesus wanders on forty second street
Rummaging in garbage cans for food to eat
And I write songs never to be sung
There is a glory in being forever young

Have you heard I went insane?
Too much torment too much pain
I curse the sun and laugh at the rain
In the wild domain of the brain

Winner Takes All

I can hear the dragon's breath
And feel the chilly hand of death
Is it sunrise or is it sunset?
Is it ending or the best yet?

Back against the wall
The bully's in the hall
Will it be rise or fall?
In winner takes all

Dealing from the bottom of the deck
Just who you trying to protect?
Queen of hearts has no crown
Going up while I'm going down

Back against the wall
The bully's in the hall
Will it be rise or fall?
In winner takes all

Wheels spin and in comes the sin
Lose your soul you cannot win
God is love but what is love?
You're the only one I'm thinking of

Back against the wall
The bully's in the hall
Will it be rise or fall?
In winner takes all

In the carnival of fools the lions are cruel
The clown is downtown seeking a tool
You pimp your mind and what do you find?
All I ever wanted was a woman who was kind

So it's almost one in the morn
Is the genius being born?
Or will they laugh me to scorn?
Two hearts cause the one was torn

Back against the wall
The bully's in the hall
Will it be rise or fall?
In winner takes all

Words

Googling Indonesia on my phone
Wondering about the time zone?
Big A laying down the melody
Dreaming how things could be

Words are words let it be
I believe we all should be free
Not a slave to religion
Not a slave to money
Words are words let it be

Manic magic late in the night
Thirty seconds and all is right
From God right through my hand
It's a gift don't you understand?

Words are words let it be
I believe we all should be free
Not a slave to religion
Not a slave to money
Words are words let it be

Thirty years of scribbling down my notes
In a one-man election you get all the votes
If it ain't commercial call it avant garde
Einstein couldn't write a hit it's far too hard

Miracles come from hard work
Mark is the boss what a jerk
Three minutes to fortune and fame
Playing in a silly little lover's game

Words are words let it be
I believe we all should be free
Not a slave to religion
Not a slave to money
Words are words let it be

Words Of The Wise

Memories from faded photographs
All the tears and all the laughs
Proving to the children we were young
Remembering all the songs we sung

Words of the wise
The truth and the lies
Tear away the disguise
Words of the wise

We all have been the fool at seventeen
Sought the love of a beauty queen
Believed in that pie in the sky
God and country till the day we die

Words of the wise
The truth and the lies
Tear away the disguise
Words of the wise

I saw God sitting in all His glory
He was rapping a beautiful story
A tale of love drenched with mercy
I picked up my cross how it hurt me

Words of the wise
The truth and the lies
Tear away the disguise
Words of the wise

Broken in the brutal bliss of gray
Life was never free such a price to pay
But who is it that collects the toll?
Seek refuge in the rage of rock and roll

Words of the wise
The truth and the lies
Tear away the disguise
Words of the wise

Working Late

There's a hope like falling rain
It's how I cope feeling vain
That one day the seeds I sow
Will take deep root and grow

Here I am again working late
For fame and fortune I wait
Longing for that eternal date
Here I am again working late

And Debbie has a career
Or at least it does appear
But me I'm trying to survive
Outside of the nine to five

Here I am again working late
For fame and fortune I wait
Longing for that eternal date
Here I am again working late

Lusting for sweet inspiration
Trusting to meet my destination
I walk Pam's dog in the heat
Freedom always has a taste sweet

Here I am again working late
For fame and fortune I wait
Longing for that eternal date
Here I am again working late

Jon Jeter writes on Mister Zimmerman
We all try to do the best we can
And I feel like a rolling stone
Typing late night all alone

Here I am again working late
For fame and fortune I wait
Longing for that eternal date
Here I am again working late

And here I am taking a look
The lyrics are done save the hook
If you don't get it read the book
The greatest artist is the biggest crook

You Can't Say

Can we just sing one more time
To light life up with our rhyme
Can we just have one more dance
And make more majestic romance

You can't say I love you often enough
The worlds a tumble plenty tough
But when the ride is rough
You can't say I love you – often enough

The moon sings in a lonely bar
Planet Jupitar is playing guitar
Gives a new meaning of being a star
I love you, you know who you are

You can't say I love you often enough
The worlds a tumble plenty tough
But when the ride is rough
You can't say I love you – often enough

Inca Queen wake up from your dream
Things aren't the way that they seem
I'll help you escape your crown of gold
Hurry and don't worry that we're old

You can't say I love you often enough
The worlds a tumble plenty tough
But when the ride is rough
You can't say I love you – often enough

Freedom is a state of mind
Love is being kind
And the truth of this day
Well you can't say

Pilgrims of promise praying for peace
That hatred will end and love increase
Would you give your life and more
It can't be maybe you gotta be sure

You can't say I love you often enough
The worlds a tumble plenty tough
But when the ride is rough
You can't say I love you – often enough

You Know The Story

Broken pieces of shattered lives
Only the strong survives
But every now and then
There arises from among men
A champion of us all
An answer to the higher call

I find the strength to love
In my faith in above
God in all His glory
You know the story

Eyes not looking through me
Here but in another reality
Seeing the best in the worst
A quenching of desperate thirst
A mainline of the divine
The finest of the fine

I find the strength to love
In my faith in above
God in all His glory
You know the story

The wasp's stinger has stung
Only the good die young
Killed long before your time
Compassion your only crime
You dared asked the question
Cryptic answers to mention

I find the strength to love
In my faith in above
God in all His glory
You know the story

This is for all who believes
Crucified between two thieves
Mother Mary how she grieves
Peter and James sadly leave
A story of dismal doom
Until of course the empty tomb

A Better Deal

Lay down your weapons lift up a prayer
Live life for love alone show that you care
Beat the sword into the plowshare
Where sweethearts meet I'll join you there

Life is full of pressure a harsh ordeal
But I know deep below that you can feel
Take my hand understand love is real
Search the heart do your part for a better deal

The stars of night sing in sweet harmony
Together when things are better so shall we
Heaven is above let's bring it to Earth
Every human being is of great worth

Life is full of pressure a harsh ordeal
But I know deep below that you can feel
Take my hand understand love is real
Search the heart do your part for a better deal

The bombs and missiles fill up the sky
I have to mention the question of 'why?'
The reasons for war for sure they're a lie
It's high time that we give peace a good try

Life is full of pressure a harsh ordeal
But I know deep below that you can feel
Take my hand understand love is real
Search the heart do your part for a better deal

Dream the dream nothing is too high
Everything that we lack Love will supply
A battle world for all is the battle cry
The bliss of righteousness none can deny

Life is full of pressure a harsh ordeal
But I know deep below that you can feel
Take my hand understand love is real
Search the heart do your part for a better deal

All I Speak

Jesus told me to turn the other cheek
Jesus told me to turn the other cheek
Let the words of love be all I speak
Jesus told me to turn the other cheek

Yes the Bible says blessed are the meek
Yes the Bible says blessed are the meek
Let the words of love be all I speak
Yes the Bible says blessed are the meek

I'm gonna walk the walk all through the week
I'm gonna walk the walk all through the week
Let the words of love be all I speak
I'm gonna walk the walk all through the week

I'll have hope inside no matter how bleak
I'll have hope inside no matter how bleak
Let the words of love be all I speak
I'll have hope inside no matter how bleak

Heaven's on the other side take a peek
Heaven's on the other side take a peek
Let the words of love be all I speak
Heaven's on the other side take a peek

Faith hope and love are a gentle technique
Faith hope and love are a gentle technique
Let the words of love be all I speak
Faith hope and love are a gentle technique

I Sing For Peace

I see the Lord His precious blood flows
See the secret of Love how it goes
I will do right though it cost me all
God has spoken I hear the call

I am a woman I sing for peace
May hatred and war cease
In my song is sweet release
I am a woman I sing for peace

Mother nestling a child in her arms
Keeping baby safe from all life's harms
May he live in a world without any war
Where hunger and poverty are no more

I am a woman I sing for peace
May hatred and war cease
In my song is sweet release
I am a woman I sing for peace

Grandmother looks with her tender eyes
Hear the wisdom in sympathetic sighs
She's lived long enough to see the lies
The war machine so obscene she defies

I am a woman I sing for peace
May hatred and war cease
In my song is sweet release
I am a woman I sing for peace

Gather ye ladies of every age
Together I know we can turn the page
To a new heavens and a new Earth
Remember only women can give birth

I am a woman I sing for peace
May hatred and war cease
In my song is sweet release
I am a woman I sing for peace

Love Is The Key

They bind the mind with their evil lie
Serve your country in war kill and die
They train your brain until you're insane
All the money of the world is vain

Love is the key to release
As ye seek so shall it be found
Come and join me heaven bound
I will live a life of peace
Love is the key to release

Go to college and get a degree
Major in the art of agony
Work behind a desk as a slave
Be a faithful follower to the grave

Love is the key to release
As ye seek so shall it be found
Come and join me heaven bound
I will live a life of peace
Love is the key to release

We only come down this way one time
If you don't live right it's a wicked crime
Smell the flowers and resist the higher powers
Understand you're in command of all your hours

Take sweet time to walk off of the path
Let your words rhyme and ignore the wrath
Let there be a merry song in your heart
And never let righteousness depart

Love is the key to release
As ye seek so shall it be found
Come and join me heaven bound
I will live a life of peace
Love is the key to release

My Song

Let the waters wash away our wrong
Let the waters wash away our wrong
I'm going to sing my song loud and strong
Let the waters wash away our wrong

Let the Love shine down all the day long
Let the Love shine down all the day long
I'm going to sing my song loud and strong
Let the Love shine down all the day long

Take my hand I want you to belong
Take my hand I want you to belong
I'm going to sing my song loud and strong
Take my hand I want you to belong

I'll fight for what's right all the yearlong
I'll fight for what's right all the yearlong
I'm going to sing my song loud and strong
I'll fight for what's right all the yearlong

We'll march for peace please come march along
We'll march for peace please come march along
I'm going to sing my song loud and strong
We'll march for peace please come march along

Putting it all together birds of a feather flock together
We'll sing and bring the good news no matter the weather
Let the waters wash away our wrong
I'm going to sing my song loud and strong
Let the Love shine down all the day long
I'm going to sing my song loud and strong
I'll fight for what's right all the yearlong
I'm going to sing my song loud and strong
We'll march for peace please come march along
I'm going to sing my song loud and strong

We Too Are The USA

I walk down Wall Street I see the golden calf
The upper one percent ain't the better half
If you want to see America there is more
We hate all the fighting and embrace the poor

There's something I need to say
We too are the USA
Don't let the war mongers have the day
We too are the USA
With folded hands we pray
We too are the USA

We're farmers working the land with honest hands
We're the Natives existing in ragtag bands
There is love in our heart and peace in our soul
Hear our cry we defy evil seeking control

There's something I need to say
We too are the USA
Don't let the war mongers have the day
We too are the USA
With folded hands we pray
We too are the USA

Sister brother father mother
Everybody love one another
United we stand divided we fall
Come down and answer the call
There's something I need to say
We too are the USA

No matter what's behind the future is ours
There is a heaven of love beyond the stars
We have come to serve to lift up those in need
We strive to be true in every word and deed

There's something I need to say
We too are the USA
Don't let the war mongers have the day
We too are the USA
With folded hands we pray
We too are the USA

You Are Always There

God you gave us the Earth to live and share
God you gave us the Earth to live and share
I am never alone you are always there
God you gave us the Earth to live and share

God you gave us a heart to love and care
God you gave us a heart to love and care
I am never alone you are always there
God you gave us a heart to love and care

God you gave us voice to lift up holy prayer
God you gave us voice to lift up holy prayer
I am never alone you are always there
God you gave us voice to lift up holy prayer

Living is for giving we are aware
Living is for giving we are aware
I am never alone you are always there
Living is for giving we are aware

I will fight for what's right oh yes I dare
I will fight for what's right oh yes I dare
I am never alone you are always there
I will fight for what's right oh yes I dare

A Bit Of Lady Luck

I had lost everything except the blues
Even the Mormon didn't have good news
Went to the casino put my last dollar down
Lost it all I was leaving this dingy old town

And that's when you walked in
Looking like the ultimate win
A bit of lady luck God it's true
A bit of lady luck yeah it's you

My heart raged bursting into blazing flame
I had to win I was playing love's game
I knew I was never going to be the same
I unleashed the dragons that none could dare to tame

And that's when you walked in
Looking like the ultimate win
A bit of lady luck God it's true
A bit of lady luck yeah it's you

I'll climb the mountain I'll swim the deep sea
I'll try to write some decent poetry
I was reading Shakespeare my dearest Juliet
I got deep fear I just needed the winning bet

And that's when you walked in
Looking like the ultimate win
A bit of lady luck God it's true
A bit of lady luck yeah it's you

I looked at my cards do you understand
The queen of hearts it was the winning hand
Let's go to the chapel and become man and wife
Elvis gave his blessing and we started new life

And that's when you walked in
Looking like the ultimate win
A bit of lady luck God it's true
A bit of lady luck yeah it's you

A Flight Of Fancy

It seems Wednesday always comes before Thursday
I was just wondering who made it that way
When it comes Sunday we get on our knees to pray
All was fine until I found out my wife was gay

The Warlocks went and changed their name
No matter the music was still the same
A flight of fancy do you get the point
A flight of fancy let's smoke a joint

The leprechauns and fairies had a real big fight
It was a real shame because they were so tight
I'm going to Alabama just cause I like the name
I traded a boring job for some fortune and fame

The Warlocks went and changed their name
No matter the music was still the same
A flight of fancy do you get the point
A flight of fancy let's smoke a joint

The slaves are still seeking emancipation
Red Cloud don't think this is a great nation
Good Lord I'd surrender all for some salvation
A knock on the door before the interrogation

The Warlocks went and changed their name
No matter the music was still the same
A flight of fancy do you get the point
A flight of fancy let's smoke a joint

Here is the climax we've all been waiting for
If you got cash for the bash you're sure to score
I'd sing the blues but the reds are good news
Life is strife with contradicting clues

The Warlocks went and changed their name
No matter the music was still the same
A flight of fancy do you get the point
A flight of fancy let's smoke a joint

A New Song

I remember December with a bitter freeze
Love can bring the strongest down to their knees
I was missing your kisses so tender and sweet
I needed a victory life was one long defeat

I have a song shiny and new
A little red some yellow and plenty blue
I have a song shiny and new
And I'll sing it for you

Bottom's a bummer like a drummer in a punk band
My heart raced as we embraced hand in hand
Sometimes the only answer is fighting through the pain
With fear looming near my brain struggled to stay sane

I have a song shiny and new
A little red some yellow and plenty blue
I have a song shiny and new
And I'll sing it for you

A sacred chord a clever word laying down the beat
The sun rises in the skies shedding some heat
Heaven is a place of grace a refuge for the human race
If you deal all the cards someone gets the ace

I have a song shiny and new
A little red some yellow and plenty blue
I have a song shiny and new
And I'll sing it for you

Hey Eli is on high never asking why
Day and night from a distant height is a gray sky
Point of view is true but I will always love you
Right or wrong here is my song sing it with me too

I have a song shiny and new
A little red some yellow and plenty blue
I have a song shiny and new
And I'll sing it for you

All A Disguise

I hear the man on the t.v.
He's speaking right to me
He said we gotta fight to be free
Come on down and join the army

While the rich man wears his suit
With girls and girls looking so cute
He smiles but it's all a disguise
His life is a myriad of mad lies
He smiles but it's all a disguise

I've been fighting for the truth
I became aware when I was a youth
Rules for fools in the schools
Shaping me into one of their tools

While the rich man wears his suit
With girls and girls looking so cute
He smiles but it's all a disguise
His life is a myriad of mad lies
He smiles but it's all a disguise

Hey say hey
Tomorrow is today
Don't dare pray
Action is the way
Hey say hey
Tomorrow is today

There are chains of paper and gold
Step right in line do as you're told
Stop to think all is insane
Freedom ain't free it comes with pain

While the rich man wears his suit
With girls and girls looking so cute
He smiles but it's all a disguise
His life is a myriad of mad lies
He smiles but it's all a disguise
He can't answer any of the why's
His life is a myriad of mad lies
He smiles but it's all a disguise

Allen's Song

Aces can be high aces can be low
Life is hard when you just don't know
There's so much more than keeping score
I've told you many times before

You always played the game to win
And that Allen was your sin
You gotta die before you begin
And here I go blowing like the wind

I was always afraid my mind paranoid
Before I could fly I was destroyed
Couldn't let go couldn't hold on
But now yesterday is gone

You always played the game to win
And that Allen was your sin
You gotta die before you begin
And here I go blowing like the wind

Two losers with a dream that was you and I
Now you sell drugs that don't make you high
Once we searched for the reason why
I found the Truth and you found a lie

You always played the game to win
And that Allen was your sin
You gotta die before you begin
And here I go blowing like the wind

Wine woman and song
Love is what's strong
Take your money take your gold
Cause brother you got sold

When you wake up in your father's place
You look in the mirror it ain't your face
When you become the unknown stranger
Remember I warned you of the danger

You always played the game to win
And that Allen was your sin
You gotta die before you begin
And here I go blowing like the wind

An Endless Metaphor

The fire is burning hot and steady
Pretty soon the coffee will be ready
You know I like it hot black and strong
Like the ladies inside of my song

Life is an endless metaphor
A kiss is nice but I want more
A little woman a little whore
Life is an endless metaphor

Midnight speaks listen as the moon screams
Darkness is the domain of endless dreams
I reach for you hoping for the best
One way or another I'll be blessed

Life is an endless metaphor
A kiss is nice but I want more
A little woman a little whore
Life is an endless metaphor

The dragon chases the rainbows end
More than a lover you are my best friend
The chariots they are swinging low
Soon will be the time you need to go

The cup is empty not one more drop
Tears are free and they never do stop
In every sigh of goodbye a new crop
A gift from heaven falling from atop

Life is an endless metaphor
A kiss is nice but I want more
A little woman a little whore
Life is an endless metaphor

Well Sylvia I cannot pretend
That I will walk alone the final bend
You will be missed that I know for sure
Love is love an endless metaphor

Life is an endless metaphor
A kiss is nice but I want more
A little woman a little whore
Life is an endless metaphor

Apocalypse

The merchants of greed are sharpening their blades
See the soldiers marching in endless parades
Don't you know that profits soar when there's a war?
It's a trick that's been used many times before

Darling give me one last kiss on the lips
Here comes the apocalypse
The dreaded moment when time slips
Welcome to the apocalypse

They made our rivers their private open sewer
While the wild life's getting fewer and fewer
They saved a dollar and destroyed Mother Earth
When there's nothing to eat what's your money worth?

Darling give me one last kiss on the lips
Here comes the apocalypse
The dreaded moment when time slips
Welcome to the apocalypse

See the fake news is on every channel
Go and sing the blues this is our funeral
Real soon thinking will be the worst kind of crime
All the poets today they can't even rhyme

Darling give me one last kiss on the lips
Here comes the apocalypse
The dreaded moment when time slips
Welcome to the apocalypse

I am the resistance as I sing this song
Together I know we can right every wrong
When we have life there's hope for a better day
Oh yes my friend a better day so I pray

Darling give me one last kiss on the lips
Here comes the apocalypse
The dreaded moment when time slips
Welcome to the apocalypse

Doe A Dear

I'm a dear near shedding sacred fear
Angry fists furious and queer
Or a gazelle galloping in hell
Time takes tomorrow who can tell

If I were to be an animal
More pure than a human soul
If I were to be a wild beast
Only on the grass would I feast
If I were to be an animal

Doe a dear a female dear
The time of love is near
The time of love is here

Lions have pride human's genocide
An angry red wave of the tide
Dark dolphins swim heroes one and all
We were equals before the fall
We were equals before recall

If I were to be an animal
More pure than a human soul
If I were to be a wild beast
Only on the grass would I feast
If I were to be an animal

Doe a dear a female dear
Scream dream without fear
The time of love is here
See heaven signs appear

Hyenas in Ethiopia south of the Nile
Refugees exiles guilty without trial
Migrating flocks with no place to land
Earth is to share please understand

Give me a line with nine syllables
Cages are for prisons not animals
Doe a dear it resonates clear
Sweet Jesus what's happening here?

If I were to be an animal
More pure than a human soul
If I were to be a wild beast
Only on the grass would I feast
If I were to be an animal

Doe a dear a female dear
Ray a golden way to fight
Go on and on and have no fear
Doe a deer and female dear

At The Back Of The Bus

Many colors but the world is blind
Black and white that's what I find
I just want a home that's good and kind
Hatred is sacred you're out of your mind

We're sitting at the back of the bus
The first shall be last so says Jesus
I don't really know why there's a fuss
We're sitting at the back of the bus

You judge a man by the color of his skin
The darker the shade the greater the sin
Never mind the content of a person's heart
Never mind we'll tear the world apart

We're sitting at the back of the bus
The first shall be last so says Jesus
I don't really know why there's a fuss
We're sitting at the back of the bus

Out in the ghetto the temperature is on the rise
We're tired of the false promises and endless lies
We'll make our own solution we'll organize
In the end my friend we'll catch you in surprise

In hushed whispers we plot and plan
Listen to me because I am a man
Hatred is the policy of the weak
Learn the power of turning the cheek

We're sitting at the back of the bus
The first shall be last so says Jesus
I don't really know why there's a fuss
We're sitting at the back of the bus

At The Law Office

Empty words filling me with hollow praise
I am seeking to know the end of my days
The sun rises and then it will always set
I remember your love and then I forget

Working down at the law office
Where all is wonderful bliss
God I can't take more of this
Working down at the law office

Ma'at made love to me under the apple tree
She had golden chains promising liberty
Somewhere I forged in iron a new reality
I love you I wonder do you love me?

Working down at the law office
Where all is wonderful bliss
God I can't take more of this
Working down at the law office

Baba O'Reilly danced an ancient Irish jig
I was a one-man blues band playing a gig
Every Tom Dick and Harry got a demo
I would have cum but I never got the memo

Working down at the law office
Where all is wonderful bliss
God I can't take more of this
Working down at the law office

Insanity is vanity come and chose your poison
Making money is the ultimate kind of sin
They sleep in the park it breaks my heart
Living in America is a delicate art

Working down at the law office
Where all is wonderful bliss
God I can't take more of this
Working down at the law office

Atlantic City

I was falling calling out your sweet name
The cards had been marked in the crooked game
All the chips were stacked high on the table
Swaying her hips she's a legend from a fable

She's looking pretty in Atlantic City
I was happy that she was with me
All eyes fell on the raving beauty
We're sitting pretty in Atlantic City

Forever is still counted second by second
In the dream Love's supreme so I reckoned
In the casino the rules are written slanted
She loved me but took my heart for granted

She's looking pretty in Atlantic City
I was happy that she was with me
All eyes fell on the raving beauty
We're sitting pretty in Atlantic City

The smoke was strong and something was wrong
On the radio they played a slow dance song
I refused the alcohol as last hand took all
I had a full house queens and kings I recall

She's looking pretty in Atlantic City
I was happy that she was with me
All eyes fell on the raving beauty
We're sitting pretty in Atlantic City

When you have the losing hand there's still your gun
Poker is like war it only matters that you won
Hand in hand we fled with the alarms ringing loud
I didn't care I was aware it wasn't our crowd

She's looking pretty in Atlantic City
I was happy that she was with me
All eyes fell on the raving beauty
We're sitting pretty in Atlantic City

So here we are a band forever on the run
We laugh writing songs about the things we've done
Fact and fiction truth is still but a state of mind
By definition the future leaves the past behind

She's looking pretty in Atlantic City
I was happy that she was with me
All eyes fell on the raving beauty
We're sitting pretty in Atlantic City

Baby You're The Best

When I hear a sad song I think of you
And all the things that we've been through
We had more than our fair share of the test
And baby I gotta say that you're the best

Hey there sweet Syl
I love you and always will
Close your eyes take a rest
Cause baby you're the best

We were two strangers lost on the road
We came together to share our load
You and me, me and you we were a happy two
But baby today I say I'm so blue

Hey there sweet Syl
I love you and always will
Close your eyes take a rest
Cause baby you're the best

Up and down all-around hand in hand
Life is full of things we can't understand
God have mercy how it hurts me
To see you now a lost ship on the sea

Hey there sweet Syl
I love you and always will
Close your eyes take a rest
Cause baby you're the best

Heaven is calling you're halfway there
Lost counting the cost in an empty prayer
May the Lord have mercy on your soul
God knows life has taken its toll

Hey there sweet Syl
I love you and always will
Close your eyes take a rest
Cause baby you're the best

Black And Beautiful

Hey woman you really got some soul
Black as the midnight sky and beautiful
You're a song and baby I want to sing
Give me the blessings only a woman can bring

Black and beautiful baby that's you
Black and beautiful a dream come true
Black and beautiful love me do
Black and beautiful baby that's you

You're the sweetest string on my guitar
In an endless heaven the brightest star
My only wish is to make you believe
That as you give so shall you receive

Black and beautiful baby that's you
Black and beautiful a dream come true
Black and beautiful love me do
Black and beautiful baby that's you

Some people they love and let them go
I offer your forever an endless show
Take my hand these words ain't pretend
Lover and wife my eternal best friend

Black and beautiful baby that's you
Black and beautiful a dream come true
Black and beautiful love me do
Black and beautiful baby that's you

The world unleashes such a harsh lesson
Jim Crow teaches wicked oppression
Revolution is the word on the street
The solution is marching to the beat

I got dreams baby higher than the sky
You only live once give it your best try
I need somebody like you by my side
Someone I can cherish with all my pride

Black and beautiful baby that's you
Black and beautiful a dream come true
Black and beautiful love me do
Black and beautiful baby that's you

Born To Lead The Revolution

They always said that I was a child of the sixties
From the tie-dies to the issues that pricks me
In God we trust so I was born at the right time
Greed is wicked lust torn by my write rhyme

I was born to lead the revolution
Peace and love is the solution
Don't digress into confusion
I was born to lead the revolution

In the fraternity house they had pot coke and booze
They had intricate plans the best way to lose
Cause between love and mammon look what they choose
I just know Mikey is sad softly singing the blues

I was born to lead the revolution
Peace and love is the solution
Don't digress into confusion
I was born to lead the revolution

Sometimes it hurts so bad I simply go insane
Trying to understand that we ain't fighting in vain
You got to make every step following the ideal
You go to make every step vividly real

I was born to lead the revolution
Peace and love is the solution
Don't digress into confusion
I was born to lead the revolution

Love is the course
Love is the source
We don't need force
Love is the source

Don't let them fool you with their intricate lies
Look past the suit you got the devil in disguise
Money is the biggest scam every created
The banks feed on greed it can't be debated

I was born to lead the revolution
Peace and love is the solution
Don't digress into confusion
I was born to lead the revolution

Cam Girl

She was the star of the private show
Wicked secrets that none should know
Despite a wig and fake name
All the boys knew her shame

See the cam girl cum
Where is God's kingdom?
Fame only finds some
See the cam girl cum

She sells her body for spare change
The blue bloods find that strange
But they never had that hunger
No they never knew that hunger

See the cam girl cum
Where is God's kingdom?
Fame only finds some
See the cam girl cum

So here I write these words on the edge of poverty
Wondering if the thundering is a reality
So if you hear this song say yourself a little prayer
And remember that the cam girl she's always there

Hear her orgasm it's totally fake
But hey baby you can really shake
You always give more than you take
Going beyond the point that you break

See the cam girl cum
Where is God's kingdom?
Fame only finds some
See the cam girl cum

And the evangelists on the television
Deplore the whore as vile sin
Purity is the lesson so properly taught
Until the moment that they are caught

See the cam girl cum
Where is God's kingdom?
Fame only finds some
See the cam girl cum

Camera Click

They all use aliases just to be on the safe side
One underage actress and everybody gotta hide
But hey that's just the way it is in the flick
You get that extra pay if you can make it sick

Camera click let's get a smile
Love is what makes life worthwhile
Here we go baby in sweet style
Camera click let's get a smile

She was a real beauty but so are they all
She had a dream and heard Los Angeles call
All she found was a hungry stomach and empty mind
Then there was this older man acting so kind

Camera click let's get a smile
Love is what makes life worthwhile
Here we go baby in sweet style
Camera click let's get a smile

Stills gave them a little bit of thrills
The booze mixed well with the pills
Still she was some kind of star
You're my baby that's who you are

Hell is something that we all know firsthand
From the outside everything was exciting and grand
A million men lusted over her every move
She was the queen of them all with everything to prove

Camera click let's get a smile
Love is what makes life worthwhile
Here we go baby in sweet style
Camera click let's get a smile

Chasing A Dream

I fell in the love with the hopping jaw dropping teeny bopping queen
She was the cosmic star playing guitar on the movie screen
I found I was on the rebound forgetting Poly Styrene
I said hey baby don't tell me maybe just where have you been?

Here I am chasing a dream
Life it ain't all that it seem
Forget the milk here's the cream
There I go chasing the dream

You never know tomorrow the wind might blow in sorrow
I sat front row at the show the striptease at the go-go
The ladies hot the beer so cold I forgot that I was old
At six in the morning my head was scorning my soul was sold

Here I am chasing a dream
Life it ain't all that it seem
Forget the milk here's the cream
There I go chasing the dream

As long as you have cash they'll let you crash the private party
The brains in your head the whores in your bed you're such a smarty
A life at ease you do as you please careful you'll catch a filthy disease
On her knees not to pray I heard her say I never tease

Life is a grind lust is in the mind
As you seek so shall you find
The glowing lights the great unknown
So tired of being all alone
Hell comes in many a shade
All is well as long is the bill is paid

Twenty years brings horrible fears you shall reap what you sow
All the truth they taught you in your youth well it ain't so
Love is a grand mystical force until the point of your divorce
Though many are gone life goes on for the better or worse

Here I am chasing a dream
Life it ain't all that it seem
Forget the milk here's the cream
There I go chasing the dream

Cold War Blues

Capitalism is marching dreaming of mammon
The depths of Africa is suffering from famine
The Russian bear wants to tear the world apart
Because communism exists in the core of his heart

There is a time you must pay your dues
Sitting in fear singing cold war blues
Insanity it comes in a myriad of hues
Angel of death bringing cold war blues

You're damned if you don't and you're damned if you do
There's going to be a battle to divide the world into two
And all I want to do is sing my songs of peace
May God brings us the love to make all this hatred cease

There is a time you must pay your dues
Sitting in fear singing cold war blues
Insanity it comes in a myriad of hues
Angel of death bringing cold war blues

I'm leaving on a jet airplane
Gotta go or I'll go insane
Off to America the land of the free
Off to America and opportunity
Fair well Uganda fair well
About my future who can tell?
It may be heaven it may be hell
Fair well Uganda fair well

Nuclear stalemate terrorizes the strongest of men
It seems that Armageddon is coming round again
When will we learn the lessons of a love pure?
When will we be able to sleep in a place secure?

There is a time you must pay your dues
Sitting in fear singing cold war blues
Insanity it comes in a myriad of hues
Angel of death bringing cold war blues

Controlled Opposition

He was a little too handsome to be a freak
And he never smiled turning the other cheek
During the day he would man the barricade
Never knowing in truth we were being played

Controlled opposition
Satan's secret sin
Betrayal from within
Controlled opposition

Deep December and we turned up the heat
Revolution filled our cup tasting sweet
Our 'comrade' never took a big drink
And after a while I started to think

Controlled opposition
Satan's secret sin
Betrayal from within
Controlled opposition

Well he's could quote a little bit of Marx
But there were just some outlandish remarks
About war heroes and the American way
I see it now clearer then a sunny day

Controlled opposition
Satan's secret sin
Betrayal from within
Controlled opposition

Paranoia well that word is too strong
Still deep down I knew he didn't belong
I kept watching with a cautious eye
Until the day I caught him in a lie

Controlled opposition
Satan's secret sin
Betrayal from within
Controlled opposition

Cornfield Mafia Harvest

Here I go on a manic mystery move
I got something that I need to prove
There are cornfields in the Midwest
And honey mother nature is the best

Here we go the reaper is calling
Great powers will soon be falling
How will you stand up in the test?
This is the Cornfield Mafia harvest

Go east young man says the Sioux
God Lord help us the sky ain't blue
Woody Guthrie's ghost is lurking near
And red my friend I never did fear

Here we go the reaper is calling
Powers will soon be falling
How will you stand up in the test?
This is the Cornfield Mafia harvest

I remember when I was a tiny boy
We were leaving Illinois
We got lost on the highway
Endless fields full of corn
Those plants stood proud and tall
Round and round as I recall

God planted a seed into my heart
Love it was in the form of art
Fifty years through hell and worse
Was it a blessing or a curse?

Here we go the reaper is calling
Powers will soon be falling
How will you stand up in the test?
This is the Cornfield Mafia harvest

Dancing For The Dollar Bill

She dreams of having a dream
Something to wake her from her scream
There a fuzzy line before fantasy
But baby is downright nasty

Dancing for the dollar bill
Giving the customer a thrill
Setting them up for the kill
Dancing for the dollar bill

Hear the beat the rhythm rages
We display them of all ages
See them older seem them younger
Whatever feeds the men's hunger

Dancing for the dollar bill
Giving the customer a thrill
Setting them up for the kill
Dancing for the dollar bill

Oh darling what I wanna know is do you do a little more?
I'm looking from some pretty momma to rack up the score
Dancing is fine romancing divine but I want you to be mine
Can we rock and rage behind the stage or am I crossing the line?

The money is good but not great
In the business of love full of hate
Someday she plans for her escape
Even if you oblige it's still rape

Dancing for the dollar bill
Giving the customer a thrill
Setting them up for the kill
Dancing for the dollar bill

Got no future trying to forget the past
No telling how long this will last
Too much pride to do suicide
Where's the rainbow bridge to the other side?

Dancing for the dollar bill
Giving the customer a thrill
Setting them up for the kill
Dancing for the dollar bill

Dark Eyes

Son of a sharecropper from Mississippi
Well-schooled in the cruelness of history
Come here boy do this and with a grin
Good Lord I live in the land of sin

I see the world through dark eyes
We're taught little white lies
I can see past your disguise
I see the world through dark eyes

Grandma she dreams of some better days
Withered and gray on her knees in praise
Just something better for the young
A happier song that could be sung

I see the world through dark eyes
We're taught little white lies
I can see past your disguise
I see the world through dark eyes

Education it is the ticket to ride
Salvation is only on the other side
No surrender gotta live off of hope
The world is crashing it's so hard to cope

I see the world through dark eyes
We're taught little white lies
I can see past your disguise
I see the world through dark eyes

I see crosses burning and men with hearts full of hate
I see liberals turning saying son you just gotta wait
Mansions of glory tell the story of our slavery
To change the world we need hearts of bravery

Off on the trail looking for something new
Gotta prevail dreams sometimes come true
Life is a trip and you only get one chance
And I was never one to sit out on a dance

I see the world through dark eyes
We're taught little white lies
I can see past your disguise
I see the world through dark eyes

Darrell And The Corn Field Mafia

He came with an offer I could never refuse
A song of glory infused with the blues
I just needed to surrender my soul
I just needed to give up complete control

Hey Darrell the grass grows tall
Hey Darrell why don't you call?
Hey Darrell am I going to fall?
I'm getting no answer no answer at all

Hold on Harry you're going to be a star
Never mind if you can play the guitar
Smile for the camera follow the script
Sunday you're a Blood Monday a Crypt

Hey Darrell the grass grows tall
Hey Darrell why don't you call?
Hey Darrell am I going to fall?
I'm getting no answer no answer at all

There's the dude who wrote Dylan's stuff
We serve him rum and coke it's enough
He likes to play poker but he can't bluff
Do as we say cause we play it rough

Hey Darrell the grass grows tall
Hey Darrell why don't you call?
Hey Darrell am I going to fall?
I'm getting no answer no answer at all

Did you hear about the lip-synching politician?
They found him guilty of the greatest of sin
Inside of his heart there existed a shred of decency
It's a rare crime that hasn't happened recently

The money comes and the money leaves
The television evangelist fully believes
Wall Street worships the golden calf
If you can't cry sweetheart then please laugh

Hey Darrell the grass grows tall
Hey Darrell why don't you call?
Hey Darrell am I going to fall?
I'm getting no answer no answer at all

Every Saint

Sign outside reads come as you are
In the glory of the sun what's a star?
You gotta learn when to fold when to fight
The bottom line is treat everybody right

I've lost a battle a time or two
Outnumbered what was I to do?
Every saint began as a sinner
How good you gotta be to be a winner?
Every saint began as a sinner

In the church of madness they speak babble
Our congregation is riffraff and rabble
Hear the choir singing Accapella blues
The story of love is pure good news

I've lost a battle a time or two
Outnumbered what was I to do?
Every saint began as a sinner
How good you gotta be to be a winner?
Every saint began as a sinner

Sylvia she drifted away to lose her mind
Gerard is cool but he could be more kind
Half of the contest is knowing what's right
Knowledge alone won't help you Friday night

I've lost a battle a time or two
Outnumbered what was I to do?
Every saint began as a sinner
How good you gotta be to be a winner?
Every saint began as a sinner

I ain't pretty but please take a look inside
From the God of Love none can hide
My friend don't pretend death ain't the end
I am so happy to call Jesus my friend

I've lost a battle a time or two
Outnumbered what was I to do?
Every saint began as a sinner
How good you gotta be to be a winner?
Every saint began as a sinner

Fantasy

Tuning an electric guitar at the dingy bar
Singing blues paying dues gonna be a star
He sacrifices his heart he offers his soul
Hear hell's bells ringing death's toll

Every punk is drunk on fantasy
Singing la la la let it be
Welcome to rock and roll reality
Every punk is drunk on fantasy

Fame is around the corner so he prays
A game of lost and found these days
It's strictly a part time gig for now
But he's gonna make it big somehow

Every punk is drunk on fantasy
Singing la la la let it be
Welcome to rock and roll reality
Every punk is drunk on fantasy

See the legions of zombies marching in line
They'll kill in war or whore just to sign
But he don't care he's on a mission divine
Rock and roll reality he claims it mine

Every punk is drunk on fantasy
Singing la la la let it be
Welcome to rock and roll reality
Every punk is drunk on fantasy

So we rage on stage a song for the new age
Life is eternal turning page after page
Between the amphetamines and the blaring light
He smiles in the trial getting it just right

Every punk is drunk on fantasy
Singing la la la let it be
Welcome to rock and roll reality
Every punk is drunk on fantasy

Feeling Blue

I went back to read the sacred note
A little secret someone special wrote
The paper was faded ripped and gray
It brought me back to yesterday

Feeling blue as the sky
Feeling blue like I want to die
Feeling blue and I don't know why
Feeling blue as the sky

The treasure chest was overflowing
With dismal dark thoughts knowing
That you were never coming back
That's when the blue turned black

Feeling blue as the sky
Feeling blue like I want to die
Feeling blue and I don't know why
Feeling blue as the sky

They say drinking gin is a sin
But how else can this poor boy win?
Miracles are only in the Good Book
And you never gave me a second look

Feeling blue as the sky
Feeling blue like I want to die
Feeling blue and I don't know why
Feeling blue as the sky

So here I am writing this song
Wondering how everything went so wrong
Just another dream never to come true
Oh yes I'm feeling wickedly blue

Feeling blue as the sky
Feeling blue like I want to die
Feeling blue and I don't know why
Feeling blue as the sky

Folk Singer

You were sweetness with a guitar
A rising rage a shooting star
The rose is pretty with her thorn
We cannot choose the way we are born

Folk singer with a folk song
Doing right is never wrong
Keep on going be strong
Folk singer with a folk song

A war was raging the country afire
Peace and love such a worthy desire
In fighting history history was made
A pretty nickel you got paid

Folk singer with a folk song
Doing right is never wrong
Keep on going be strong
Folk singer with a folk song

Well the years they roll on by
We all laugh and we all cry
And there is an answer to 'why?'
But they only tell you the grand lie

Folk singer with a folk song
Doing right is never wrong
Keep on going be strong
Folk singer with a folk song

The scenes change but the story stays
It is always the poor man who pays
Alas we all pass naked as we came
All this hate and killing is a shame

Folk singer with a folk song
Doing right is never wrong
Keep on going be strong
Folk singer with a folk song

Forest Street

They were slipping into Friday
Listening to the guitar man play
For a moment everything's okay
So much that words could never say

Where are the trees on Forest Street?
Crowded with houses and places to eat
Sometimes in victory there's defeat
Where are the trees on Forest Street?

Two lovers talk with their eyes
In life we wear a permanent disguise
Walking between the truth and lies
Drinking thinking brand new alibis

Where are the trees on Forest Street?
Crowded with houses and places to eat
Sometimes in victory there's defeat
Where are the trees on Forest Street?

Sky is gray clouds gather for rain
After the fire lingers more pain
Life is a gamble who can refrain
Or even define what is sane

Where are the trees on Forest Street?
Crowded with houses and places to eat
Sometimes in victory there's defeat
Where are the trees on Forest Street?

Laughter and voices clutter my ear
The time of my departure draws near
One final sip from my coffee cup
When the show ends you've had enough

Where are the trees on Forest Street?
Crowded with houses and places to eat
Sometimes in victory there's defeat
Where are the trees on Forest Street?

Gideon

I hung with Gideon we smoked dope
We shared our dreams mainlining hope
If you never knew the streets be still
Down here the law is conquer and kill

Gideon well he wrote a Bible
From page one it was all survival
Love is another word for denial
Gideon well he wrote a Bible

I played guitar and he played bass
Queen Anne sang with her pretty face
We were a match short of heaven
We had sins never to be forgiven

Gideon well he wrote a Bible
From page one it was all survival
Love is another word for denial
Gideon well he wrote a Bible

Words flow like a raging roaring stream
You gotta fight if you want to dream
Nobody hands anything to the poor
Except for excuses and endless war

Gideon well he wrote a Bible
From page one it was all survival
Love is another word for denial
Gideon well he wrote a Bible

Gideon burned like a torch in the night
You lose the second you quit the fight
Was it over dose or suicide?
Gideon was gone and how I cried

Gideon well he wrote a Bible
From page one it was all survival
Love is another word for denial
Gideon well he wrote a Bible

Waiting on Revelation for my crown
For Gideon the curtain went down
Angels well maybe they are true
But it was only demons Gideon knew

Gideon well he wrote a Bible
From page one it was all survival
Love is another word for denial
Gideon well he wrote a Bible

God Bless The USA

He was the all-American boy so wonderful
She was the all-American girl so beautiful
They saluted the flag and had sex in the car
She was in the band and he played the guitar

God bless the U.S.A.
If you got money you're okay
Nothing more to say
Have a very nice day
God bless the U.S.A.

If you can play the chords I'll write the words
The man from the army demanded to be heard
Sign on the line and then your soul is mine
Just like the priest but less than divine

God bless the U.S.A.
If you got money you're okay
Nothing more to say
Have a very nice day
God bless the U.S.A.

Well hell is for children and we all have to sin
You never know the truth when you begin
The politician has a forked tongue and a grin
The game is rigged so you can never win

God bless the U.S.A.
If you got money you're okay
Nothing more to say
Have a very nice day
God bless the U.S.A.

Dreams they fade into a song of desperation
Wherever I am it's not my intended destination
You can only say so much until you're slain
In the struggle I guarantee you a dose of pain

God bless the U.S.A.
If you got money you're okay
Nothing more to say
Have a very nice day
God bless the U.S.A.

God Says

The genius says one and one is three
And obediently we bow the knee
Open your eyes tell me what you see
Open your heart give your love to me

And God says blessed are the meek
And God says turn the other cheek
And God says better to give than receive
But mankind he don't believe

And this song is played in honky-tonk bars
By drunken singers with second hand guitars
All is fine so pour me another beer
Look in the mirror find your greatest fear

And God says blessed are the meek
And God says turn the other cheek
And God says better to give than receive
But mankind he don't believe

Up is down while they say left is right
Wherever you turn there awaits a fight
All the worlds' riches mean nothing to the poor
It was never about winning they fixed the score

And God says blessed are the meek
And God says turn the other cheek
And God say better to give than receive
But mankind he don't believe

Anarchy is reality
Control is futility
To take as you need
Death is senseless greed
Right conquers wrong
And this is a song

Alabama Jack plucks his banjo solo
I read the book of secrets that you don't know
Swing your partner round and round and round
When you lose it all happiness is found

And God says blessed are the meek/ And God says turn the other cheek
And God says better to give than receive/ But mankind he don't believe

Grant

On the eight track you had both left and right
The bass and drums they needed to be tight
When I can't write I jot down words like these
Before I implore the Lord upon bended knees

And Grant they played you for the fool
Life full of strife welcome to the school
The A&R man he was anything but cool
Let time pass in history you'll rule

We'd smoke cigarettes by your oxygen tank
Money in your heart and cash in the bank
Best of all Jesus he was a very good friend
In heaven we sing forever without an end

And Grant they played you for the fool
Life full of strife welcome to the school
The A&R man he was anything but cool
Let time pass in history you'll rule

You tell me of memories of a fantasy
In life we never become all we can be
But if you can smile it's all worthwhile
And Grant you played the game with style

And Grant they played you for the fool
Life full of strife welcome to the school
The A&R man he was anything but cool
Let time pass in history you'll rule

They took the best lines damn them to hell
With crooked smiles fluent lies they tell
So fortune and fame it never came
It ain't winning but how you play the game

And Grant they played you for the fool
Life full of strife welcome to the school
The A&R man he was anything but cool
Let time pass in history you'll rule

Growing Up (At Seventeen)

Sitting here waiting for the phone to ring
I would rather be doing anything
Between false promises and harsh demands
Seventeen and nobody understands

Growing up it's something to do
Growing up I'm missing a clue
Growing up what will life bring?
Growing up thank God I can still sing

The future is coming with a black sun
Money to be made and killing to be done
I just want to be free and find a love true
I look at the world 'What's wrong with you?'

Growing up it's something to do
Growing up I'm missing a clue
Growing up what will life bring?
Growing up thank God I can still sing

I'm fighting hard but who is the foe?
Half of the battle is things I don't know
They sure have played me for the fool
Forging my mind so I can be their tool

Growing up it's something to do
Growing up I'm missing a clue
Growing up what will life bring?
Growing up thank God I can still sing

I promise I will resist I will rebel
I long to make heaven out of this hell
At seventeen I have dreams of light
At seventeen I will make it right

Growing up it's something to do
Growing up I'm missing a clue
Growing up what will life bring?
Growing up thank God I can still sing

He Wore The Uniform

I remember John he would say hello to me
He served in Vietnam he was history
And he would ask for a dollar or two
So he could get his service dog some food
I always gave him a dollar or two
What else could I do?

And he had that faraway look in his eyes
As if he was in a play wearing some disguise
When I saw him a million questions would form
He was a soldier he wore the uniform

Well on Church Street we would protest the war
Like they did so many times before
And John he never did join our ranks
And John he never gave us any thanks
To peace love and understanding I am true
What else could I do?

And he had that faraway look in his eyes
As if he was in a play wearing some disguise
When I saw him a million questions would form
He was a soldier he wore the uniform

And one time I gave him a dollar bill
My curious tongue didn't stay still
I said I heard you served John
Did you get see any action?
He pointed to a scar on his head
With a dead look 'See this' he said

I have dreams fueled by the noblest ideal
I have a vision of Love I need to make real
Silence is consent and silence equals death
So with scream and whisper I'll give my breath
Every choice begs some toll that is due
I shall pay what else could I do?

And he had that faraway look in his eyes
As if he was in a play wearing some disguise
When I saw him a million questions would form
He was a soldier he wore the uniform

I killed the man who I fought understand
I snapped his neck with my two hands
John's face was dead somber and grim
With pity my eyes looked on him
So I gave him a dollar or two
What else could I do?

And he had that faraway look in his eyes
As if he was in a play wearing some disguise
When I saw him a million questions would form
He was a soldier he wore the uniform

God with all my heart do I hate this thing called war
It is a widow maker something I greatly deplore
God with all my heart do I hate this thing called war
And I will do all that I can so it will be no more
For John the hour it has passed it is too late
But for the next generation love must replace hate
So I send my call out searching for ears true
What else could I do?

And he had that faraway look in his eyes
As if he was in a play wearing some disguise
When I saw him a million questions would form
He was a soldier he wore the uniform

Hello Baby Hello

I came by late today but I still came by
Every time I see you I have to cry
If you're there then I know you're aware
And if you're gone it gives me a scare

Hello baby hello
I'm hoping that you are well
So sorry to see you in hell
Hello baby hello

Well I guess it's the best for the both of us
Hey look didn't they crucify Jesus?
Hold my hand they say heaven's past the door
I just wish that I could be sure

Hello baby hello
I'm hoping that you are well
So sorry to see you in hell
Hello baby hello

Well it's time to spread love and peace
Who cares if the money supply will increase?
Filthy green papers featuring evil men
When you learn the truth you can't go back again

Hello baby hello
I'm hoping that you are well
So sorry to see you in hell
Hello baby hello

And all the rock stars are doing the very best that they can
After Woody and Seeger most didn't give a damn
Maybe they'll write a tune or support some cause
But we need to stand up and demand some just laws

Well they were singing in the room downstairs
Linda was dancing she don't have any cares
And I wonder if you even heard it at all
And I wonder if you even heard it at all

Hello baby hello
I'm hoping that you are well
So sorry to see you in hell
Hello baby hello

Hopes And Fears

She was a dangerous darling blonde freak
With acoustic guitar and poetic speak
Every day we fade a little bit more
And we don't even have time to keep score

Peace love and understanding
Life is so demanding
With a million eager ears
Sharing our hopes and fears

If you don't go up you can't go down
Let me take you to the poor side of town
They sing the blues in perfect harmony
As they struggle just to be free

Peace love and understanding
Life is so demanding
With a million eager ears
Sharing our hopes and fears

One day these words will live to testify
That I knew the truth and told a lie
God and country please serve them well
What do you say about the highway to hell?

Peace love and understanding
Life is so demanding
With a million eager ears
Sharing our hopes and fears

And so old folk singers fade to gray
Even Dylan had lived a better day
While Biggie and Tupac rest in peace
I just want the endless wars to cease

Peace love and understanding
Life is so demanding
With a million eager ears
Sharing our hopes and fears

I Love Your Body

You're so hot that I can feel your steam
A midnight princess straight from a dream
I want to make you moan I want to make your scream
Sugar is sweet the coffee is hot and oh the cream

I love your body body body and your sex
I love the way you move move move and vex
I love your body body body and your sex
I love the way you move move move and vex

This song has been dancing all around inside my head
Is it wrong to want you prancing around inside my bed?
Riding the morning train my thoughts turn to you
I'm a poor boy caught in fantasy what am I to do?

I love your body body body and your sex
I love the way you move move move and vex
I love your body body body and your sex
I love the way you move move move and vex

All the girls strut their stuff up and down Broad Street
Sometimes I feel the temptation to take a bite to eat
But they're all chop meat and you're filet mignon
I want to devour you and chew the bone when you're gone

I love your body body body and your sex
I love the way you move move move and vex
I love your body body body and your sex
I love the way you move move move and vex

Bennet got me singing a song of the purest blues
Seems life is bringing the wrong of paying endless dues
Kelly makes me smile but it only lasts a little while
But you my darling are the sexology of survival

I love your body body body and your sex
I love the way you move move move and vex
I love your body body body and your sex
I love the way you move move move and vex

I Want To Find A Place Where I Belong

I'm just a runaway who never had a home
From here to there is where I roam
A broken heart always on my own
The street is the only friend I've known

I would like to sing a love song
I want to find a place where I belong
I don't want nobody to do me wrong
I want to find a place where I belong

I'll take your hand if it's for free
But darling you got to take all of me
The good the bad and even the beauty
When you look at me what do you see?

I would like to sing a love song
I want to find a place where I belong
I don't want nobody to do me wrong
I want to find a place where I belong

I once had friends but only in name
They made promises only for their shame
I burned my cards life tore me in two
The queen of clubs she abandoned me too

It takes courage to smile to try to make life worthwhile
Some people are barely getting by others they live in style
I've seen the rich I've seen the poor and there is no cure
It seems we all have sweet dreams of just a little bit more

I would like to sing a love song
I want to find a place where I belong
I don't want nobody to do me wrong
I want to find a place where I belong

Forgive me if I doubt all you say
Between the bars and scars I'm gray
Night reins the pains they hang high
Could you please save me from my lie?

I would like to sing a love song
I want to find a place where I belong
I don't want nobody to do me wrong
I want to find a place where I belong

I Whispered Into Her Ear

I woke up on a day I couldn't remember
Maybe it was the never of December
I was lying naked in my bedroom
Lingering in the air the sweetest perfume

I whispered into her ear
And said what she needed to hear
I whispered into her ear
And kissed away her aching fear

She was an angel or perhaps a demon
Ruby red lipstick proved I wasn't dreaming
There is a difference between truth and lies
And lust is really love in disguise

I whispered into her ear
And said what she needed to hear
I whispered into her ear
And kissed away her aching fear

Carnal pleasures come in double measures
You drink your fill and you make the kill
The engine works on built up pressures
In the race of the chase lies the thrill

Empty and aching I lie alone
I am a man but I have never grown
Here is my song wrong or right
I'd do it again any Saturday night

I whispered into her ear
And said what she needed to hear
I whispered into her ear
And kissed away her aching fear

I'm A Dreamer

We all have wings but some never fly
They stand on the Earth and look at the sky
But me I got a rocket ship ready to go
Commence the countdown let the engines blow

I'm a dreamer lost in a fantasy
And you my love mean all to me
Together is the only way to be
I'm a dreamer lost in a fantasy

Say goodbye to all those you hold dear
Tomorrow is coming dismiss every fear
Life is wide open the galaxy has no end
Give me your hand my lover and friend

I'm a dreamer lost in a fantasy
And you my love mean all to me
Together is the only way to be
I'm a dreamer lost in a fantasy

We'll go to a place kind where we have some peace of mind
To a planet of grace deep in outer space where none are blind
Where war is a concept that hasn't even been created
Where harmony and brotherhood rule and none are hated
They say my sweet darling that dreams don't come true
Well whoever said that baby they never met you

Give me a kiss for good luck and something more
In ten seconds this spaceship is going to soar
Have no fear when you hear the engines roar
The game is over one nothing is the final score

I'm a dreamer lost in a fantasy
And you my love mean all to me
Together is the only way to be
I'm a dreamer lost in a fantasy

In Your Mind

Daddy was never the same after the war
His empty eyes I wish they would say more
Something died long before the proper time
War may not be illegal but it's a crime

What do you find in your mind?
I see the blind leading the blind
Sanity and love they're left behind
What do you find in your mind?

Pearl was a girl of the finest style
I would give the world just to see her smile
She flew to L.A. and a star was born
But it ain't Hollywood it was porn

What do you find in your mind?
I see the blind leading the blind
Sanity and love they're left behind
What do you find in your mind?

We're all flesh and blood body and soul
The juggernaut in an onslaught for control
In a great grind the spirit of truth they bind
Let love rule, in your mind, in your mind

Johnny had a brilliant brain keen and quick
He wanted to be an engineer real slick
But he went crazy somewhere along the way
Now he sits and writes poetry all day

What do you find in your mind?
I see the blind leading the blind
Sanity and love they're left behind
What do you find in your mind?

Robert wanted to rule the rock and roll show
But he got bogged down with the booze and blow
Fame faded as he found out what was real
Now he plays guitar at the bar for a meal

What do you find in your mind?
I see the blind leading the blind
Sanity and love they're left behind
What do you find in your mind?

Josh Ain't Cool Anymore

Walter wasn't popular nobody pretends
But he did have a couple of friends
There was Josh, Tom and his older brother John
My oh my how fast have the years gone

Josh ain't cool anymore
Wasn't sure about before
But now there ain't no cure
Josh ain't cool anymore

They would sit together over a couple of beers
They were young punks with grown up fears
They didn't trust the system they knew the deal
That high school history wasn't really real

Josh ain't cool anymore
Wasn't sure about before
But now there ain't no cure
Josh ain't cool anymore

Well Walter and John they left this place
And Josh has lost every trace of grace
He turned from being cool to the perfect fool
I say this but I'm not trying to be cruel

Josh ain't cool anymore
Wasn't sure about before
But now there ain't no cure
Josh ain't cool anymore

Well they would listen to Bob Dylan sing
So wise but they didn't know a thing
It's not the position when you start the race
It's how much you help the human race

Josh ain't cool anymore
Wasn't sure about before
But now there ain't no cure
Josh ain't cool anymore

So Josh it's all about dollars and cents
When God judges you you'll have no defense
You're just a whore who likes endless war
I've seen this story so many times before

Josh ain't cool anymore
Wasn't sure about before
But now there ain't no cure
Josh ain't cool anymore

Kelly

Kelly sits at her desk with two kinds of candy
She got a pretty vase of flowers thanks to Andy
With a window with a view she silently dreams
Life is what you make of it not what it seems

Hunter was never told his mother rock and rolled his mother rock and rolled
She used to be brave and bold Kelly she rock and rolled Kelly rock and rolled
Hunter was never told Kelly rock and rolled Kelly rock and rolled
Hunter was never told Kelly rock and rolled Kelly rock and rolled

Early in the morning Hunter gets ready for school
Kelly would be happy if he became anything but a fool
Life has many lessons and most of them cruel
What does Kelly care she's aware she's cool

Hunter was never told his mother rock and rolled his mother rock and rolled
She used to be brave and bold Kelly she rock and rolled Kelly rock and rolled
Hunter was never told Kelly rock and rolled Kelly rock and rolled
Hunter was never told Kelly rock and rolled Kelly rock and rolled

Friday night drinking some light beer at her bar
If you can't be a star be happy with who you are
She hears the music play a song from distant yesterday
Kelly laughs and takes a sip she's doing okay

Hunter was never told his mother rock and rolled his mother rock and rolled
She used to be brave and bold Kelly she rock and rolled Kelly rock and rolled
Hunter was never told Kelly rock and rolled Kelly rock and rolled
Hunter was never told Kelly rock and rolled Kelly rock and rolled

Laughing Linda

She's the last card an ancient ace
The future is past with some hard grace
God He numbers all of your hairs
But I wonder if anyone else cares

Laughing Linda laughs all day
Laughing Linda always at play
Laughing Linda hear me pray
Laughing Linda laughs all day

Playing bingo listening to Ringo Star
The answer to the mystery ain't far
If you seek then you also shall find
Wonders of yesterday in her mind

Laughing Linda laughs all day
Laughing Linda always at play
Laughing Linda hear me pray
Laughing Linda laughs all day

Tomorrow is built on shaky ground
Wisdom is common sense so profound
Full steam ahead never looking before
As you live you can give a little more

Laughing Linda laughs all day
Laughing Linda always at play
Laughing Linda hear me pray
Laughing Linda laughs all day

Pretty soon we'll come to high noon
Whistling away with a pleasant tune
A kiss goodbye I promise to cry
Try mercy forget the alibi

Laughing Linda laughs all day
Laughing Linda always at play
Laughing Linda hear me pray
Laughing Linda laughs all day

Liberty

Dixie is still singing her sweet song
God bless America tell me what went wrong
Down to the Walmart getting some food to eat
Three men of darker skin drawing the heat

Caught in a thought of liberty
In the hell of my cell I am free
Fall to the call of let it be
Caught in a thought of liberty

The cold air shuffles in from the riverside
Love and only love can cross the great divide
There's a reason for everything under the sun
A million billion winners one number one

Caught in a thought of liberty
In the hell of my cell I am free
Fall to the call of let it be
Caught in a thought of liberty

Late at night hypocrisy flows free
You can see my face but do you see me
Every story has a beginning and end
If you fail you can prevail just pretend

Caught in a thought of liberty
In the hell of my cell I am free
Fall to the call of let it be
Caught in a thought of liberty

Major Tom dropped the bomb on the crazies
Outmoded it exploded into a trillion daisies
The asylum has invisible walls
How come the kingdom nobody recalls

Caught in a thought of liberty
In the hell of my cell I am free
Fall to the call of let it be
Caught in a thought of liberty

Life Is A Never Ending Show

Dreams come true don't you know?
Here I am singing at the Apollo
I've come from the land of sorrow
And I still have many miles to go

Life is a never-ending show
Like a river you see time flow
In the heavens clouds blow
Life is a never-ending show

The world is an endless song
I am here yes I truly do belong
In my music there is a tale to tell
A story of glory with a little hell

Life is a never-ending show
Like a river you see time flow
In the heavens clouds blow
Life is a never-ending show

My people have walked down a road of woe
My people once ruled the world don't you know?
Freedom is a word seldom heard with a smile
My goal is to emancipate your soul in this trial

The lights are bright on this night
I'm feeling fine everything's a delight
Dreams come true don't you know?
Here I am singing at the Apollo

Life is a never-ending show
Like a river you see time flow
In the heavens clouds blow
Life is a never-ending show

Dreams come true don't you know?
Here I am singing at the Apollo

Life is a never-ending show
Like a river you see time flow
In the heavens clouds blow
Life is a never-ending show

Life Is A Party

Bopping and hopping from the streets to the dance floor
Full ahead no stopping still seeking something more
Hitting the beat searching for mister wonderful to meet
Arms swaying feet tapping tongue singing a song sweet

Life is a party see the fool grin
Up and down lose and win
Having a good time ain't no sin
Life is a party welcome in

Days are magic and nights utterly fantastic
The key to living is giving the perfect trick
Walking the school halls or under disco mirror balls
Memory is an illusion the mind recalls

Life is a party see the fool grin
Up and down lose and win
Having a good time ain't no sin
Life is a party welcome in

When you're young you want to be old
You never wanna do what you are told
When you're old you wanna be young
Because the song of your life has been sung

When you're in the grove you gotta prove you're for real
All of the men are looking to seal the big deal
Gotta be quick in your mind to know what you wanna find
For me I want a tall handsome man fine and kind

Life is a party see the fool grin
Up and down lose and win
Having a good time ain't no sin
Life is a party welcome in

Lords Of The Hollow

Walk the walk talk the talk that's what they say
I'm a midnight demon hunting my prey
Every footstep fills another letter
And let me tell you brother it's getting better

We are the Lords of the Hollow
We take the lead we never follow
See how the eagle kills the sparrow
We are the Lords of the Hollow

Flying high in the sky past the stratosphere
It's live and let die without any fear
I've waited a lifetime just to flap my wings
I'm ready roaring soaring seeing what life brings

We are the Lords of the Hollow
We take the lead we never follow
See how the eagle kills the sparrow
We are the Lords of the Hollow

There she is the definition of love
She's the one everybody's dreaming of
Keeping cool I start to drool taking aim
In a flash of fire my desire bursts into flame

We are the Lords of the Hollow
We take the lead we never follow
See how the eagle kills the sparrow
We are the Lords of the Hollow

Tomorrow's something that will never come
We are kings and rock and roll our kingdom
Hot gals fast cars and a good portion of soul
We're radicals revolting against ground control

We are the Lords of the Hollow
We take the lead we never follow
See how the eagle kills the sparrow
We are the Lords of the Hollow

Lost In Space

When I was a child God's words were written in stone
And hatred was the only religion I had known
The language of love was spoken in foreign verse
And the blessings of the state was their curse

I was lost in space
Never knowing grace
Turning the other face
I was lost in space

The theatre was in town and I decided to attend
I was lonely my shadow was my only friend
I sought truth in the words the actress said
I believed and received but she wound up dead

I was lost in space
Never knowing grace
Turning the other face
I was lost in space

I drifted with the wind blowing in blowing out
My spirits were lifted by Jesus but I had my doubt
The hypocrites were circling like buzzards in the sky
They had all the answers but the questions were a lie

I was lost in space
Never knowing grace
Turning the other face
I was lost in space

And Gerard refused to believe a syllable
He looks at the world we're all the fool
I can't decide if he's kind or cruel
In the devil's box there's many a tool

So here I go with death my certain reality
The men in arms do their harms with savage brutality
I was watching the skies hoping for a celestial sign
When I realized that this life I lived was mine

I was lost in space
Never knowing grace
Turning the other face
I was lost in space

Love Is In Command

I feel your love whenever you are near me
Happy smile and bright eyes I see clearly
Every second I hold on so dearly
I say hello somehow I know you hear me

You're a million miles away I understand
You're a million miles away I hold your hand
Life never works out the way you planned
But I know Love is in command

I whisper sweet nothings into your space
Life is love and love is a form of grace
The hardest mile is the one you walk alone
You are the best woman I've ever known

You're a million miles away I understand
You're a million miles away I hold your hand
Life never works out the way you planned
But I know Love is in command

An iron cross searing hot
All the good time never forgot
Give and take take and give
Live is the only way to live

A cat's whisper our dreams will never end
Forever my lover forever my friend
Hold on baby this is the long goodbye
When I kneel in prayer I ask God why

You're a million miles away I understand
You're a million miles away I hold your hand
Life never works out the way you planned
But I know Love is in command

Love Just Walked In The Door

Back in sixty two the angel blew his horn
In joyful bliss a child of promise was born
Hope and change were the lyrics of the new song
We were young we were beautiful we were strong

And love just walked in the door
Just like the time before
Searching for the perfect score
Love just walked in the door

Born before her time the essence of the perfect rhyme
Your always guilty if you're at the scene of the crime
The men of shame passed the blame to the sacred lamb
In the valley of the shadow of death I am

Running guns currency of the third world nation
He walked away without pay for salvation
The promoter smiled the ticket sales rose
You ain't nothing if you can't afford the shows

And love just walked in the door
Just like the time before
Searching for the perfect score
Love just walked in the door

Whatever isn't real has to be a lie
Searching heaven for the big guy in the sky
Jesus he preached good news while singing the blues
Go far be a star but you pay your dues

And love just walked in the door
Just like the time before
Searching for the perfect score
Love just walked in the door

Doctor Dave is good but he could never save
You'll get your rest when you settle in the grave
One by one the work is done we shall overcome
Open your eyes be wise enter God's kingdom

And love just walked in the door
Just like the time before
Searching for the perfect score
Love just walked in the door

Love Machine

I had a dream I made a love machine
It didn't pollute it was fully green
My machine-made thoughts and prayers become real
The only fight that is right is for the ideal

Love machine love machine
Makes you happy even if you're mean
It run on nothing the engine is clean
Love machine love machine

Peace was declared all wars came to an end
The worst of enemies embraced as friends
Rich misers sold all and gave to the poor
Hatred and evil didn't exist any more

Love machine love machine
Makes you happy even if you're mean
It run on nothing the engine is clean
Love machine love machine

I knew that all of this was fantasy
That I would wake up to dark misery
I would put the love machine in my heart
That in this wicked world I would do my part

Love machine love machine
Makes you happy even if you're mean
It run on nothing the engine is clean
Love machine love machine

So here I am singing this simple song
If you hear it please try to right a wrong
Love is the finest thing we have in this place
So show a little mercy and show some grace

Love machine love machine
Makes you happy even if you're mean
It run on nothing the engine is clean
Love machine love machine

Love One Another

Captain Neil was sailing in deep space
Searching for a faint ray of love and grace
He was smiling strumming his guitar
Sometimes near and sometimes far
Life is hard if you don't know who you are

Earth she is my home and my mother
Why can't we love one another?
We are all family I am your brother
Think of all the good we could discover
Why can't we love one another?

Peter passed on to heaven's kingdom
Finally free he had overcome
There is a beauty in the righteous fight
A blessing of doing what's right
It is like living in day or in night

Earth she is my home and my mother
Why can't we love one another?
We are all family I am your brother
Think of all the good we could discover
Why can't we love one another?

What are we doing with the life God gave?
Only a few ticks until the final grave
We could build towers that touch the sky
Instead we wage war to kill and die

Roger was confused but still quite clear
I was not born to live with hate or fear
What is this about building us a wall?
We were born free as I recall
Now is the moment and here is the call

Earth she is my home and my mother
Why can't we love one another?
We are all family I am your brother
Think of all the good we could discover
Why can't we love one another?

Love Will Never Die

Good friends who walked with me
Through laughter and agony
Together we will grow old
Tomorrow is yet to be told

Heaven will always be high
The cup cannot run dry
You do not fail if you try
And love will never die

Playing the game of remembering
There is no surrendering
Forgive all wrong and move on
One day we too will be gone

Heaven will always be high
The cup cannot run dry
You do not fail if you try
And love will never die

In the glory of my youth I searched the truth of grace
I saw the hatred and the love in the human race
I was raised and praised by the voice of the divine
I knew full well come high hell that the choice was mine

Lend a hand to those to come
The task it is never done
The wheel is forever in spin
And quitting the lethal sin

Heaven will always be high
The cup cannot run dry
You do not fail if you try
And love will never die

Love Will Prevail

She is made of silicone and titanium steel
At night all alone the wisdom is so real
Love is the tutor and the lesson profound
As you seek as you sow so shall it be found

Love will prevail
And so goes the tale
Love it cannot fail
Love will prevail

The soldiers are marching in close ranks
They sacrifice heart and soul for no thanks
In the parade her eyes fall on her love
He is her man he is all she thinks of

Love will prevail
And so goes the tale
Love it cannot fail
Love will prevail

War has been declared the world is in fright
What happens in the darkest of the night?
Dreams come true but nightmares too
She would sacrifice all for the two

Love will prevail
And so goes the tale
Love it cannot fail
Love will prevail

This is the long goodbye
She does her best not to cry
Her only question is 'Why?'
She don't want him to die

How did the world get to this dark place?
What about the gentler aspects of graces?
She sits like Buddha full of reflection
 It is hard to believe when you need protection

Love will prevail
And so goes the tale
Love it cannot fail
Love will prevail

More Than The Money

In Silicon Valley lies the Dragon's Lair
At the political rally they scream a prayer
Gonna shoot a rocket ship to the planet Mars
While the in crowd plays their electric guitars

The robot never had a soul
More than the money its control
Follow the greed to see the goal
More than the money its control

Free love acid rock new kids squatting on the block
When you find the truth it's one hell of a shock
The temple of Midas is empty so they say
Boys will be boys it's best to let them play

The robot never had a soul
More than the money its control
Follow the greed to see the goal
More than the money its control

Tanya gonna fly to L.A.
Free the poor without pay
They're all guilty hear them say
The truth don't matter anyway

Collateral damage the numbers are lies
A war on terror it's the devil in disguise
The engineer boasts about his new jet plane
And drowns his sorrow with fine wine and cocaine

The robot never had a soul
More than the money its control
Follow the greed to see the goal
More than the money its control

The circles broken the pyramids in place
Useless eaters are what makes the human race
A machine kills clean and never asks for a raise
Full steam ahead we're soaring for better days

The robot never had a soul
More than the money its control
Follow the greed to see the goal
More than the money its control

My Life

Well I opened up the door looking for some more
A child of the universe under a curse for sure
Looking for love searching from heaven to below
Never clever she was ever traveling too slow

I photo shopped my life
Now I got a beautiful wife
I cut out all of the strife
I photo shopped my life

In the bar there you are a rage upon the stage
Like a lion prancing dancing locked up in a cage
I had the key but afraid to open the lock
Looking from above were the gods of love and rock

I photo shopped my life
Now I got a beautiful wife
I cut out all of the strife
I photo shopped my life

My mama gave me drama since the day I was born
On the cross I took a loss my body completely torn
Walking on water in my name this bloody slaughter
Babylon the Whore is bound once more I bought her

We took a chance nothing was well running like hell
Only the blind prophet could stop it so I tell
In the chase there is the grace of unending thrill
You're caught when you're bought sold out ready for the kill

I photo shopped my life
Now I got a beautiful wife
I cut out all of the strife
I photo shopped my life

So here we are so far bouncing from star to star
If you have juice turn loose your electric guitar
Somewhere out there in all this wrong is a great song
In my arms safe from harms is just where you belong

I photo shopped my life
Now I got a beautiful wife
I cut out all of the strife
I photo shopped my life

Oh Baby Love Me

See the clown downtown with guitar in his hand
He plays the blues a language you fluently understand
Down at the crossroads he made himself a deal
But the devil ain't the only one looking for a soul to steal

And he sings oh baby love me
And he sings oh baby love me
But tomorrow I'll be free
But tonight oh baby love me

Smoking a cigarette while he mumbles the words wrong
Sometimes too soft and sometimes much too strong
She smiles knowing that she can get her own way
For every fool a rule they have a price to play

And he sings oh baby love me
And he sings oh baby love me
But tomorrow I'll be free
But tonight oh baby love me

Lights and stages might be the rages for those who dream
But to him his life so grim is freed by her scream
Flesh and fetishes fantasy is released in a single word
He plucks all the strings but never plays the chord

And he sings oh baby love me
And he sings oh baby love me
But tomorrow I'll be free
But tonight oh baby love me

The hat is full of tossed coins and crumpled dollar bills
With all his skills taking pills helps his thrills
In the end he'll leave with his friend full of skills
Hear him sing the chosen king of broken wills

And he sings oh baby love me
And he sings oh baby love me
But tomorrow I'll be free
But tonight oh baby love me

On The Radio

Turn the dial until you smile
Search the church it's worthwhile
Changing frequency with a twist
She's an angel of amethyst

It's gotta be good if it's on the radio
Like the wind you can see her blow
Dancing romancing at the go-go
It's gotta be good if it's on the radio

Listen to the D.J. chatter
Saying things that don't matter
 Turn up the volume to ten
Finish your prayers with an amen

It's gotta be good if it's on the radio
Like the wind you can see her blow
Dancing romancing at the go-go
Its gotta be good if it's on the radio

Payola blues the song to rule
They'll take you right back to school
It's all about the green fool
The whore and the bore had a duel

It's gotta be good if it's on the radio
Like the wind you can see her blow
Dancing romancing at the go-go
It's gotta be good if it's on the radio

And Mother Mary she's doing the Vatican rag
The priest got lucky with the nun hear him brag
Meanwhile the sermon is on the evils of rock and roll
Tell me mister what can a man give for his soul?

Flap your wings it's time to fly
One final kiss then goodbye
We'll always have our special song
Playing on the radio strong

Paradise

I remember the days before you were born
Between love and duty the solider he was torn
In a final goodbye in love he took it all
In the morning he answered his country's call

The sound of the bugle brings her to tears
Not knowing is the worst of her fears
Life zooms by and they don't even think twice
There's a price in defending paradise

Well they all said that you got your father's eyes
You will be born and raised on identical lies
The truth is the truth there cannot be compromise
Wounded in battle can you hear his bitter cries?

The sound of the bugle brings her to tears
Not knowing is the worst of her fears
Life zooms by and they don't even think twice
There's a price in defending paradise

War is hell and the fires never fade away
At church the reverend said he'd pray
How quickly the finest are forgotten
Johnny our hero becomes Johnny Rotten

And daddy he can't play a game of baseball
Daddy has no legs he cannot walk at all
In the morning he answered his country's call
In the evening sleep so much he cannot recall

The sound of the bugle brings her to tears
Not knowing is the worst of her fears
Life zooms by and they don't even think twice
There's a price in defending paradise

Wall Street bankers have what money can buy
The keep their sacred truth by repeating the lie
They'll salute the veteran and whisper with scorn
I was like that long before you were born

The sound of the bugle brings her to tears
Not knowing is the worst of her fears
Life zooms by and they don't even think twice
There's a price in defending paradise

Raise Your Voice

We are citizens of Babylon freedom is a lie
We are citizens of Babylon can you hear our cry
Endless war is no cure it only serves greed
We are citizens of Babylon in desperate need

If you don't like the system then raise your voice
If you don't like the system you still have a choice
In satanic wisdom see lady folly rejoice
If you don't like the system then raise your voice

The ways of love they sing a sweeter song
In the ways of love you don't do any wrong
Carry your cross speaks words of righteousness
In the ways of love it is our duty to resist

If you don't like the system then raise your voice
If you don't like the system you still have a choice
In satanic wisdom see lady folly rejoice
If you don't like the system then raise your voice

I am talking to all of the people we must unite
I am talking to all of the people it's time to fight
Don't let your children be slaves all their lives
Listen here only in fear the system survives

Follow your heart do your part lend a hand
Emancipate your mind it's time to take a stand
The four winds are blowing from a distant land
The forces of freedom are marching with the band

If you don't like the system then raise your voice
If you don't like the system you still have a choice
In satanic wisdom see lady folly rejoice
If you don't like the system then raise your voice

Refugee

The bombs exploding brought in the morn
Heart mind and soul all twisted and torn
Hell was screaming real loud hate will prevail
Look around and you will see evil's tale

Just a refugee trying to flee
It could be you it could be me
Can't you just feel their agony?
Just a refugee trying to flee

Down on Wall Street see the market soar
Drunk on blood it's Babylon the Whore
All they see are the digits on the chart
They got a cash register for a heart

Just a refugee trying to flee
It could be you it could be me
Can't you just feel their agony?
Just a refugee trying to flee

House in ruins no reason to stay
They walk the lonely road the winding way
Belly empty and their mind transfixed with fear
The sound of soldiers ominously near

Just a refugee trying to flee
It could be you it could be me
Can't you just feel their agony?
Just a refugee trying to flee

Not welcome is the message spoken
On the roam no home spirit broken
As you have done unto the least of these
Hopes and prayers it puts you on your knees
God have mercy on the refugees

Just a refugee trying to flee
It could be you it could be me
Can't you just feel their agony?
Just a refugee trying to flee

Repent

Here I am down to my last dime
And a dime ain't worth much these days
Working for a living it's a crime
I keep searching for somebody who pays
Enough for food and rent
Repent, repent, repent

I'm in the mood to sing the blues
I'll sit on a bench with a tin can
Say mister you got some good news
How about some master plan
I'm looking for a savior heaven sent
Repent, repent, repent

I saw a woman from a magazine
I said hi baby hello how are you
Don't you know she caused a scene?
What's a lonely man to do?
Get away woman that I resent
Repent, repent, repent

My buddy and I were sipping some wine
Sitting in the park enjoying the sun
Everything was going along fine
Until the bottle was all done
He wouldn't fork over his fifty cent
Repent, repent, repent

Well the devil came looking for my soul
He promised me the sun and moon
I've been on that road paid the toll
I said I ain't following no time soon
We started a great big argument
Repent, repent, repent

Here I am down to my last song
My fingers are sore my throat dry
Everything that could just went wrong
I feel like I could up and die
Maybe tomorrow won't be so bent
Repent, repent, repent

Rock And Roll Soldier

I was born bursting out in a rebel yell
I gave mommy and daddy some living hell
Dancing and romancing my lightning was white
Romancing and dancing through the entire night

I'm a Rock and roll soldier
Turn it louder be bolder
Rock and roll soldier
Getting better getting older

See how in the dark the fire burns much brighter
Baby I'm a lover and baby I'm a fighter
The world spins the devil grins the sinner sins
I'm holding four hot aces let's see who wins

I'm a Rock and roll soldier
Turn it louder be bolder
Rock and roll soldier
Getting better getting older

Armed with a guitar you know just who you are
Electricity crying flying to a star
Unleashing the force which is the source of all
We're learning past secrets things we can't recall

I'm a Rock and roll soldier
Turn it louder be bolder
Rock and roll soldier
Getting better getting older

Putting magical dust in the equation
Love and lust will both lead you to salvation
Come here hot momma kiss me right on my lips
When we become one you know how time just slips

I'm a Rock and roll soldier
Turn it louder be bolder
Rock and roll soldier
Getting better getting older

Rocket Ship To Ride

Engines glowing red hot feel them revving up
Sin hits the spot there's real firewater in my cup
The night is still young the hunger it aches
Ain't no maybe lady I have what it takes

Got me a rocket ship to ride
We ain't gonna be denied
Do it for love do it for pride
Got me a rocket ship to ride

Music is loud the band's out of control
Baby let's lose this crowd and search for our soul
Black is the color of imagination
The curse of the universe is salvation

Got me a rocket ship to ride
We ain't gonna be denied
Do it for love do it for pride
Got me a rocket ship to ride

I can tell that you've graced outer space a time or two for sure
What I need to know before we go is are you ready to soar?
Pretend is the friend of those who can't reach their fantasy
So Miss Jane let me put it plain do you want to ride with me?

Here we go my love let the countdown commence
When you got nothing to lose it all makes sense
The lights are low and I can feel the fire glow
Me and you a private two front row to the show

Ten, nine, eight, seven, six
Pick up some sticks
Five, four, three, two, one
Blastoff has begun – are you having fun?

Got me a rocket ship to ride
We ain't gonna be denied
Do it for love do it for pride
Got me a rocket ship to ride

Sacrifice

Day fades to night, night passes to day
All is a grand eternal gray
I am paying my dues the toll is high
But I'll rock and roll until I die

This world is full of sacrifice
Honey you gotta pay the price
Take my best advice
If you can refrain don't toss the die
This world is full of sacrifice

She's a psychopath fuming with wrath
Say hey lady go take an ice-cold bath
The loudest voice is never right
For peace and love I will always fight

I walked through the village by the Pequannock River
I was searching for a lover a savior to deliver
There was Jesus hanging on his cruel cross
If you want something better it comes through loss

This world is full of sacrifice
Honey you gotta pay the price
Take my best advice
If you can refrain don't toss the die
This world is full of sacrifice

I hear the bombs exploding in my mind
Somewhere I left my innocence behind
Support the troops for the sake of greed
I lament this world was never meant to bleed

This world is full of sacrifice
Honey you gotta pay the price
Take my best advice
If you can refrain don't toss the die
This world is full of sacrifice

Sad Eyes

I saw your picture on the magazine
The rage of the age a beauty queen
Your face was painted pretty with lies
And oh the sorrow in your sad eyes

Sad eyes you got them sad eyes
I see past your disguise
It's the truth that the world denies
Sad eyes you got them sad eyes

When I knew you fame was but a dream
You had some plan a clever scheme
A rocket ship ride past the stars
A simple chord on electric guitars

Sad eyes you got them sad eyes
I see past your disguise
It's the truth that the world denies
Sad eyes you got them sad eyes

So tell me honey now that it's real
Did the devil get the better of the deal?
The grass is green but the sky is gray
Are you wishing for yesterday?

Sad eyes you got them sad eyes
I see past your disguise
It's the truth that the world denies
Sad eyes you got them sad eyes

You don't come round no more
Ain't no loving like before
Life really don't have a cure
A wreck ship on the ocean floor

Every move never are you alone
You eat the meat toss away the bone
You tried to call me on the telephone
Just to tell me that your missing home

Sad eyes you got them sad eyes
I see past your disguise
It's the truth that the world denies
Sad eyes you got them sad eyes

Salah

I met Salah down at the Sandalwood
They like a brown man when they're good
Salah was a refugee from Palestine
Salah he was a good friend of mine

Hey Salah the world turns
Life changes and one learns
Simple lessons like fire burns
Hey Salah the world turns

Well we busted our asses bussing tables
Salah explained history just some fables
At the end of the day we had a good time
It seemed the words all had a rhyme

Hey Salah the world turns
Life changes and one learns
Simple lessons like fire burns
Hey Salah the world turns

Well Sue liked to screw or give head
And Jim's boyfriend he knocked us dead
You liked to hang with Tony and Gary
Those two pipsqueaks were real scary

Hey Salah the world turns
Life changes and one learns
Simple lessons like fire burns
Hey Salah the world turns

Hey Salah now don't you do me wrong
Come look for me when you hear this song
We'll talk about the future and the past
Friends are friends and love will last

Hey Salah the world turns
Life changes and one learns
Simple lessons like fire burns
Hey Salah the world turns

Seeking Grace

See the king on a hill with a crimson brow
No past no future there's only the now
If you trust the lust you're bound to bust
But give me your sweet kiss if you must

I am a sinner seeking grace
A member of the human race
I am a sinner seeking grace
How can I get out of this place?

For thousands of years an empty fight
Pilgrims wandering searching for the light
And if could I would have made it right
Still I will follow the lord of love and might

I am a sinner seeking grace
A member of the human race
I am a sinner seeking grace
How can I get out of this place?

The refugees kept inside a barbwire fence
None of the few clues make any sense
I am hungry I am tired I am weary
See the scared face of my child so teary

I am a sinner seeking grace
A member of the human race
I am a sinner seeking grace
How can I get out of this place?

If you don't have a song I have one to share
If you don't have a hope I'll offer a prayer
I've heard your story it's one I share
We shall overcome oh yes I will dare

I am a sinner seeking grace
A member of the human race
I am a sinner seeking grace
How can I get out of this place?

Serving Is Its Own Reward

When you see me in my dream don't wake me up
Don't tempt me sir with some coffee cup
I'll by riding the dragons in the stratosphere
Yeah you'll know that the rapture is getting near

Tip your hat to the Lord
Serving is its own reward
I'm standing on the word
Serving is its own reward

Many years ago I stopped counting the cost
I've been through the jungle never getting lost
Cause Jesus is a light shining oh so bright
And it don't matter I'm blind in endless night

Tip your hat to the Lord
Serving is its own reward
I'm standing on the word
Serving is its own reward

Michael where have you gone you've gotten old
I learned a lesson never do as you're told
It took forty years of wandering the desert land
Maybe Peter is somebody who could understand

Tip your hat to the Lord
Serving is its own reward
I'm standing on the word
Serving is its own reward

I am the poet man you see how all the words rhyme
I was born well ahead of the proper time
I'm taking requests so nothing could go wrong
Sad thing is that I only know how to play one song

Tip your hat to the Lord
Serving is its own reward
I'm standing on the word
Serving is its own reward

Sisters

Say woman why they call you girl?
Say woman you're a black pearl
Say woman there is a solution
Say woman try a little revolution

We are sisters one and all
We are sisters who hear the call
Empires rise and kingdoms fall
We are sisters one and all

Hey there we ain't going to submit
This thing called freedom is counterfeit
I am going to be just how I desire
I am a flame together we're a fire

We are sisters one and all
We are sisters who hear the call
Empires rise and kingdoms fall
We are sisters one and all

They want us to cook and clean
And at night be a sexual machine
Well let me tell you I got a mind
And brother I'm leaving you behind

We are sisters one and all
We are sisters who hear the call
Empires rise and kingdoms fall
We are sisters one and all

Jim Crow don't you know it's wrong
We gotta do more than just sing a song
The Black Panther Party of defense
Let me tell you that makes perfect sense

We are sisters one and all
We are sisters who hear the call
Empires rise and kingdoms fall
We are sisters one and all

Slavery On The Plantation

They give you a number when you're born
With a slap hello you begin to mourn
Dreams abound but only while you sleep
There are secrets but will you look deep

Here we are yes we are slaves on the plantation
For you and me all that's free is salvation
Nine to five to stay alive that's our destination
Here we are yes we are slaves on the plantation

At the library the signs keep control
For law and order we sacrificed our soul
The streets ain't clean there's too much crime
And worst of all the poets don't rhyme

Here we are yes we are slaves on the plantation
For you and me all that's free is salvation
Nine to five to stay alive that's our destination
Here we are yes we are slaves on the plantation

Freedom is a grand illusion
Money a demonic delusion
Always gotta look away
Be careful what you say
Tomorrow is another day
Here's the piper time to pay

It's a high-tech digital world
Girl meets boy machine meets girl
Soon the human race will be obsolete
Flesh and blood well it can't compete

Here we are yes we are slaves on the plantation
For you and me all that's free is salvation
Nine to five to stay alive that's our destination
Here we are yes we are slaves on the plantation

Slow Song

Dreams are like chasing the moonshine
I love you so will you ever be mine?
A summer night everything is divine
Here we are under the stars walking the line

And the band plays the slow song
All is perfect nothing is wrong
In my arms is where you belong
While the band plays the slow song

The singer he's speaking to me and you
Saying in his words a lesson so true
See the carriage rolling down a road of gold
I just might give you a kiss if I can be bold

And the band plays the slow song
All is perfect nothing is wrong
In my arms is where you belong
While the band plays the slow song

Well the crowd is getting empty and thin
Making love is a beauty transcending sin
Every forever begins with the first hello
Together we have many miles for us to go

And the band plays the slow song
All is perfect nothing is wrong
In my arms is where you belong
While the band plays the slow song

On the road of eternity we walk
Hand in hand sweet nothings our talk
The infinite path is a journey without end
The lessons of blessing you can't fully comprehend

And the band plays the slow song
All is perfect nothing is wrong
In my arms is where you belong
While the band plays the slow song

Spare Parts

I was born in a junkyard my momma's home
I was baptized in a hub cap made of chrome
Running with the dogs gunning on the prowl
Late at night feeling right you can hear me howl

Baby I'm just spare parts
A technical respectable piece of art
Won't you come and fine tune my heart
Baby I'm just spare parts

Well I ain't fit to speed down on the highway
To fill my need I always do it my way
I ain't no fancy luxury Mercedes Benz
I'm looking for a lover who can be friends

Baby I'm just spare parts
A technical respectable piece of art
Won't you come and fine tune my heart
Baby I'm just spare parts

Well God he made them in every kind of style
Life is snappy I'm happy with just a smile
I ain't one to judge beauty is a point of view
But darling one thing I know is that I love you

Baby I'm just spare parts
A technical respectable piece of art
Won't you come and fine tune my heart
Baby I'm just spare parts

Never mind the rust the dust and the lust
My tires are flat so they ain't gonna bust
We'll take that ride to nowhere going so slow
Wind in your hair without a care let it blow

Baby I'm just spare parts
A technical respectable piece of art
Won't you come and fine tune my heart
Baby I'm just spare parts

Tale Of Babylon

I'm an angel of glory with a story before me
In Leviticus I found Jesus to bore me
"Thou shall not kill" engraved into the stone
Why won't they listen or at least leave me alone?

Here is the tale of Babylon
In a moment to be gone
Love will move on
Here is tale of Babylon

Down in the new land grand came the genocide
So much for the Bible and all that pilgrim pride
But the faithful linger with a ring upon their finger
The proud W.A.S.P unleashes a nuclear stinger

Here is the tale of Babylon
In a moment to be gone
Love will move on
Here is tale of Babylon

We got babies murdered before they're born
With fifty channels of various porn
The red white and blue is flying high
Death to darkie is their battle cry
On the street the blue kill in the hood
But apple pie really tastes so good

Lucifer is laughing behind the Vatican walls
Only the wicked hear the truth of his calls
Lies and lies the disguise right before our eyes
You'll all find the truth when Babylon dies

Here is the tale of Babylon
In a moment to be gone
Love will move on
Here is tale of Babylon

The Blues

I was born singing the Memphis blues
The nurses went on strike over union dues
It was straight milk I was doing so fine
Heaven had me and heaven was mine

This is a song about the blues
Dark and light all of the hues
Blue it is the bluest of the blues
This is a song about the blues

A little boy hearing daddy play guitar
The road went forever and forever is far
Maybe it is true what they say about Emmylou
I looked at the yellow sun the sky was blue

This is a song about the blues
Dark and light all of the hues
Blue it is the bluest of the blues
This is a song about the blues

Well I don't want this to sound too rude
If there's a God He's one funky dude
Destiny is a word for lacking all the clues
You can have red I only want the blues

This is a song about the blues
Dark and light all of the hues
Blue it is the bluest of the blues
This is a song about the blues

Well I met Jesus Christ on Forty Second Street
He was bumming for a dime to get food to eat
He pointed to the porno, it's hard to compete
I whipped out my guitar and we did a duo sweet
And we sung la la la I really love you
And we sung la la la I'm feeling so blue
And we sung la la la for the chosen few
And we sung la la la I'm feeling so blue

This is a song about the blues
Dark and light all of the hues
Blue it is the bluest of the blues
This is a song about the blues

The Champion

I am ashamed of the things I've done
Not every day was a victory won
It was a struggle since my walk begun
The victory alone belongs to God's son

He is the champion of the human race
Lift him up to the highest place
He is the champion look into his face
You will find mercy and grace

Some days I'm soaring high as the sky
Other times I feel like I want to die
Every battle every day I draw near
Put your trust in Jesus and have no fear

He is the champion of the human race
Lift him up to the highest place
He is the champion look into his face
You will find mercy and grace

Straying to the left straying to the right
Bruised and battered its been a fight
But Jesus he's been through what I've been
He's lived the life and He's had no sin

He is the champion of the human race
Lift him up to the highest place
He is the champion look into his face
You will find mercy and grace

One day we'll meet the Lord in the air
Forgive me savior my single prayer
With the sheep let me gather on your right
To praise Jesus forever my delight

He is the champion of the human race
Lift him up to the highest place
He is the champion look into his face
You will find mercy and grace

The Essence Of Love

On Easter we got eggs and a chocolate bunny
And grandma slipped me a card with money
But those are memories faded in the past
You see this world wasn't meant to last

Late at night my words flow like a river
Another fight with no savior to deliver
Jesus he's still hanging on the cross
The essence of love is about taking a loss

Well we buried uncle Ziggy he was first
And poor old grandma it hit her worst
No mother should have to bury her son
I think of the wars and the evil we done

Late at night my words flow like a river
Another fight with no savior to deliver
Jesus he's still hanging on the cross
The essence of love is about taking a loss

Mom was next and dad followed the same year
When Walter perished I felt death near
He was a distant person a brother only in name
Walter never lived and it was truly a shame

Late at night my words flow like a river
Another fight with no savior to deliver
Jesus he's still hanging on the cross
The essence of love is about taking a loss

So here I sit looking at the crooked trail
If you give it your best well you cannot fail
One day I'm going to harvest what I've sown
I pray that the seeds of my love have grown

Late at night my words flow like a river
Another fight with no savior to deliver
Jesus he's still hanging on the cross
The essence of love is about taking a loss

The Heartland

In the heartland we are gentle and kind
In the heartland love is what you'll find
When things get tough we say a prayer
There's always enough because we share

We are middle America with a song
We are middle America brave and strong
We are the heartland a place of grace
We are the heartland America's face

Early to rise we got ourselves a job to do
The fields are green and the sky is blue
We work hard and back up what we say
Cause there's more to us than just the pay

We are middle America with a song
We are middle America brave and strong
We are the heartland a place of grace
We are the heartland America's face

Lord knows we've had our share of hard times
We faced floods and droughts and the bankers' crimes
Trouble is something that will make you or break you
And here in the heartland we always make it through

In the heartland our music touches the soul
We got country mixed with rock and roll
So come on take a chance and go to the dance
Cause in the heartland we know how to romance

We are middle America with a song
We are middle America brave and strong
We are the heartland a place of grace
We are the heartland America's face

The Journey Of Life

I walked on the old street
Dirt and rocks under my feet
Was a time when life was sweet
And the circle was complete

The journey of life is one way
For every blessing a price to pay
There are things too wonderful to say
The journey of life is one way

Age came with worries great
And love has faded to hate
No more is the child's mind
Youth I had left far behind

The journey of life is one way
For every blessing a price to pay
There are things too wonderful to say
The journey of life is one way

But how I long to return
To forget all I came to learn
To look at the world anew
And see the secrets true

The journey of life is one way
For every blessing a price to pay
There are things too wonderful to say
The journey of life is one way

I am walking I will walk evermore
I need to return to what I had before
Is it possible to even open the door?
I know somehow that Love is the cure

My legs weary my shoes worn
I am old looking to be reborn
My soul ravaged my heart torn
After every night comes the morn

The journey of life is one way
For every blessing a price to pay
There are things too wonderful to say
The journey of life is one way

The Muse (Leadbelly's Song)

He was the midnight sun shining ever bright
Every note was light defining what was right
A crusader conquering with song and rhyme
A forgotten serenader belonging to another time

Leadbelly was fused with the muse
A folk singer immersed in the blues
Singing bringing the good news
Leadbelly was fused with the muse

His deep voice declared the prayer of the downtrodden
I keep rejoicing aware why the rich man wants him forgotten
He's like reverse gravity pushing those up on the bottom
He strums his guitar working harder than picking cotton

Leadbelly was fused with the muse
A folk singer immersed in the blues
Singing bringing the good news
Leadbelly was fused with the muse

A champion in a land that made him a second-class citizen
In this world they take you for everything that they can
But Leadbelly was really glad to sing his sweet song
All the while with a smile he dreamed that he could belong

Leadbelly was fused with the muse
A folk singer immersed in the blues
Singing bringing the good news
Leadbelly was fused with the muse

Well time has passed and Leadbelly's ghost roams the land
Searching churches and honky-tonk bars for those who understand
And so I sing this song in memory of folk music's king
I laugh with the spirit of Leadbelly hoping for a better thing

Leadbelly was fused with the muse
A folk singer immersed in the blues
Singing bringing the good news
Leadbelly was fused with the muse

The Rocket Star

Here I am and I ain't got a song
I can't even pretend that I'm strong
I'm wondering what I did so wrong
Never did fit in never did belong

And you are the rocket star
Electric poison on your guitar
If you try you'll go far
Cause you are the rocket star

I'm so blue that I'd borrow a line
I'd do anything just to make you mine
Shall we have caviar with our wine?
Spring in Paris is always divine

And you are the rocket star
Electric poison on your guitar
If you try you'll go far
Cause you are the rocket star

Bumming strumming here I go a slumming
The preacher says I'll be overcoming
Heaven is the lie to make you do well
And if that don't work there's always hell

For better or worse embrace the curse
I'll have a whiskey bar in my hearse
This may be a rock and roll fantasy
But don't you know it's real as steel to me

And you are the rocket star
Electric poison on your guitar
If you try you'll go far
Cause you are the rocket star

Every broken heart needs a good friend
Every song needs a classic end
If you can't make it you can just pretend
There hope to cope just around the bend

And you are the rocket star
Electric poison on your guitar
If you try you'll go far
Cause you are the rocket star

The Small Man

I chain smoke those menthol cigarettes
Life well yeah I got some regrets
See the three legged horse place your bets
When we reach tomorrow today forgets

I'm the small man with the small mind
In blunder I'm the wonder of human kind
For some reason time left me behind
I'm the small man with the small mind

I salute the flag America wrong or right
I'll boast and brag in the thick of the fight
Never mind the Beatles and Jesus Christ
For the golden bull of Wall Street I sacrifice

I'm the small man with the small mind
In blunder I'm the wonder of human kind
For some reason time left me behind
I'm the small man with the small mind

I was talking to Joe backstage at the show
He wasn't too cool but he had real good blow
The name of the band was the band
If you knew Levon Helm you would understand

I'm the small man with the small mind
In blunder I'm the wonder of human kind
For some reason time left me behind
I'm the small man with the small mind

I cursed God eye to eye and spit in His face
I tore up the Bible and refused His grace
All the kid did was turn the other cheek
Never knew the crew could be so meek

I'm the small man with the small mind
In blunder I'm the wonder of human kind
For some reason time left me behind
I'm the small man with the small mind

There are no pictures of you and me as one
When the plate is empty you are truly done
Love or hate in the end the cold grave waits
All are equal in the shadows of heaven's gates

I'm the small man with the small mind
In blunder I'm the wonder of human kind
For some reason time left me behind
I'm the small man with the small mind

The White Queen Of Oz

She is the pristine dream folly of frigid tears
An endless world of dreams full of fears
Have pity for the mistress she tries to be kind
Mommy is like Tommy deaf dumb and blind

She's the white Queen of Oz Brian Cole
She's the white Queen of Oz got no soul
She's the white Queen of Oz in control
She's the white Queen of Oz no heart only an empty hole

Where does the black bird go to hide in the cold snow
How much do you get when you pass go?
Pink Floyd filled the void and they built a red brick wall
When Jesus screamed on the cross I heard the call

She's the white Queen of Oz Brian Cole
She's the white Queen of Oz got no soul
She's the white Queen of Oz in control
She's the white Queen of Oz no heart only an empty hole

I am forgetting as I slowly remember
I am I Am I am singing a slow lament
I am regretting I can't be but remember
Cuban missile crisis Khrushchev did repent
He saved the world halleluiah amen
And Kennedy scored with the whore Marilyn

Man on the moon where is the technology?
Constitution but who are really free?
Black man can kill the yellow man ever gladly
Now you know why I love the Muslim Ali

She's the white Queen of Oz Brian Cole
She's the white Queen of Oz got no soul
She's the white Queen of Oz in control
She's the white Queen of Oz no heart only an empty hole

These Are Things

Every ghetto defender got a rap in the hood
I can't be no pretender cause they ain't no good
Demeaning woman using some vulgar name
They're just dreaming they can play this game

And Tupac was killed by the state
Cause he embraced love over hate
John Lennon met the same fate
These are things you can't debate

The land of the free and I can't speak my mind
Full speed ahead leaving the masses behind
We gotta plenty of money to spend on war
But only empty promises for the poor

And all the politicians live a lie
They don't care if you live or die
The common man he just gotta wait
These are things you can't debate

America was built on slavery and genocide
Something the history books try to hide
Things only change when we organize
Don't get fooled they only speak in lies

Manifest Destiny is insane
Slavery was built on pain
Look at the hell they did create
These are things you can't debate

They're destroying the world for this thing they call money
Robbing every joy from girl and boy it ain't funny
The future is mortgaged for the luxury of the elite
See the devil laughing it makes the picture complete

They say these are just how things are
Go buy yourself an electric guitar
Play all day until you become a star
Stay true to the heart and you'll go far

Rock and roll is the dream
Rock and roll is supreme
The moment is now you ain't late
These are things you can't debate

Tired Of Fighting

Two amigos on the run for some fun
Drinking rum thinking the day is done
They went down to the river in the sky
But the shelves of heaven were all dry

I was marching in the grand band
When heroes were in high demand
Another war well God be damned
We're tired of fighting understand

Fire rockets bursting on the fourth of July
The vet hits the ground afraid to die
If you want a piece of hell sign the line
Don't you pretend that everything's fine

I was marching in the grand band
When heroes were in high demand
Another war well God be damned
We're tired of fighting understand

Say hey Bruce the juice is turning you loose
Just waking bones shaking from abuse
We won the war now can we celebrate?
Victory is when there's no more hate

I was marching in the grand band
When heroes were in high demand
Another war well God be damned
We're tired of fighting understand

The bankers and the weapon makers created wicked schemes
While the teenager is lost in the fantasy of wet dreams
Besides on the television commercial it ain't as bad as it seems
Until basic training charging with bayonet fixed in screams

Say Charlie why can't we achieve some peace
I sit in prison waiting for release
Not knowing that the key is in my fist
All you gotta do is just resist

I was marching in the grand band
When heroes were in high demand
Another war well God be damned
We're tired of fighting understand

To Be A Star

Every teen beauty queen who shared the dream
Knows what it means to shout and scream
They tantalize innocent eyes with paradise
But their precious advice comes with a price

Ah Lord I want to be a star
Sing out my heart with this guitar
I can make it, make it real far
Ah Lord I need to be a star

Well Niki sings to the old and gray
It may be a drag but its decent pay
Still she dreams of her name in light
If you quit the struggle you lose the fight

Ah Lord I want to be a star
Sing out my heart with this guitar
I can make it, make it real far
Ah Lord I need to be a star

Well Levi looks on his future almost gone
Niki is another hot body to dream upon
But in this modern age where we're aware
A dirty old man must lust with tender care

Ah Lord I want to be a star
Sing out my heart with this guitar
I can make it, make it real far
Ah Lord I need to be a star

So Niki sings and we give polite applause
It's like buying war bonds helping the cause
There ain't room for two in number one
And it's victory or defeat when it's all done

Ah Lord I want to be a star
Sing out my heart with this guitar
I can make it, make it real far
Ah Lord I need to be a star

To Set The Soul Free

The guitar was muted like a polluted river
Looking for a cute star who could deliver
Well they were rocking in their wheel chairs
Jamming in the dining room downstairs

Singing songs to set the soul free
Living in a distant memory
Tomorrow never come let it be
Love is here to set the soul free

Old men with old eyes they have hunger
For some piece of meat decades younger
But it's all fantasy if you ain't got money
Cause the obscene green gets you honey

Singing songs to set the soul free
Living in a distant memory
Tomorrow never come let it be
Love is here to set the soul free

I put all of my songs into one big book
Twenty dollars if you want to take a look
But right now we're trying to survive
And dreams and screams are simply jive

Singing songs to set the soul free
Living in a distant memory
Tomorrow never come let it be
Love is here to set the soul free

Read the Bible for some survival
Who's walked the Earth without a trial
Billionaires offer prayers to empty space
While the poor are secure in endless grace

Singing songs to set the soul free
Living in a distant memory
Tomorrow never come let it be
Love is here to set the soul free

Tomorrow Is Around The Bend

The road is rolling long and wide
Hand in hand you're by my side
Every step seems like a new day
I am so glad to be on my way

Tomorrow is around the bend
Joy and love will never end
You are my love my best friend
Tomorrow is around the bend

I've seen pain fall like endless rain
I cursed the darkness empty and vain
My mind wandered in realms insane
But to have you I'd do it again

Tomorrow is around the bend
Joy and love will never end
You are my love my best friend
Tomorrow is around the bend

The poet spoke in perfect rhyme
Law officers practice vile crime
I heard Jim Morrison wasn't dead
But ain't nothing as exciting
As taking you to bed

Tomorrow is around the bend
Joy and love will never end
You are my love my best friend
Tomorrow is around the bend

There's a stairway to heaven to climb
Hear the bells of freedom chime
Speak the truth why live a lie?
We're all going to meet God
We're all going to die

Tomorrow is around the bend
Joy and love will never end
You are my love my best friend
Tomorrow is around the bend

We All Want To Be Loved By Some One

He was a singer singing songs about being free
She was a waitress who also sang harmony
Picking at his guitar as she rambled behind the bar
When you're in heaven you don't need to go far

We all want to be loved by some one
To be kissed when the day is done
Walking hand in hand in the setting sun
We all want to be loved by some one

Well everyone said they made a lovely pair
When they performed they hadn't a single care
But when the music ended her duties would call
Decide what you want cause you can't have it all

We all want to be loved by some one
To be kissed when the day is done
Walking hand in hand in the setting sun
We all want to be loved by some one

Well he longed to be a star it was his fantasy
She was a hurt woman founded in reality
He promised one day that he would come to return
But she knew it so true that the fire would burn

We all want to be loved by some one
To be kissed when the day is done
Walking hand in hand in the setting sun
We all want to be loved by some one

He left it all to heed the call of his dream grand
She cried but how could he ever understand
That late at night when they held each other tight
It was the only thing in the universe that was right

We all want to be loved by some one
To be kissed when the day is done
Walking hand in hand in the setting sun
We all want to be loved by some one

What Do You Know

When the castles of gold crumble
When the runner falls to stumble
When the body is dust in the grave
It is too late to try to save

Ride the wheel it turns and turns
So many books nobody learns
Round and round here we go
Tell me what do you know?

On Wall Street the market is bull
The punk on junk is so cool
The bankers lust to kill and rule
And the soldier he plays the fool

Ride the wheel it turns and turns
So many books nobody learns
Round and round here we go
Tell me what do you know?

A vagrant once had this message of love and loss
He left his throne just to take up some wicked cross
A crown of thorns and a fistful full of scorn
Hung between two thieves his spirit was torn

So the pen it leaves some ink
And I wonder can you think?
At the end we all have to let go
So tell me what do you know?

Ride the wheel it turns and turns
So many books nobody learns
Round and round here we go
Tell me what do you know?

What Have We Done To Paradise?

Angles of death are circling in the sky
After the first bomb you don't ask why
Any kind of answer would be a lie
Tell me honest are you afraid to die?

What have we done to paradise?
Sold it to the sinner for the highest price
God is great but we don't take His advice
What have we done to paradise?

The land of the free waging endless war
This is a movie that I've seen before
Rome rose only to fall in the fire
Come on baby can't we take it higher?

What have we done to paradise?
Sold it to the sinner for the highest price
God is great but we don't take His advice
What have we done to paradise?

Love is dead we worship lust instead
In Babylon even the poor are overfed
We worship the golden calf of mammon
While in Africa they suffer endless famine

What have we done to paradise?
Sold it to the sinner for the highest price
God is great but we don't take His advice
What have we done to paradise?

There are cracks in the foundation the towers sway
No turning back salvation is for another day
We've destroyed the planet smashed all of the guitars
We're escaping to a gig on the planet mars

Three and a half kids with a two-car garage
In the small-town big fish seem to be large
Over the rainbow lies what could have been
Look around see the wages of our sin

What have we done to paradise?
Sold it to the sinner for the highest price
God is great but we don't take His advice
What have we done to paradise?

What's She Doing In This Place?

The flowers are plastic and the drinks warm
In the evening she's the coming storm
Lustful looks feed dreams starved so close to death
Forget tomorrow's sorrow take a deep breath

Behind her painted face
There lies a heart of grace
What's she doing in this place?
This sultry siren from outer space
What's she doing in this place?

She's singing tunes from a forgotten year
The danger of the stranger lurking near
Ignorance is bliss you miss all the fear
In rage on stage all is crystal clear

Behind her painted face
There lies a heart of grace
What's she doing in this place?
This sultry siren from outer space
What's she doing in this place?

He song is all wrong but her dress real tight
In the eyes of the guys dynamite
If you ask for a dance there's a chance she might
Forever until never starts tonight

Behind her painted face
There lies a heart of grace
What's she doing in this place?
This sultry siren from outer space
What's she doing in this place?

From the hot spotlight straight into your soul
With each chord there's a struggle for control
Music is a healer and the song strong
Just like heaven with everything wrong

Behind her painted face
There lies a heart of grace
What's she doing in this place?
This sultry siren from outer space
What's she doing in this place?

Wishing On A Star

The middle of the metal came to rust
Hear my riddle of fame or bust
But every line has two sides
In the hot spotlight our hero hides

Here I go wishing on a star
If only I could sing and play guitar
But you know exactly who you are
Here I go wishing on a star

Enter in Lady Lace with disgrace
A warrior woman from time and space
She's the Inca Queen in carnal form
The bass guitar thundered like a storm

Here I go wishing on a star
If only I could sing and play guitar
But you know exactly who you are
Here I go wishing on a star

The dog is old but he clings to life
Children of sin from more than one wife
Heroes ain't born no heroes are made
And you young man were always well paid

Here I go wishing on a star
If only I could sing and play guitar
But you know exactly who you are
Here I go wishing on a star

With the sick flick everybody will score
Silicone Sally is a sensational whore
She's the rage back stage in a cage
What's the deal Neil are you new age?

Here I go wishing on a star
If only I could sing and play guitar
But you know exactly who you are
Here I go wishing on a star

Wonders

Down in the valley money grows on trees
Swing singing with the funky chimpanzees
Its logical Doctor Watson can't you see
The world formed and conformed to anarchy

Wonders with arms open wide
Welcome welcome come inside
See the miracle man walk on the tide
Wonders with arms open wide

They got guns and more weapons galore
Only professional dancers allowed on the floor
I got front row tickets for the championship fight
If you ain't got the card disregard the invite

Wonders with arms open wide
Welcome welcome come inside
See the miracle man walk on the tide
Wonders with arms open wide

Sally I'm sinking the water is filling in fast
I ain't got a future and I've done spent my past
Some men they hide screaming in plain sight
But we all heed the call of the final midnight

Wonders with arms open wide
Welcome welcome come inside
See the miracle man walk on the tide
Wonders with arms open wide

Swing your partner round and round
Where is the answer to be found?
Watch out you're walking on holy ground
In the quiet of the riot hear the sound

I see the future with telescopic eyes
When you get high you can see past all the lies
We're all human beings something to consider
The power of love is all that will deliver

Wonders with arms open wide
Welcome welcome come inside
See the miracle man walk on the tide
Wonders with arms open wide

Words From The Future (Dedicated To Rhyming Paul Simon)

The laser beams screams in the depleted forest
Welcome in Tom don't drop a bomb my guest
Green and blues are the hues they give some clues
Grunting soldiers frag paying their dues

Words from the future we're still alive
Jimi Hendrix was electric jive
Jim was slim and couldn't open the door
Words from the future no one wins in war

Pete Seeger was a hero a zero star
Had a banjo instead of a guitar
And now Aleena Zahir is right here
Righteous in bliss knowing no fear

Words from the future we're still alive
Jimi Hendrix was electric jive
Jim was slim and couldn't open the door
Words from the future no one wins in war

The draft was a laugh until the riots broke out
Richer sons headed to war sowed seeds of doubt
In Europe Stallone cried a pathetic moan
I'm so far to the left my right is now unknown

Sweetheart I love you come and please take my hand
Peace love and compassion come understand?
Vietnam was never to be our land
I say Henry Kissinger to hell be damned

Words from the future we're still alive
Jimi Hendrix was electric jive
Jim was slim and couldn't open the door
Words from the future no one wins in war

You Live Until The Day You Die

The genie was in a bottle of rum
Playing slide guitar and bass drum
Three wishes and so the fable goes
Only the joker man really knows

Hear the harmonica played by the swordfish
There's a paranoia fueling all you accomplish
I rode my emu today the river was dry
You live until the day you die

The melody was really upbeat
Napoleon had his final defeat
You can change the past if you try
All you gotta do is just lie

Hear the harmonica played by the swordfish
There's a paranoia fueling all you accomplish
I rode my emu today the river was dry
You live until the day you die

The fiddler on the roof needed proof
After the war the poets were aloof
All we want is some love and grace
That would save the human race

Hear the harmonica played by the swordfish
There's a paranoia fueling all you accomplish
I rode my emu today the river was dry
You live until the day you die

So we sing the song and the lyrics change
Don't pretend my friend something's strange
They have their crosses waiting
You see them smile but they're hating

Hear the harmonica played by the swordfish
There's a paranoia fueling all you accomplish
I rode my emu today the river was dry
You live until the day you die

You Pick Up The Pieces

The lady at the carnival had green hair
She lived show to show powered by prayer
Broken hearts broken dreams such a sad song
What do you do when everything's wrong?

You pick up the pieces and try some more
You never surrender you fight the war
Never give in cause you can win for sure
You pick up the pieces and try some more

Pregnant at sixteen life seemed to end
A hard road trouble around every bend
A baby isn't easy when you're all alone
In nine months good Lord how you've grown

You pick up the pieces and try some more
You never surrender you fight the war
Never give in cause you can win for sure
You pick up the pieces and try some more

Family is those who show love and care
When you have a need they are always there
So she took off to live a life on the road
There were plenty to help carry her load

You pick up the pieces and try some more
You never surrender you fight the war
Never give in cause you can win for sure
You pick up the pieces and try some more

So now she's the lady running the game
Gone is the world of permanent shame
Give her a dollar and then you can play
The world never ends in yesterday

You pick up the pieces and try some more
You never surrender you fight the war
Never give in cause you can win for sure
You pick up the pieces and try some more

You're A World Away

I was looking for grace on Sylvan place
Someway the save the whole human race
I noticed that it was only a one-way street
So I fled with dread in utter defeat

You're a world away
So sad for me to say
I am night you are day
You're a world away

The dragons were gathering at Mickey's bar
The troll of rock and roll played bass guitar
I said to my shadow I know who you are
If you follow the circle you're bound to go far

You're a world away
So sad for me to say
I am night you are day
You're a world away

The rat in the cage was overflowing with rage
Crazy Horse of course will turn the page
The book is forever without any end
No matter what you got Jesus as a friend

You're a world away
So sad for me to say
I am night you are day
You're a world away

Van the man Morrison he used to be cool
Till he climbed the hill with a cruel fool
But I won't cast the first stone oh not me
Live and let live singing let it be

You're a world away
So sad for me to say
I am night you are day
You're a world away

So after the verse comes the chorus to sing
If you'll be the queen then I'll be the king
My first command will be freedom for the land
Oh mister Bojangles don't you understand

You're a world away
So sad for me to say
I am night you are day
You're a world away

A Bitter Lullaby

Hello my name is Mother Jones roses are red
I weep for all my children who haven't been fed
No jackets for the cold and no shoes for the frost
Prosperity has come but with a bitter cost

My name is Mother Jones
I sing a bitter lullaby
Kings sit on thrones
While workers perish and die
Could you give me an honest answer why?
I sing a bitter lullaby

I was a seamstress and a wage slave in my youth
I awoke from America's dream into the truth
Early to rise working hard while the rich sleep late
I've seen with my own eyes good cause for me to hate

My name is Mother Jones
I sing a bitter lullaby
Kings sit on thrones
While workers perish and die
Could you give me an honest answer why?
I sing a bitter lullaby

They can break the body they can come steal the soul
But a righteous Spirit only God can control
And God Allmighty has seen their houses of prayer
And God Allmighty has never set foot in there

My name is Mother Jones
I sing a bitter lullaby
Kings sit on thrones
While workers perish and die
Could you give me an honest answer why?
I sing a bitter lullaby

I am a mother of the abused kin to the poor
I preach revolution a necessary cure
We'll strike to be free from starvation wages
And move away from these so called golden ages

My name is Mother Jones
I sing a bitter lullaby
Kings sit on thrones

While workers perish and die
Could you give me an honest answer why?
I sing a bitter lullaby

Money is paper human beings alive
You sip your rum while we can just barely survive
Your possessions are too many your wealth immense
Yet you lust for more your greed it just makes no sense

My name is Mother Jones
I sing a bitter lullaby
Kings sit on thrones
While workers perish and die
Could you give me an honest answer why?
I sing a bitter lullaby
From the grave hear my cry
I live though I die
I sing a bitter lullaby

In Remembrance of the IWW

I sing a song for the martyr true
Who gave more than life to me and you
Brave men and yes women too
They teach us what to do

The AFL is the boss' tool
Unskilled labor was not a fool
Exploited what is there to do?
Form the IWW

In this world of endless fight
There is a standard wrong and right
To give, to share, to live as one
Love is the victory won

Brave workers fighting for a decent life
Bayoneted by the soldiers knife
Government is on the owners pay
Stick together it's our only way

Thrown in jail some shot dead
Looked down on by the well bred
But fight they did, that they done
Many a victory they have won

In this world of endless fight
There is a standard wrong and right
To give, to share, to live as one
Love is the victory won

Call us red, that is we
A worker for a just society
One Big Union for one and all
One Big Union answer the call

In this world of endless fight
There is a standard wrong and right
To give, to share, to live as one
Love is the victory won

We sang in the jails and we sang in the street
We sang in sorrow and we sang so sweet
We sang a song of hope for just a little more
We sang so our voices they could not ignore

We're singing now it shall never stop
The sounds of factories the harvesting of crop
What we sang was righteous and true
In remembrance of the IWW

My Wobbly Girl

My Wobbly Girl is a fine looking lass
A pretty pearl see her shine working class
My Wobbly Girl is a very good find
And her best feature is her Wobbly mind

My Wobbly Girl I love you
My Wobbly Girl my heart is true
We never sing the blues
Cause we always pay our dues
My Wobbly Girl I love you

My Wobbly Girl please promise never to part
You've built a tunnel deep into my heart
My Wobbly Girl workers built everything
Even the gold crown on the head of the king

My Wobbly Girl I love you
My Wobbly Girl my heart is true
We never sing the blues
Cause we always pay our dues
My Wobbly Girl I love you

My Wobbly Girl the whole world is ours to share
My Wobbly Girl your love always pays fair
My Wobbly Girl you have courage so brave
You'll fight with all your might to free the wage slave

My Wobbly Girl I love you
My Wobbly Girl my heart is true
We never sing the blues
Cause we always pay our dues
My Wobbly Girl I love you

My Wobbly Girl I want you to be my wife
My Wobbly Girl I offer you all my life
I promise never to treat you less than me
My Wobbly Girl we'll have a Wobbly family

My Wobbly Girl I love you
My Wobbly Girl my heart is true
We never sing the blues
Cause we always pay our dues
My Wobbly Girl I love you

Never Alone

When the suns shines bright
But you think it's night
When sadness is all you've known
Remember you're never alone

You're stuck below bottom
Believing you're forgotten
When your song is a sorrowful moan
Remember you're never alone

We stick together
No matter the weather
Come worse or better
We stick together

Emptiness is what you see in the sky
All truth became an empty lie
Weeds is all the garden has grown
Remember you're never alone

We have the philosophy
Of total equality
Even if you can't understand
Take our helping hand

Your future is only black
Yesterday will never come back
Today is a torturous moan
Remember you're never alone

All we have we share
With all our love we care
Your welcome inside
You won't be denied

Occupy

Merchants of Greed control the money in the bank
They got evil a plenty plotting in their think tank
The business of war is booming based on a lie
Commercial propaganda can't silence our cry

High time to occupy
Here we come beating a drum
We shall overcome
High time to occupy

Local police try to beat us in a savage fight
Practice free speech it's a constitutional right
A land for the people by the people its truth
Our ideals are real hear the appeals of our youth

High time to occupy
Here we come beating a drum
We shall overcome
High time to occupy

Listen, hasten one and all
A cry to defy duty does call
Global warming feel the heat
Fracking we must defeat
Meltdown and nuclear waste
Solar power I like its taste
Mother Earth stop the rape
When the world dies none can escape

Laws are only words on paper written by power
We face the abyss this is now the final hour
Love is a command from the mouth of God supreme
Slay the system wisdom screams ending a dark dream

High time to occupy
Here we come beating a drum
We shall overcome
High time to occupy

One Family

Hand in hand through desert over ocean
Take command put the plan into motion
Join the cause pause to sing in harmony
The whole wide world we are one family

Sing with me
We are one family
Forever free
We are one family

Don't pick up a gun don't believe the lie
The leaders deceive I'm telling you why
They seek control and material gain
Riches and profits from poor people's pain

Sing with me
We are one family
Forever free
We are one family

I never met you or talked eye to eye
Why should I hate you yes please tell me why
We are human you are just like me
White or black it's a fact just one family

Sing with me
We are one family
Forever free
We are one family

Missiles destroy war is an effort vain
The generals are evil and insane
Charge they yell as they sit safe far away
Sister, brother, Love one another today

Sing with me
We are one family
Forever free
We are one family

I'm willing to share to help you succeed
We need no weapons or Merchants of Greed
Together we can build a new reality
You and me joined we are one family

Sing with me
We are one family
Forever free
We are one family

Patricia

A flower child from nineteen sixty four
She turned on to love and protested war
A grown woman a mother kids of her own
Peace is the only path she's ever known

Patricia come out to play
We'll make a better world I say
Let us unite and join the fight
Everyone knows we're in the right
Come on Patricia let's build a delight

Oppression is a devil many a face
An evil menace plaguing the human race
Until all are free we all wear chains
Until all are well we all feel the pains

Patricia come out to play
We'll make a better world I say
Let us unite and join the fight
Everyone knows we're in the right
Come on Patricia let's build a delight

Teach us so we can learn I hear the call
These wicked old men I wish they would fall
They claim truth but their actions are a lie
Share and care as the gobble down the pie

Patricia come out to play
We'll make a better world I say
Let us unite and join the fight
Everyone knows we're in the right
Come on Patricia let's build a delight

Kindness is never understated
Men's theories so hotly debated
Hatred disguised in high institution
Love your neighbor a simple solution

Patricia come out to play
We'll make a better world I say
Let us unite and join the fight
Everyone know we're in the right
Come on Patricia let's build a delight

Patricia's wisdom your silver hair
The lesson to learn is to act as you care
A new generation to carry the cross
Promise me your Love will never be lost

Patricia come out to play
We'll make a better world I say
Let us unite and join the fight
Everyone knows we're in the right
Come on Patricia let's build a delight

Piggy, Piggy, Piggy

Piggy, piggy, piggy nice and fat
Fine overcoat a black top hat
Goes to the theatre looking so fine
See the whole farm wish it was mine

Piggy, piggy, piggy eats his feed
Gobbles on up more than he does need
Only thinks about fat number one
Won't be nothing left when he's done

Piggy, piggy, piggy wants some more
Got a wife, a mistress and a whore
It is very hard to fill the cup
When you can't keep the gosh darn thing up

Piggy, piggy, piggy has no friend
People are just a means to an end
Darkness lives inside of his black soul
His only dream is complete control

Piggy, piggy, piggy speaks with lies
Never tells the truth, he never tries
Changes his story to fit the times
Never admits to his evil crimes

Piggy, piggy, piggy slaughter day
So much evil now it's time to pay
Piggy, piggy, piggy time to stop
You'll really make a nice pork chop

Secret Agent FBI

Sun glasses on a cloudy day
He never goes far away
Always nervous and in fear
Clinging close and near

He's the guy
Secret Agent FBI
James Bond is a lie
A far, far cry
From Secret Agent FBI

His overcoat is gray
Talks with nothing to say
Prays to god amen
Fascists called G-Men

He's the guy
Secret Agent FBI
James Bond is a lie
A far, far cry
From Secret Agent FBI

Tax dollars down the pipe
Always the mysterious type
Recording every move made
And he's so highly paid

He's the guy
Secret Agent FBI
James Bond is a lie
A far, far cry
From Secret Agent FBI

I wish the act would end
Why won't you be a friend?
A sacred hatred in his soul
Why do you desire complete control?

He's the guy
Secret Agent FBI
James Bond is a lie
A far, far cry
From Secret Agent FBI

The Worker Shall Rise

Help wanted ads they no longer exist
It'll get better politicians insist
Take a look at history for our guide
If we stick together we can't be denied

You say heaven is beyond the skies
Take a back seat I can hear your lies
The worker shall rise, the worker shall rise
In the heat of the street hear our cries
The worker shall rise, the worker shall rise

Living in the parks wandering the street
Longing for some warmth or a morsel to eat
They took it serious when banks went broke
Now that it's the people they laugh like a joke

You say heaven is beyond the skies
Take a back seat I can hear your lies
The worker shall rise, the worker shall rise
In the heat of the street hear our cries
The worker shall rise, the worker shall rise

Share the wealth our slogan ringing so true
Power to the people that means me and you
Capitalism the religion of greed
Socialism giving as there is a need

You say heaven is beyond the skies
Take a back seat I can hear your lies
The worker shall rise, the worker shall rise
In the heat of the street hear our cries
The worker shall rise, the worker shall rise

Big business bribes everyone taking lead
The government is sick everyone got greed
The common man has a plan of solution
Brothers and sisters time for revolution

You say heaven is beyond the skies
Take a back seat I can hear your lies
The worker shall rise, the worker shall rise
In the heat of the street hear our cries
The worker shall rise, the worker shall rise

Abraham Raised The Knife

Your feeling blue cause things ain't working out
Wondering if God loves you there's plenty of doubt
Let me tell you plainly let me make you aware
We have a cross to bear and a message to share

I gotta tell you something about life
Abraham raised the knife
To kill the only child of his wife
Don't you know that Abraham raised the knife

God is good and God is great and God He's never late
But human beings well we never want to wait
I guarantee when all that remains is your final prayer
God Almighty will loose the chains and fill you with care

I gotta tell you something about life
Abraham raised the knife
To kill the only child of his wife
Don't you know that Abraham raised the knife

Trust in Him when all seems lost
Trust in Him don't you count the cost
Give Him the praise He's faithful and true
Give Him the praise He really loves you

Precious child awaiting you is a priceless reward
When things get wild hold on trust in the Lord
Angels are watching and the Good Shepherd near
So be brave and bold do as your told without fear

I gotta tell you something about life
Abraham raised the knife
To kill the only child of his wife
Don't you know that Abraham raised the knife

Africa Shall Rise

This is a call to all who love one another
I am your sister and you are my brother
A new dawn is coming the rays break through
The turning of the wheel do you feel it too?

Listen with your ears see with your eyes
Don't pay attention to the enemy's lies
Like an eagle soaring through the skies
I declare beware Africa shall rise

She is our mother the womb of humanity
Man was born in a land grand and free
Great civilizations of grandest glory
Yes we were slaves but hear the whole story

Listen with your ears see with your eyes
Don't pay attention to the enemy's lies
Like an eagle soaring through the skies
I declare beware Africa shall rise

There is a spirit singing a song in our heart
We are all servants you must do your part
Rise up seize the moment answer the call
For the sake of the children give it your all

Listen with your ears see with your eyes
Don't pay attention to the enemy's lies
Like an eagle soaring through the skies
I declare beware Africa shall rise

They are dancing in the street laughing in the air
God Almighty hears our desperate prayer
Africa Love is the key for the chains that bind
Come find the truth and free your mind

Listen with your ears see with your eyes
Don't pay attention to the enemy's lies
Like an eagle soaring through the skies
I declare beware Africa shall rise

African Man

From the slums of the barrio
A song plays on the stereo
The rapper slaps the blues
Do you have any good news?

African man they stole your mind
African man slavery is not kind
African man are you blind?
African man break free – from the chains that bind

Money is a paper cut thin
Greed is the worst sin
God Almighty he is just
God Almighty in Him I trust

African man they stole your mind
African man slavery is not kind
African man are you blind?
African man break free – from the chains that bind

On Chancellor Avenue they pump in the dope
Hear the singing bringing songs of endless hope
If we meet the test with our best we shall cope
Hear the singing bringing songs of endless hope

Are you a man or are you not
Don't let the past be forgot
African man you ruled the Earth
Africa the land of all our birth

African man they stole your mind
African man slavery is not kind
African man are you blind?
African man break free – from the chains that bind

Aleena Zahir

I am a patriot in the cause of the universal man
To love to fight to unite that is our grand plan
I shall decide how to define my destiny
Africa I embrace won't you be one with me?

Let it be said Brenda is dead
I am a woman who's been born again
Let it be said Brenda is dead
Aleena Zahir she lives instead

As a little girl there was so much I did not understand
I wondered why we did not rule our own land
As a child I could see the right I could see the wrong
Now as a woman I boldly sing out my song

Let it be said Brenda is dead
I am a woman who's been born again
Let it be said Brenda is dead
Aleena Zahir she lives instead

The parasite he sucks the cream leaving the bile
He comes with God's religion and Satan's smile
Listen mister I took a look at the sacred book
God is good and the businessman he's a crook

Let it be said Brenda is dead
I am a woman who's been born again
Let it be said Brenda is dead
Aleena Zahir she lives instead

Let the wave wash Africa in a baptism of fire
For what is just for what is right that is our desire
We must learn to live in a way without any fear
I am the mistress of the muse I am Aleena Zahir

Let it be said Brenda is dead
I am a woman who's been born again
Let it be said Brenda is dead
Aleena Zahir she lives instead

All I Need Is A Chorus

The Gnostic coveted mysterious rhyme
He read chilling thrillers of true crime
Charles Manson never really did kill
And all the armies they do God's will

All I need is a chorus and a funky beat
All I need is a chorus tender and sweet
All I need is a chorus to make it complete
All I need is a chorus and a bite to eat

Saint Augustine was of darker skin
In a place where race was not a sin
He stole his words from heaven divine
His rage on the page written so fine

All I need is a chorus and a funky beat
All I need is a chorus tender and sweet
All I need is a chorus to make it complete
All I need is a chorus and a bite to eat

Oh give me a woman with a loyal heart
Who can write a song to top the chart
Marketing is the talent to strike it big
If you can fake it you can take the gig

All I need is a chorus and a funky beat
All I need is a chorus tender and sweet
All I need is a chorus to make it complete
All I need is a chorus and a bite to eat

Jerry seems obsessed with the blues
In his dreams he's blessed by accurate news
I find the masses to be totally blind
I took of my glasses what did I find?

All I need is a chorus and a funky beat
All I need is a chorus tender and sweet
All I need is a chorus to make it complete
All I need is a chorus and a bite to eat

An Old time Folk Singer

Winter is here with my hair white like snow
Wisdom is more than the facts you know
I strum the chords and sing the melody
Overcome by the words that set you free

Just an old time folk singer singing my song
Here I am still trying to right every wrong
Day is passing to night but I'm still going strong
Just an old time folk singer singing my song

I've seen the times change from bad to worse
Eyes that see are a blessing but also a curse
I lift my voice loud protesting endless war
Just like I did in all of those years before

Just an old time folk singer singing my song
Here I am still trying to right every wrong
Day is passing to night but I'm still going strong
Just an old time folk singer singing my song

I pray for the children
The victims of our sin
I cry for the children
Over and over again

My voice may sound sweet but my heart is sour
Remember people you hold all of the power
Always waiting until it is our hour
As the cancer of hatred comes to devour

Just an old time folk singer singing my song
Here I am still trying to right every wrong
Day is passing to night but I'm still going strong
Just an old time folk singer singing my song

Dreaming For Africa

Listen brothers listen sisters hear this song
Our land is calling we need to be strong
On the winds can't you hear the call?
It is calling you it is calling us all

I am dreaming for Africa – wake up
I am dreaming for Africa – get up
I am dreaming for Africa – stand up
I am dreaming for Africa – wake up

Get off your knees praying time in done
It is time to arise for we shall over come
There is a mighty victory that must be won
The solution of revolution is has begun

I am dreaming for Africa – wake up
I am dreaming for Africa – get up
I am dreaming for Africa – stand up
I am dreaming for Africa – wake up

From north to south from east to west
We are one people and this is our test
Will you be slaves and play the fool?
No pity for our masters they're wicked and cruel

I am dreaming for Africa – wake up
I am dreaming for Africa – get up
I am dreaming for Africa – stand up
I am dreaming for Africa – wake up

Victory I can feel the surging of the power
Victory man it is real now is our hour
Sleeping giant it is the time to awake
Victory is there it is for us to take

I am dreaming for Africa – wake up
I am dreaming for Africa – get up
I am dreaming for Africa – stand up
I am dreaming for Africa – wake up

Edward Jones

Newark is a city where they got pity to share
Second class or third rate they're well aware
Rich man he don't venture down to the south
Cause without guns he ain't got no mouth

Where you gonna sleep tonight Edward Jones
Where are you gonna lay your tired bones
They got plenty of money for endless war
But strange they got no spare change for the poor

Poverty is there Valerie sleeps in an abandoned car
Chancellor Avenue shows slavery's deep scar
And in the suburbs it is a whole world away
Pale face don't venture to the hood okay

Where you gonna sleep tonight Edward Jones
Where are you gonna lay your tired bones
They got plenty of money for endless war
But strange they got no spare change for the poor

The states police conduct the drug raid
With machine guns still afraid
In our great society still forgotten
The open sore of America's sin

They can put a man on the moon to plant the flag
On the bigger bang of the bomb they boast and brag
But with the poor it's don't you be so lazy
And God forbid if you happen to go crazy

Where you gonna sleep tonight Edward Jones
Where are you gonna lay your tired bones
They got plenty of money for endless war
But strange they got no spare change for the poor

Endless Rain

An old man chewing on stale bread
At night he has nowhere to lay his head
Society blindly races down the road
One day I dare say it will explode

Sugar snaps and candy cane
Living life in the endless rain
When you hurt you feel the pain
Living life in the endless rain

The acrobats labor long into the night
With great precision all must be right
At the show they don't use any nets
One mistake makes eternal regrets

They paint a smile on the clown's face
Were after laughter says the human race
Walter could never learn to relax
He had no wisdom just endless facts

Sugar snaps and candy cane
Living life in the endless rain
When you hurt you feel the pain
Living life in the endless rain

Down the corridor all the doors are locked
Welcome to the madhouse why are you shocked?
Write us a poem with clever rhymes
Truth and honesty are the greatest crimes

Sugar snaps and candy cane
Living life in the endless rain
When you hurt you feel the pain
Living life in the endless rain

Where is Diane when you need her most?
She published a story hear her boast
To hell with the infidel says the monk
The priest at the feast is hooked on junk

Sugar snaps and candy cane
Living life in the endless rain
When you hurt you feel the pain
Living life in the endless rain

The old man is sleeping in his chair
Unaware of prayer he has no care
Surely this world was meant to share
If we both get to heaven I'll meet you there

Sugar snaps and candy cane
Living life in the endless rain
When you hurt you feel the pain
Living life in the endless rain

I Am Aleena

Hear my voice I am the advocate of the poor
I sing for freedom I sing against war
Mother Africa she will rise as before
Good times are near knocking on the door

I am Aleena from the Uganda wild
I am Aleena an African child
I fight for all yearning to be free
I am Aleena the champion of liberty

My hands are busy planting the seeds
We must work hard to meet our needs
I shall not go down without a fight
We are the generation to make it right

I am Aleena from the Uganda wild
I am Aleena an African child
I fight for all yearning to be free
I am Aleena the champion of liberty

I want you to sing this song with me
I want you to walk by my side
I want you to sing this song with me
Africa is our mother say it with pride

We shall build temples for the God of Love
He will answer with blessing from above
The Almighty will smile and turn the page
We are walking to a blessed age

I am Aleena from the Uganda wild
I am Aleena an African child
I fight for all yearning to be free
I am Aleena the champion of liberty

Immigration Blues

Here I am a punk without a clue
Madly lost in love with you
If Ron Redman will just let us be
We'll wander the world wild and free

Joni she shines like the sun
Jesus on the cross ain't fun
Immigration blues it's all wrong
Immigration blues is my song

Oh when you get the letter in the mail
They investigate each detail
They're setting you up to fail
Just so big money can prevail

Joni she shines like the sun
Jesus on the cross ain't fun
Immigration blues it's all wrong
Immigration blues is my song

I'm too stressed to be blessed
My lawyer I've second guessed
So we jump through the hoops
With ice cream of hope in double scoops

Good Lord pale face you stole the land anyway
So tell me why Sylvia can't stay?
I'm saying it right now there's a price to pay
And you see tomorrow well that's my day

Joni she shines like the sun
Jesus on the cross ain't fun
Immigration blues it's all wrong
Immigration blues is my song

Madelyn she never called back
And you can't even rely on Jack
The devil he even froze my phone
Emptiness is being alone

Joni she shines like the sun
Jesus on the cross ain't fun
Immigration blues it's all wrong
Immigration blues is my song

Living A Lie

I had a beer with the engineer
World peace was his biggest fear
Wouldn't settle well with his career
And retirement was looming near

These are the days of living a lie
For the love of God and the battle cry
Enter in the greatest sin is asking why
These are the days of living a lie

There sat a poet crying in his drink
He had a brain but let the heart think
All I feel is real if I put it in ink
But I dare not say so to the shrink

These are the days of living a lie
For the love of God and the battle cry
Enter in the greatest sin is asking why
These are the days of living a lie

At the library I found books galore
On the virtue of love and the glory of war
All written by well-educated men
Praise the nation and say your amen

These are the days of living a lie
For the love of God and the battle cry
Enter in the greatest sin is asking why
These are the days of living a lie

She was far from a star or a beauty queen
But I took the feast for the beast was clean
She giggle saying whisper secrets obscene
I said I love you fearing being mean

These are the days of living a lie
For the love of God and the battle cry
Enter in the greatest sin is asking why
These are the days of living a lie

Long Ago

I'm a million years from the Isle of Wight
Is it a sin to smile and ask for a fight?
Free love free music but you pay for your dope
Tomorrow can only come if we have hope

Beautiful little girl on the piano
I wonder if the world will ever know
Secrets from so long ago
Yeah we keep it secret
From long, long ago

The fragile woman is confident in folly
Nothing in this ordeal is real but Lusting Lolly
Santa Clause cums once a year he's not jolly
The fragile woman she clutches her dolly

Beautiful little girl on the piano
I wonder if the world will ever know
Secrets from so long ago
Yeah we keep it secret
From long, long ago

Maybe they say it's all wrong
But by God we got us a song
Commercialism is a wicked beast
Some they starve while others feast
And I'd like to give you a just world
So sings the beautiful little girl

You are yesterday and I am just forever
Do you find my words kind and clever?
I hear your story from the combination of chords
Music is a language without any words

Beautiful little girl on the piano
I wonder if the world will ever know
Secrets from so long ago
Yeah we keep it secret
From long, long ago

Lord Have Mercy

The tunnels are leaking the bridges shake
Ain't got no sugar to bake a cake
Armies are marching to settle the score
The bankers stand cheering endless war

Lord have mercy I just want to write a song
Instead in my head I ponder all that is wrong
Sweet Jesus who can forget Calvary
Hate and the state are our worst enemy

The man of perdition has endless ambition
Void of a soul his only goal is to win
Soon the black ink of censorship will be employed
Watch what you teach free speech will be destroyed

Lord have mercy I just want to write a song
Instead in my head I ponder all that is wrong
Sweet Jesus who can forget Calvary
Hate and the state are our worst enemy

If I was a prophet I'd send the alarm
Evil is deceitful like a friend with charm
The rise and fall tells all we need to know
Head the lesson nuclear weapons are ready to blow

Lord have mercy I just want to write a song
Instead in my head I ponder all that is wrong
Sweet Jesus who can forget Calvary
Hate and the state are our worst enemy

The psychiatrist tried to resist and went insane
No matter how tall the wall it's built in vain
The young have the future the old have the past
At the turning of the clock neither will last

Lord have mercy I just want to write a song
Instead in my head I ponder all that is wrong
Sweet Jesus who can forget Calvary
Hate and the state are our worst enemy

Love Will Win The Day

The man from the bank got a heart of stone
A material soul Love he's never known
Africa your spirit is gentle and sweet
Africa come rise up to your feet
Africa there is work to be done
Africa there is a battle to be won

Hey hey hey hey
Listen to what I say
Hey hey hey hey
Love will win the day

Let us unite and become one nation
Let us unite freedom is our destination
Africa five fingers alone they are weak
But a fist my friend that will speak
It is time to take the pen to make our story
Africa this rhyme shall lead us into glory

Hey hey hey hey
Listen to what I say
Hey hey hey hey
Love will win the day

Justice is the fuel that makes the light burn
Straight and narrow we shall never turn
If you stumble I will be at your side
In the face of evil we will not hide
Unleash the shackles I refuse to be a slave
I believe in the power of love to save

Hey hey hey hey
Listen to what I say
Hey hey hey hey
Love will win the day

Mary Magdalene

On La Rue Avenue she stands underneath the street light
Survival is a stronger force then wrong or right
She's thin as sin cause the heroin has a mighty bite
If you love fantasy ask her cause she just might

And Jesus kicked back with Mary Magdalene
She was at the cross to see salvation begin
All the Pharisees were blind as night
Mary Magdalene she was the Lord's delight

Lusting Lolly paid double so he had no trouble at all
Like starving birds to bread they were led to the fall
Say sweet Anne I'm a man can you make me feel?
With a wiggle and a giggle she let out a squeal

And Jesus kicked back with Mary Magdalene
She was at the cross to see salvation begin
All the Pharisees were blind as night
Mary Magdalene she was the Lord's delight

Well the preacher had a feature talking on good clean fun
He's a hypocrite full of shit so said the nun
And Lolly wrote a large check for the collection plate
The priest took the cash to by some hash to celebrate

And Jesus kicked back with Mary Magdalenc
She was at the cross to see salvation begin
All the Pharisees were blind as night
Mary Magdalene she was the Lord's delight

The symphony never ends but my friends the song will change
God bless my soul soon rock and roll will sound strange
But love sex and desire is an endless fire burning
If you feel blue head to La Rue Avenue for your yearning

And Jesus kicked back with Mary Magdalene
She was at the cross to see salvation begin
All the Pharisees were blind as night
Mary Magdalene she was the Lord's delight

All About The Money

Trying to say I love you in a million ways
Each song I sung giving you some elegant praise
I said to my soul with a little bit of doubt
It's time me and my second hand guitar sell out

I love you, yes I do honey
But it's all about money
It may sound funny
It's all about the money

I felt the hunger I wasn't getting younger
She said flowers are for free and a bee stung her
A walk in the park all was dark no more power
Don't pay the water bill and you cannot shower

I love you, yes I do honey
But it's all about money
It may sound funny
It's all about the money

Mistress Money she's just a piece of paper
Free your mind and you shall escape her
So says the grand Poet to the Poor
Understand he don't want poverty anymore
Eternal is this endless class warfare
While most of us are truly unaware

Writing lyrics into the late hours of the night
Sanity and vanity two mighty powers fight
I'm thanking on line banking for all the updates
I heard someone say good things come to he who waits

I love you, yes I do honey
But it's all about money
It may sound funny
It's all about the money

Nine To Five

Nobody messes with the psychopath
Nobody tells him he needs a bath
You can't chase the dragon unless you're high
On the weekend they all give it a try

It's nine to five just to survive
Eyes open, are you alive?
Nonsense and expensive jive
It's nine to five just to survive

Careers and fears make laughter and tears
What can you show for all you years?
A room with a view and a title or two
What's wrong with the world- Why it's you

It's nine to five just to survive
Eyes open, are you alive?
Nonsense and expensive jive
It's nine to five just to survive

Business school a master's degree
Climbing the ladder of society
Dressing for style with a fake smile
You wonder is it all worthwhile
Never time to think or second guess
How could it be life is such a mess?

Bullies they can sense any fear
Tiny tyrants tougher than they appear
Power flows down is that perfectly clear?
If you disagree simply get out of here

It's nine to five just to survive
Eyes open, are you alive?
Nonsense and expensive jive
It's nine to five just to survive

On The Radio

At Jersey Mike's there ain't too much happening
The counter girls stand with fingers snapping
Keeping the beat to a song from long ago
They dream dreams only the poor can know

Here we go on the radio
Music it locks the flow
Always in all way it's a show
Here we go on the radio

Nobody wants a job paying minimum wage
Money seems to be the eternal rage
And the owner he takes the lion's share
They call it capitalism and it ain't fair

Here we go on the radio
Music it locks the flow
Always in all way it's a show
Here we go on the radio

Love lost is better than having none
Some girls give twirl just for the fun
How much fulfillment is there in slicing meat?
She sings along strong in a song so sweet

Here we go on the radio
Music it locks the flow
Always in all way it's a show
Here we go on the radio

The record producer I can see him strut
You can be sure that he'll take his cut
And the musicians don't even got on the label
I'm eating my ham and cheese at my table

Here we go on the radio
Music it locks the flow
Always in all way it's a show
Here we go on the radio

Reclaim Your Glory

You are a child of darker skin
I see a light radiating within
Rebuke the notion of original sin
Go to the waters be born again

Come and reclaim your glory
It is up to you the end of the story
I fight for you I fight for me
Come and reclaim your glory

Empires they rise and empires fall
I hear in the distant Africa's call
From around the world we must unite
It is the time to make things right

Come and reclaim your glory
It is up to you the end of the story
I fight for you I fight for me
Come and reclaim your glory

The drums are beating from the mountain top
The drums are beating they never do stop
The drums are beating from the savannah plain
The drums are beating from the depths of pain
The drums are beating the clouds will rain
The drums are beating life will not be in vain

The future is coming around the bend
Past and future let them be your friend
Walk along your ancestors' trail
Reclaim your glory you cannot fail

Come and reclaim your glory
It is up to you the end of the story
I fight for you I fight for me
Come and reclaim your glory

Rock And Roll

I woke up inside a rock and roll song
Chasing the dragon I could do no wrong
The choir was on fire with radiant heat
A place of grace where love and fantasy meet

Rock and roll is endless glory
Reveals your souls tells the story
Rock and roll is what you feel
Rock and roll is what is real

The guitar solo full of electric shock
The line to the show went around the block
From heaven Jimi looked down with a smile
Beyond the strife of life it was all worth while

Rock and roll is endless glory
Reveals your souls tells the story
Rock and roll is what you feel
Rock and roll is what is real

There is a hunger the artist needs
A heart of wonder see how it bleeds
Creativity is a woman to romance
You'll never score if you don't take a chance

The crowd screams as my dreams are all fulfilled
My heart is racing while my spirit thrilled
After the encore the crowd demanded more
I was mainlining heaven perfectly pure

Rock and roll is endless glory
Reveals your souls tells the story
Rock and roll is what you feel
Rock and roll is what is real

See The Love

She's selling dreams but you got to pay
Got enough money she'll go all the way
Fantasy is defined by state of mind
She sees the glory it makes her blind

Pretty package with bows neatly tied
Here's a mantra don't be denied
On the cross Christ crucified
See the love arms open wide

Day by day we're all going to die
You live the truth or you live a lie
Chief criminals do white collar crime
If caught they never do any time

Pretty package with bows neatly tied
Here's a mantra don't be denied
On the cross Christ crucified
See the love arms open wide

Memoirs of a boring house wife
See the plane mundane of my life
You can only spin the sin so far
What is rock with no electric guitar

Pretty package with bows neatly tied
Here's a mantra don't be denied
On the cross Christ crucified
See the love arms open wide

A best seller she can only hope
High in the sky better than dope
Hey who am I to judge the lost
Before you jump count the cost

Pretty package with bows neatly tied
Here's a mantra don't be denied
On the cross Christ crucified
See the love arms open wide

She Forgot

She writes poems that never rhyme
A flower woman trapped in another time
She can't get the acid for free anymore
And they went and had a brand new war

She forgot what she was going to say
If she had words maybe she'd pray
No things aren't going to be okay
She forgot what she was going to say

She has more than a little bulge in the middle
There are no easy answers for life's riddle
Getting out of bed is a victory indeed
Despite all of her good will there's still greed

She forgot what she was going to say
If she had words maybe she'd pray
No things aren't going to be okay
She forgot what she was going to say

Judy I heard that cancer beat you down
Same time Sylvia was wandering around town
I should have sent a card that wouldn't have been hard
But alas all of us artists are always on guard

This is not the tomorrow she was dreaming of
There is no world peace but a shortage of love
She would quite but habits are hard to change
Her life is counterfeit does that sound strange

She forgot what she was going to say
If she had words maybe she'd pray
No things aren't going to be okay
She forgot what she was going to say

So Long Ago

Caught by thoughts drifting in like the rain
Forgotten memories lifting pleasure and pain
Crying trying to find any kind of phrase
In comes the sin of my formers days

And when I said I love you
Your answer was so cruel
When I said I love you
I felt like a fool
Don't you know
That was so long ago

Life is an endless symphony
Played out in a minor key
Angels sing in a sacred choir
While demons dance with fire

Bipolar is an endless rollercoaster ride
King of the universe with a curse to hide
My shoes are wet my mind soaked with regret
In a one horse race I placed the wrong bet

And when I said I love you
Your answer was so cruel
When I said I love you
I felt like a fool
Don't you know
That was so long ago

Pretty princess living on daddy's dime
In a world of abundance poverty is a crime
I have no doubt you'll pout about my rhyme
Say what you will still this is my time

And when I said I love you
Your answer was so cruel
When I said I love you
I felt like a fool
Don't you know
That was so long ago

So Sad To Say

Yellow form pink slip sign only in blue ink
Please conform we'll gladly tell you what to think
Wear a uniform shine your boots nice and grand
Desert Storm bombs fall in yet another land

Welcome to our pleasant little café
Order what you want as long as you can pay
Never mind what you'll find in yesterday
The buffalo are all gone so sad to say

I had a course in logic it made no sense
When I asked a question the professor took offense
The statement on the exam read repeat all I said
I could secure an "A" with a little pay or time in bed

Welcome to our pleasant little café
Order what you want as long as you can pay
Never mind what you'll find in yesterday
The buffalo are all gone so sad to say

There are billions of stars in the galaxy
In perfect order I envision anarchy
God's eye is on the sparrow He's a busy man
Snake oil salesmen sell salvation just cause he can
Gain the world and you shall lose your soul
Little tin gods beat the odds seeking control

All the Sioux are blue and you should be too
The skies and the rivers they were once blue
Today the system fails with overcrowded jails
The educated are hated for minor details

Welcome to our pleasant little café
Order what you want as long as you can pay
Never mind what you'll find in yesterday
The buffalo are all gone so sad to say

Stealing Your Muse

It was Saturday evening and the sun refused to set
Never making love to you is my life's single regret
She said I'd love to but first I got to place my bet
I lost my lovely lady to the game of roulette

Excuse me Bob Dylan for borrowing your muse
There are pieces of the puzzle we never use
I started with folk and graduated to the blues
Look out Bob Dylan I'm stealing your muse

By the slot machines the janitor cursed obscene
It's a crime to work double time just to clean
I have a sweet honey at home waiting for my love
Along came the manager he was wearing a white glove

Excuse me Bob Dylan for borrowing your muse
There are pieces of the puzzle we never use
I started with folk and graduated to the blues
Look out Bob Dylan I'm stealing your muse

The casino operates twenty four seven
With free booze it's not really heaven
Except when you score triple eleven
In my pocket I got me a little leaven
A dollar for the house one for the beast
Can't make a cake bake without yeast

The gritty streets of Sin City are pretty in the eternal eve
The nature of Mother Nature is enough to make you believe
Memory of my true love haunts the depths of my mind
Tomorrow will never come to the lonesome that are blind

Excuse me Bob Dylan for borrowing your muse
There are pieces of the puzzle we never use
I started with folk and graduated to the blues
Look out Bob Dylan I'm stealing your muse

Sylvia's Garden

There were glorious flowers red and yellow
And green in between the fruits so mellow
Sylvia's garden was truly a grand glory
Living and giving is such a great story

Sylvia's garden let the love grow
Sylvia's garden we want you to know
That you need not fear you are welcome here
Sylvia's garden year after year

Well Sylvia was a beautiful Caribbean queen
Who happened to have a thumb that was green
Every seed was a child planted with love and care
A smile of grace on her face to gladly share

Sylvia's garden let the love grow
Sylvia's garden we want you to know
That you need not fear you are welcome here
Sylvia's garden year after year

Well let it be told like all Sylvia grew old
Winter came with the snow and the bitter cold
And Sylvia got lost in dementia's fierce frost
Out of her mind she was blind to the high cost

Sylvia's garden let the love grow
Sylvia's garden we want you to know
That you need no fear you are welcome here
Sylvia's garden year after year

There is no justice in the cruel place called Earth
Some have more than they need right from birth
But the rich man he will never come to understand
The joy of the labor from a willing hand

Jesus oh Lord full of grace
Prepare Sylvia her place
In heaven a garden of endless land
Where peace and love is on hand

Sylvia's garden let the love grow
Sylvia's garden we want you to know
That you need no fear you are welcome here
Sylvia's garden year after year

The Bassman

Some people live the blues
Others have no clues
Some give while some use
But we all pay our dues

My last card of the deck
You know it's the ace man
She's a heavenly speck
From outer space man
Levert gonna lay a hurt
Cause he's the Bassman

Slide into my room
Let me lay down the boom
Don't have no gloom
Let me lay down the boom

My last card of the deck
You know it's the ace man
She's a heavenly speck
From outer space man
Levert gonna lay a hurt
Cause he's the Bassman

Spinning spells all over the radio
He's the Bassman with his own show
The engines are full we're ready to go
He's the Bassman let the bombs blow

We question God every day
He hears what you say
Listen to the music play
There's a show every Sunday

My last card of the deck
You know it's the ace man
She's a heavenly speck
From outer space man
Levert gonna lay a hurt
Cause he's the Bassman

The Lessons Of Truth

The prophet wrote his wise words in the sand
The wind blew and nobody knew the command
In heaven above I see the writing of his hand
See the teaching of love all over the land

In the blue of the ocean high
In heaven's glorious sky
In the green leaves of youth
There are the lessons of truth

The scripture is there in the children's eyes
It is born in each of us the truth and lies
Right and wrong we need to be strong
They are more than words in this song

In the blue of the ocean high
In heaven's glorious sky
In the green leaves of youth
There are the lessons of truth

Jesus was on the shores of Galilee
Let the truth make you free
Love is the way to live
When you have you should give
Love all turn the other cheek
Blessed are the poor and meek

We walk the path together no longer two but one
Singing with the ancients we shall overcome
If we never surrender than the victory is won
See the glory in the story let the work be done

In the blue of the ocean high
In heaven's glorious sky
In the green leaves of youth
There are the lessons of truth

The Love Of God And Man

Time is fading from blue to black
And yesterday it ain't coming back
Billions of people one of them is you
So I ask what will you do

The love of God and man
We're doing all that we can
Who is the master of the master plan?
Thinking of the love of God and man

Songs of freedom they are rare
And God's kingdom stands on prayer
The auction block it never did die
Will you sell out when the price is high?

The love of God and man
We're doing all that we can
Who is the master of the master plan?
Thinking of the love of God and man

Planet Earth she is mother to all
She is dying crying in a desperate call
Endless war waged by Babylon the whore
Wicked men feed on greed lusting for more
Peace love and understanding it is the cure
Peace love and understanding that's for sure

Strangers never make connection
Dangers they break protection
Wishful thoughts of defiance
Good intentions fall in silence

The love of God and man
We're doing all that we can
Who is the master of the master plan?
Thinking of the love of God and man

The Sad Ballad Of Mary Jane

My name is Marshall Law I have lived many years
From long ago I have wept countless tears
I lost my love my dear sweet Mary Jane
Every night I feel the bite of the endless pain

I sing this song it is all of me
I sing this song a sad melody
It keeps alive the sweet memory
Of Mary Jane who was all to me

When I was a youth I knew many a lass
But after a dance of two I would let them pass
But Mary Jane was a beauty beyond measure
I took her hand to understand her pleasure

I sing this song it is all of me
I sing this song a sad melody
It keeps alive the sweet memory
Of Mary Jane who was all to me

Well we got married and life moved on
In a blink of an eye Mary Jane was gone
Sometimes God is kind sometimes He is cruel
And I good sir played the part of the fool

I sing this song it is all of me
I sing this song a sad melody
It keeps alive the sweet memory
Of Mary Jane who was all to me

With a broken heart I sing this song of sorrow
For yesterday I would surrender tomorrow
But I am only a mortal far less than God
And on the road of despair I now trod

I sing this song it is all of me
I sing this song a sad melody
It keeps alive the sweet memory
Of Mary Jane who was all to me

The Story Of John And Lori

At school the kids called me all sorts of names
Wouldn't let me play in any of their games
An outcast confined to suffer in the inside
A criminal on a cross verbally crucified

Here's the story of John and Lori
I ain't writing this for no glory
The hour's late and things bore me
So I'll write the story of John and Lori

Well Lori she was a witch so they say
But the devil's price was so easy to pay
I just had to overcome all doubt and fear
So I went up to Lori and spoke loud and clear
Lori will you got out with me?

Here's the story of John and Lori
I ain't writing this for no glory
The hour's late and things bore me
So I'll write the story of John and Lori

When she started to laugh I got a scare
But she said yes and answered my prayer
I was flying on the cloud just below heaven
It was a great thing for a boy of eleven

Here's the story of John and Lori
I ain't writing this for no glory
The hour's late and things bore me
So I'll write the story of John and Lori

Well we met to get ourselves some ice cream
It was like something inside of a dream
But it finished before it really had a start
Lori ended it all and she broke my heart

Here's the story of John and Lori
I ain't writing this for no glory
The hour's late and things bore me
So I'll write the story of John and Lori

The World To Me

Fifty years old I hit my prime
Gave a body slam to Father Time
Gray in my hair makes me proud
Rock and Roll was born to be loud

Living is something to see
Giving by nature is free
Hear this song my melody
You mean the world to me

Library is full Friday afternoon
Time is running coming far too soon
Eyes of wisdom see my own demise
Stay young and beautiful pretty lies

Living is something to see
Giving by nature is free
Hear this song my melody
You mean the world to me

They're playing cards in the corner room
The psychopath preaches poems of doom
And I record it all like a master thief
We all have faith in some sordid belief

Living is something to see
Giving by nature is free
Hear this song my melody
You mean the world to me

The song my friend never does end
Always something around the next bend
All I need is a fantastic hook
And a silicone sister with the look

Living is something to see
Giving by nature is free
Hear this song my melody
You mean the world to me

This Is A Song Of Revolution

Wake up drink up there is a cup full of fine wine
It is a drink from the ancient hand of the divine
It is an elixir full of power it is a dose of might
We hold the future this hour we will make it right

This is a song of revolution
That is our solution
Freedom by evolution
This is a song of revolution

We the masses are the hands of this great land
United undivided we are all do you understand?
As a mighty wave of the ocean let us cleanse all
From Uganda to Africa can you hear this call?

This is a song of revolution
That is our solution
Freedom by evolution
This is a song of revolution

I look into the eyes of the children who are yet to be born
I look into the heart of the grandmothers ripped and torn
I will not behave like a slave for God made us free
Fight with all of your might to seize our liberty

This is a song of revolution
That is our solution
Freedom by evolution
This is a song of revolution

To Tell The Truth

Barefoot walking on the sands by the ocean blue
In the child's eyes the ancient lands are new
Wonders of the colors to dazzle and amaze
I pray today that he will know better days

Lost in time lost in youth
It is no crime to tell the truth
It is no crime to tell the truth
It is our duty to tell the truth

On the seas there sails a ship like long before
Heading to the New World a distant shore
Slaves ships may they sink to ocean floor
May mankind know tyranny no more

Lost in time lost in youth
It is no crime to tell the truth
It is no crime to tell the truth
It is our duty to tell the truth

She sings the song of our land of Africa so strong
Our pride is glowing knowing it is not wrong
As the phoenix we shall ascend the to heaven
Feeling good is not a sin to be forgiven

Lost in time lost in youth
It is no crime to tell the truth
It is no crime to tell the truth
It is our duty to tell the truth

Neocolonialism is the name of the shameful game
See the pirates see the thugs it is the same
For the young one he is laughing wild and free
I shall raise the cry and try for harmony

Lost in time lost in youth
It is no crime to tell the truth
It is no crime to tell the truth
It is our duty to tell the truth

Vanessa

Every punk is a walking talking piece of art
Hear Vanessa humming strumming her part
A rebel giving hell living in momma's house
Roars like a lion and fights like a mouse

Vanessa well she's one of a kind
Troubled child with a troubled mind
Somebody the word has left behind
Vanessa when you look what do you find?

Beauty is something that none can define
I don't care about good hair I like mine
Big booty but if your snooty we won't talk
See there with tender care Vanessa's Mohawk

Vanessa well she's one of a kind
Troubled child with a troubled mind
Somebody the word has left behind
Vanessa when you look what do you find?

Roger Roger I heard you lost your way
That you got old and sold for the pay
But you won't be playing the temple gig
That's the beauty of being bigger than big

And Vanessa well she dreams as we all do
Youth is an illusion where a delusion is true
Hey listen to what I say ride the peace train
War and Babylon the Whore are all in vain

Vanessa well she's one of a kind
Troubled child with a troubled mind
Somebody the word has left behind
Vanessa when you look what do you find?

Courage is getting out of bed and doing your thing
You don't gotta be an opera star to sing
In the rat race only grace will take you far
I say that today Vanessa is a living star

Vanessa well she's one of a kind
Troubled child with a troubled mind
Somebody the word has left behind
Vanessa when you look what do you find?

Visions Of Madonna

She wrote a note wishing me well
Goodbye was the reason why I could tell
The letter said feel better in a rhyme
Maybe I'll drop by from time to time

Visions of Madonna riding a pale horse
The marriage was great until the divorce
The rivers run the most natural course
And we never promised for better or worse

The world is a great big place
What is love if there is no grace?
Sorry I can't say this to your face
I just need some time and space

Visions of Madonna riding a pale horse
The marriage was great until the divorce
The rivers run the most natural course
And we never promised for better or worse

Well the poets began to organize
Refusing confusing truth and lies
But deception is the key to art
And my true love she broke my heart

Visions of Madonna riding a pale horse
The marriage was great until the divorce
The rivers run the most natural course
And we never promised for better or worse

I walked the beach by the ocean's roar
Life's ultimate lesson is far from pure
Give and take make and break don't ask why
Cause all the honest answers are a lie

Satellites are circling in the sky
They'll remain in vain long after we die
Science is a mistress calculating and cruel
And I play the part of the perfect fool

Visions of Madonna riding a pale horse
The marriage was great until the divorce
The rivers run the most natural course
And we never promised for better or worse

Wake Up Africa

The king is sleeping the hour is late
The time is changing we cannot wait
For the love of all that is good and right
For the love of man we rise to fight

Wake up Africa the time is here
Wake up Africa have no fear
Wake up Africa salvation is near
Wake up Africa the time is here

Long ago we were the highest high
Then the pale man came with his lie
But the clock is turning to our time
Now is the moment to end the crime

Wake up Africa the time is here
Wake up Africa have no fear
Wake up Africa salvation is near
Wake up Africa the time is here

Be brave for you must lead the way
Be brave come to save the day
Courage let it dwell deep inside
You are from Africa feel the pride

Let wisdom guide you on the path
We seek no vengeance or wrath
Justice is the cause of the hour
United none can stop our power

Wake up Africa the time is here
Wake up Africa have no fear
Wake up Africa salvation is near
Wake up Africa the time is here

Wake Up Black People

The smack and crack are holding you back
Can't you see that you're under attack?
Sleeping late long into the woeful day
Listen up I've got something to say

Wake up black people or you will die
Wake up black people hear my cry
Wake up black people give it a try
Wake up black people or you will die

Bankers don't care if you die of starvation
They would gladly sacrifice our whole nation
Armies come and inflict great devastation
All they offer is some phony salvation

Wake up black people or you will die
Wake up black people hear my cry
Wake up black people give it a try
Wake up black people or you will die

Why is your history some forgotten mystery?
You have a great heritage oh listen to me
Africa is where mankind had their start
Africa is your mother with love in her heart

Wake up black people or you will die
Wake up black people hear my cry
Wake up black people give it a try
Wake up black people or you will die

Reclaim your fame reclaim your name
Be a man if you can or feel the shame
Don't let the chains bind your mind
The sun is shining are you truly blind?

Wake up black people or you will die
Wake up black people hear my cry
Wake up black people give it a try
Wake up black people or you will die

Wallflower

I am a woman the men ignore
But I have dreams and so much more
Of a man who is handsome and true
And skies that are forever blue

I would like you to dance with me
Could you take a chance on me?
I want you to hold me so tight
And then give me a kiss good night

Do you know the pain of loneliness?
I am guilty but I did not transgress
So sad I cry as the hours pass by
Asking the good Lord the reason why

I would like you to dance with me
Could you take a chance on me
I want you to hold me so tight
And then give me a kiss good night

I have dreams so big and grand
I wonder if you can understand
Night passes sadly hour after hour
I live the life of the wallflower

I would like you to dance with me
Could you take a chance on me
I want you to hold me so tight
And then give me a kiss good night

When I'm Manic

When I'm manic the voices sing a sweet song
The world is a mystery and I can do no wrong
Visions of glory I tell the story in a rhyme
When I'm manic you can't convict me of a crime

And don't laugh at the poor fool
Trying to obey the golden rule
They indoctrinate in high school
In college they sharpen the tool

I had a big laugh in room eight and a half
Snorting cocaine and drinking wine from a carafe
Psycho and Hypo they were such a dubious pair
Throwing the dice as if they had not a care

And don't laugh at the poor fool
Trying to obey the golden rule
They indoctrinate in high school
In college they sharpen the tool

The cameras are rolling with infinite eyes
To catch the exact moment you compromise
Their files are immense with ample evidence
Emotions contradict good common sense

Psychotropic medicines they can stabilize
Still you always will be someone to despise
If the trust won't convict they simply tell lies
When I'm manic I reach the highest of highs

And don't laugh at the poor fool
Trying to obey the golden rule
They indoctrinate in high school
In college they sharpen the tool

Who Will You Listen To?

Mother Wisdom her song is lifted on the wind
She says that there is hope just around the next bend
See the harlot called foolishness with lush red lips
Mocking with laughter come kiss the apocalypse

Who will you listen to?
What are you going to do?
Be faithful and true
Who will you listen to?

Jesus on the cross Father forgive them for what they do
Love your neighbor love your enemy so I love you
The greedy man he wishes to take everything
To sit on a throne of gold and become our king

Who will you listen to?
What are you going to do?
Be faithful and true
Who will you listen to?

God He took the rainbow and made us His children
To live in righteousness and to forsake all sin
The devil speaks lies he cries grab all that you can
In the end my friend he is the mind behind the master plan

Some they see some are blind
The way to be is good and kind
You know that you understand
When you lend a helping hand
Together forever onward up
If you're thirsty I'll fill your cup

Who will you listen to?
What are you going to do?
Be faithful and true
Who will you listen to?

Words

Around town the sound found on the street has a funky beat
Rappers and girl slappers struggle for victory or defeat
Politicians pontificate policies perpetuating pure hate
Their truth is lies in disguise how passionately they debate

Words- they make up this song
Words- They define right and wrong
Words- Hear the poor man cry
Words – They sell you a lie

Bums out in the cold surviving from dumpster diving
A chicken in every pot they forgot who they're jiving
Rich men never go to jail if they fail they pay a fine
See the priest feast he got some line about being divine

Words- they make up this song
Words- They define right and wrong
Words- Hear the poor man cry
Words – They sell you a lie

Put letters together and move your tongue
In fuse the blues a song is sung
Rock and roll refugees with long hair
In the land of the free they don't care
Debt slaves till we enter our graves
In the end my friend only Jesus saves

Propaganda penetrates a panoply of pretense
Killing and war is evil it's a matter of common sense
The Vodka is strong you belong if you drink it straight
Don't wait articulate what you think try to relate

Words- they make up this song
Words- They define right and wrong
Words- Hear the poor man cry
Words – They sell you a lie

Writing A Song

It's almost California but not all
There's a bit of Philly as I recall
Yeah sunshine and the mellow blue
And a double heaping of I love you

Writing a song with a smile
Writing a song with Kurt Vile
Art is in heart this is survival
Writing a song with a smile

You take what you got and then you run
If you can man the plan is for fun
When the choir sings it brings joy
Love is a fire that none could destroy

Writing a song with a smile
Writing a song with Kurt Vile
Art is in heart this is survival
Writing a song with a smile

This is the part where we get really funky
Yeah, yeah, yeah, yeah, yeah
This is the part where we unleash the monkey
Oh, oh, oh, yeah, yeah, yeah
Sputnik is still orbiting the Earth or so they say
I want a dime for every crime but who will pay?

If I made you smile it was worthwhile
You become a man because of the trial
Play the guitar become a superstar
If you need lyrics I know who you are

Writing a song with a smile
Writing a song with Kurt Vile
Art is in heart this is survival
Writing a song with a smile

You're The One

Monday morning comes rise and shine
My heart is burning with love divine
The shower water is freezing cold
You're the one I'm longing to hold

I'm not a song writer
Just a fool in love
Here I am sitting here
You're the one I'm thinking of

At my desk I see your photograph
In my mind I can hear you laugh
What went wrong I still don't know
I'm begging you for another go

I'm not a song writer
Just a fool in love
Here I am sitting here
You're the one I'm thinking of

How do we define time and space
If you are near well so is grace
Equations dictate the laws of life
I wanted you to be my wife
But the numbers they add to zero
And I am far from a superhero

This son well it's my last chance
If not forever maybe a dance
The world is wild and we are free
You're the one please come back to me

I'm not a song writer
Just a fool in love
Here I am sitting here
You're the one I'm thinking of

Baby I Want To Make Love To You

Baby I want to make love to you
I want to sing you my song
Baby I want to make love to you
I won't do you any wrong

I was a sailor on the ocean blue
I had dreams
All my dreams
Were dreams of you

Baby I want to make love to you
Cover you with kisses sweet
Baby I want to make love to you
So you feel fully complete

I took a journey with no destination
I had many questions
But no answers
Nothing worth making mention

Baby I want to make love to you
I want to share my life
Baby I want to make love to you
I want you to be my wife

As a youth they sold me a lie
But I kept asking why
Why is there war
And people bitterly poor

Baby I want to make love to you
I want to sing you my song
Baby I want to make love to you
I won't do you any wrong

Devil's Pride

He was staggering drunk like marionette missing a string
It was opening night at the Met we were waiting for the fat lady to sing
She was a whore writing rock and roll lore into a score
He pushed the red button and said boys this is war

And there you sit like a stone
In a world of fantasy all alone
I wonder what's going on inside
It's only the devil and the devil's pride

Diligently at my task I had to ask who was that masked man
Hit em high hit em low hit em any way you can
Dreamers and prophets can be purchased at the local five and dime
I'd write you a love song but to rhyme is a crime

And there you sit like a stone
In a world of fantasy all alone
I wonder what's going on inside
It's only the devil and the devil's pride

In an infinite universe well there must be infinite fates
Somewhere out there lurks a world with only eights
Your eyes are supernovas just yearning to consume
Roses are only thorns until the morn that they bloom

And there you sit like a stone
In a world of fantasy all alone
I wonder what's going on inside
It's only the devil and the devil's pride

Lucifer cheats at bowling his ball is loaded
Sadly the IUD has just exploded
Have another martini feel no harm
Down in Afghanistan he left his arm

I search the church pews for a word that matches luck
Bend over baby I'll give you a massive chromium truck
On the highway to hell who tells the limit to speed
They crucified paradise a casualty of greed

And there you sit like a stone
In a world of fantasy all alone
I wonder what's going on inside
It's only the devil and the devil's pride

Evan's Song

She says there you go again with that laugh
It's definitely the better part of your better half
Love and hate are the same from different points of view
All that matters come the morning I'll be with you

And this song is for Evan yes that means you
No matter what you say the sky is still blue
Some words are always going to be true
And this song is for Evan have you got a clue?

Drums in the Congo are beating a lament
God is asking nicely please come and repent
Rock stars fade away the sky is getting dull
I'm in to win my hand trumps complete control

And this song is for Evan yes that means you
No matter what you say the sky is still blue
Some words are always going to be true
And this song is for Evan have you got a clue?

Howard says we must be nice to the police
When the climax comes the grinch finds release
Jesus Christ wears the title the Prince of Peace
And in the name of the cross wars never cease

And this song is for Evan yes that means you
No matter what you say the sky is still blue
Some words are always going to be true
And this song is for Evan have you got a clue?

Momma and daddy well they did the best they could
Until the beer drinking brawler moved in the neighborhood
You can't stay up late if you never go to sleep
When Buda calls Jesus the conversation goes mighty deep

I guess you never met a girl like me she whispers soft
I kinda give a new meaning to counting the cost
I read a book called Heather has two mommies
We gotta decide if that's better than the commies

And this song is for Evan yes that means you
No matter what you say the sky is still blue
Some words are always going to be true
And this song is for Evan have you got a clue?

Falling In Love

I remember December and your gift of surrender
Under the light with all the might I could render
I said I loved you well I'm the great pretender
I remember December and your gift of surrender

Falling in love good things take time
Falling in love trying to make the words rhyme
Falling in love I hear wedding bells chime
Falling in love good things take time

I was chasing the wind in a twisting hurricane
My eye to the sky I was egotistically vain
You were no more than a score a notch on the belt
And I never really gave a damn about how you felt

Falling in love good things take time
Falling in love trying to make the words rhyme
Falling in love I hear wedding bells chime
Falling in love good things take time

Somewhere between heaven and hell there's a place
A land down under full of wonder and glorious grace
In the battle of conquest it seemed I lost all control
I gave more than my heart I also gave you my soul

Falling in love good things take time
Falling in love trying to make the words rhyme
Falling in love I hear wedding bells chime
Falling in love good things take time

Say here we are I'm playing this song on my guitar
Walking down the road hand in hand going far
You were a keeper and the love grows deeper each day
All I can say is that I thank the Lord you came my way

Falling in love good things take time
Falling in love trying to make the words rhyme
Falling in love I hear wedding bells chime
Falling in love good things take time

Get Down On Me

Late Saturday night full of delight
I want it all and you ain't gonna fight
We go rolling and romping on the bed
Can you remember the words I said?

Get down on me baby get down on me
Get down on me lady get down on me
Get down on me darling get down on me
Get down on me baby get down on me

Dreams and screams fantasy by the moon beams
Blind in my mind nothing is as it seems
Together I am yours and you are mine
Even heaven above isn't as divine

Get down on me baby get down on me
Get down on me lady get down on me
Get down on me darling get down on me
Get down on me baby get down on me

Please please please don't tease
Take me all the way to the promised land
You ain't praying down on your knees
Life is hell but you make it all grand

You're licking your slippery lips ruby red
I know you love me though no words are said
There are perfect times when all life is still
Measure the double pleasure in the thrill

Get down on me baby get down on me
Get down on me lady get down on me
Get down on me darling get down on me
Get down on me baby get down on me

Heather

School was cruel and I was the fool
Afraid to break the simplest rule
And everybody was the devil's tool
School was cruel and I was the fool

And if I asked you to dance
Would you give me a second chance?
I ain't looking for romance
I just want to ask you to dance

Rock and roll held a redemptive scream
I only had fantasies not a single dream
Oh, the hope to escape the rape of my mind
Now that tomorrows here what did I find

And if I asked you to dance
Would you give me a second chance?
I ain't looking for romance
I just want to ask you to dance

Smile laugh let the darkness fade away
I wonder if down under are we okay
I'm talking in the philosophical sense
Life is for love not dollars and cents

And if I asked you to dance
Would you give me a second chance?
I ain't looking for romance
I just want to ask you to dance

And Myron is getting ready for the revenge of the nerd
Love and hate they are defined by more than the word
See the world crumbles as Uncle Sam stumbles down
I seek nothing at all save the call of the thorny crown

This is a June tune of the apocalypse
Women like it when you kiss their lips
Into the forever abyss time slips
I'm hanging with the Blood and Crypts

And if I asked you to dance
Would you give me a second chance?
I ain't looking for romance
I just want to ask you to dance

And I this deserves just one more verse
I have changed and I know not for the worse
Heather grace is a vineyard overflowing
Life only ends when you stop growing

And if I asked you to dance
Would you give me a second chance?
I ain't looking for romance
I just want to ask you to dance

I wonder who has the guts to sing this song
Sitting on death row wondering what's wrong
Mr. Z is a hip hypocrite who sold out
Is this song for Heather, I have my doubt

And if I asked you to dance
Would you give me a second chance?
I ain't looking for romance
I just want to ask you to dance

Jesus Is The Only One Who Answers Prayers

Every syllable of this song is synthetic blue
My teeth are fake and there are lifts in my shoe
Yeah, and I just stole that line from Mister Peter Who
But I don't really care and neither should you

This a song sung for the synthetic green
Elvis was the king and Madonna the queen
Neither could write lyrics so who cares
Jesus is the only one who answers prayers

The only thing faker than my smile is my art
This is a pop song I got a cash register as a heart
Rolling off them one-hundred-dollar bills what a thrill
Rolling off them one-hundred-dollars bills going for the kill

This a song sung for the synthetic green
Elvis was the king and Madonna the queen
Neither could write lyrics so who cares
Jesus is the only one who answers prayers

Tit and ass I ain't got no class
I'm a lovely lady a lucky lass
Buy my album dress like me
Let me mind be your reality

Stroking why'll choking baby this ain't no joking
High in the universe what's worse is what I'm smoking
Don't do as I do or even as I say just kindly pay
Cause I'm riding the unicorn steed on a grand greedy way

This a song sung for the synthetic green
Elvis was the king and Madonna the queen
Neither could write lyrics so who cares
Jesus is the only one who answers prayers

The music never really ends as least until the cash stops
I'm a whore what's more I do tricks for the cops
In Jersey everything is legal until they turn you in
I stole that line too Lord have mercy ain't it a sin

This a song sung for the synthetic green
Elvis was the king and Madonna the queen
Neither could write lyrics so who cares
Jesus is the only one who answers prayers

Joey

Joey sits at the store on Bloomfield Avenue
Life buzzes on by but he's got a great view
It's a hard world and we all gotta earn our pay
But dreaming is free so here's to a better day

In life Joey wants five stars
A double bass with triple guitars
I'm on my way to a paying gig
I'm one break away from hitting it big

He writes his words down because hey you never know
We had humble starts before playing the show
Joey looks in the mirror and sees fantasy
Hey baby there ain't no reason why that can't be me

In life Joey wants five stars
A double bass with triple guitars
I'm on my way to a paying gig
I'm one break away from hitting it big

Life is a long and winding grind
Before you start you're left behind
Ain't nothing more precious than peace of mind
If you can see you realize we're all blind

Joey's days are long and paying his dues never ends
He counts his blessings one by one health and good friends
At night Joey walks home he looks to heaven high
He might not make it but he'll give it his best try

In life Joey wants five stars
A double bass with triple guitars
I'm on my way to a paying gig
I'm one break away from hitting it big

Johnnie Valentine

Here he comes walking down the line
Much brighter than the sunshine
Like an angel singing simply divine
Who could it be but Johnnie Valentine?

As he walks on by all the girls sigh
Oh won't you come and be my guy
As he walks on by all the girls sigh
Come on Johnnie give me a try

They call my friend Johnnie ninety-nine
One short of perfection so mighty fine
Every day I say he puts it on the line
Who could it be but Johnnie ninety-nine?

As he walks on by all the girls sigh
Oh won't you come and be my guy
As he walks on by all the girls sigh
Come on Johnnie give me a try

Lea don't you worry don't trouble your mind
If Johnny left you he'd have to be blind
Because between the two you're the better find
But rhyming your name would put me in a bind

See him in the church house kneeling in prayer
Every Sunday morning I meet Johnnie there
Hoping that someone will turn water into wine
Go give it a try Mister Johnnie Valentine

As he walks on by all the girls sigh
Oh won't you come and be my guy
As he walks on by all the girls sigh
Come on Johnnie give me a try

He's the real deal pure and genuine
That's my friend Johnnie Valentine
Love and hate the two forces intertwine
We all decide says Johnnie ninety-nine

As he walks on by all the girls sigh
Oh won't you come and be my guy
As he walks on by all the girls sigh
Come on Johnnie give me a try

Laser Beam Lover

Outer space the darkness can be so cruel
Laughing ladies playing you for the fool
Well hold on cosmic cowboy there's good news
There's something blazing hot beyond the blues

She's a laser beam lover one of a kind
She's a laser beam lover she'll fry your mind
Laser beam lover she'll leave you light years behind
She's a laser beam lover the best thing to find

Her touch is the fire of the hottest flame
She's the real deal she ain't playing no game
Never mind the supernova or blackhole
Laser beam lover she got some sweet soul

She's a laser beam lover one of a kind
She's a laser beam lover she'll fry your mind
Laser beam lover she'll leave you light years behind
She's a laser beam lover the best thing to find

Venus they say it's the planet of love
Laser beam lover that's who I'm thinking of
She's fast but she knows how to take it slow
Atomic power she ain't afraid to blow

She's a laser beam lover one of a kind
She's a laser beam lover she'll fry your mind
Laser beam lover she'll leave you light years behind
She's a laser beam lover the best thing to find

See the streak blazing in the sky
That's laser beam lover and I'm her guy
My sweetheart defines being high
That's laser beam lover and I'm her guy

No time for tomorrow and the worry
I'm singing a song of eternal glory
Laser beam lover I'm bound to get burned
But that's one lesson eager to be learned

She's a laser beam lover one of a kind
She's a laser beam lover she'll fry your mind
Laser beam lover she'll leave you light years behind
She's a laser beam lover the best thing to find

Love Is Love

An orchestra of drums each with a different beat
Here I am dancing romancing light on my feet
I see the moon and stars circling in the sky
The music of madness is screaming the reason why

Love is love and hate is hate
For every good thing we must wait
The God and devil are in an endless debate
Love is love and hate is hate

The antique store had relics from the forgotten war
A thousand banjo serenaders screamed no more
When they drop the big bomb nobody ever wins
You may be lost but you can still repent from your sins

Love is love and hate is hate
For every good thing we must wait
The God and devil are in an endless debate
Love is love and hate is hate

She had a smile that was something out of a dream
Hey baby maybe you like milk but I want cream
Put your hand into mine love's the perfect crime
We'll sing tomorrow's song where all of the words rhyme

Love is love and hate is hate
For every good thing we must wait
The God and devil are in an endless debate
Love is love and hate is hate

Angels don't always have wings
They crucified the King of Kings
Only Love knows what the future brings
Today I bought a pair of wedding rings

In surrender was the victory finally won
I looked in her eyes and said baby we just begun
Heaven ain't a place heaven's a life of grace
The sign on the wall said it all 'Save the human race'

Love is love and hate is hate
For every good thing we must wait
The God and devil are in an endless debate
Love is love and hate is hate

Love Simply Flows

Its been a long time that I plucked this guitar
Always had this dream about going real far
I play for free drinks down at the corner bar
I see you every night I know who you are

You were a stranger until hello
Darkness until the sun rose
These are the ways things go
And love well love simply flows

I won't play the real slow love songs any more
Cause you're a piece of heaven and heaven's pure
I won't play the real slow love songs any more
Last time I tried you walked straight out of the door

You were a stranger until hello
Darkness until the sun rose
These are the ways things go
And love well love simply flows

I figured some man came and broke your sweet heart
With good looks and warm charm swinging is an art
You dance with the fire and you'll always get burned
Like a piece of meat over a flame you're turned

You were a stranger until hello
Darkness until the sun rose
These are the ways things go
And love well love simply flows

We never met but baby this is your song
Forgive me for coming on a little strong
Well it's time for me to have a little drink
And it's high time to meet tell me what you think

You were a stranger until hello
Darkness until the sun rose
These are the ways things go
And love well love simply flows

Never Enough

I have words but they are empty
Feel the love inside the melody
I say goodbye maybe in the next life
I'll hold you sweetly my never wife

Never enough that's the song
Never enough it's all wrong
Never enough never enough
I don't even have a bluff

There is only terror in the shadow
The harvest of the secrets we don't know
Hear the wind whistle of tomorrow
Do you have a blessing I can borrow?

Never enough that's the song
Never enough it's all wrong
Never enough never enough
I don't even have a bluff

Is God cruel or am I just a fool?
The best lessons are never taught in school
Under the bleachers life teaches
More love than the sermon the priest preaches

Never enough that's the song
Never enough it's all wrong
Never enough never enough
I don't even have a bluff

I've seen so many fold up and die
The wicked laugh while the innocent cry
I seek the cosmic beat in the tropic heat
In the end victory is defeat

Sylvie our time is fading fast
In my mind only the good will last
And Sylvie I wanna say you're the best
But it's never enough this eternal quest

Never enough that's the song
Never enough it's all wrong
Never enough never enough
I don't even have a bluff

Oliver's Madness

The ghost of Pele rages in my soccer sneakers
The twin spirit of Jimi Hendrix plays on my speakers
I got eight tracks of Jim Morrison covering Lead Belly blues
I'm wearing slippers matching Dorothy's ruby red shoes

Oliver is running on a twisty road
Endless bombing hear misery explode
Oliver Oliver this doesn't make any sense
I'd trade the universe for some shiny six pence

I got a degree from dorm sixty-two Graystone U
Rain on the brain will make you insane from my point of view
In the dungeons of Grayhawk I met a greedy grubby troll
If I had a fist full of gold dollars I'd buy your soul

Oliver is running on a twisty road
Endless bombing hear misery explode
Oliver Oliver this doesn't make any sense
I'd trade the universe for some shiny six pence

The books of psychiatric diagnoses are long
If you read the endless pages you'll see the shrinks think wrong
The Thorazine shuffle at the zombie dance we'll all rebel
You'll get a piece of heaven when you give them burning hell

Oliver is running on a twisty road
Endless bombing hear misery explode
Oliver Oliver this doesn't make any sense
I'd trade the universe for some shiny six pence

Oliver tell me what went wrong?
Oliver this is your special song
Oliver twist it's a new dance
Oliver Twist here's your last chance

Rich and poor endless war Babylon is soon to fall
Far from Gog and Magog I hear the screamin' demons call
When you hear these words remember everything that could went wrong
But it ain't about John he's gone this is Oliver's song

Oliver is running on a twisty road
Endless bombing hear misery explode
Oliver Oliver this doesn't make any sense
I'd trade the universe for some shiny six pence

Open Up Your Eyes

Here I go crying tossing roses at your feet
Your words are sighing God knows complete
I sharpened my axe on the stone wheel as well
Perhaps I'll take your head one day, who can tell

I heard you won a Nobel Prize
So did Obama, fluent in lies
You're a little boy in disguise
Mister Zimmerman open up your eyes

I made love to Melody once my bass gave a boom
Dancing with demons with grace looking to consume
Fifty years old DMX died and Prince Philip too
The future is yet to be read the past tangled up in blue

I heard you won a Nobel Prize
So did Obama, fluent in lies
You're a little boy in disguise
Mister Zimmerman open up your eyes

Your song is fading away but I'm far from done
In fact according to Jack my time has just begun
But Mister Rankin is secret cargo on a pirate ship
I misspent my youth trying to be cool instead of hip

I heard you won a Nobel Prize
So did Obama, fluent in lies
You're a little boy in disguise
Mister Zimmerman open up your eyes

The petals have faded tossed brown in the breeze
Would you rip out your heart for me, pretty please
How can you compare to the author of the morning song?
Call me Hercules only because I want to finish strong

I heard you won a Nobel Prize
So did Obama, fluent in lies
You're a little boy in disguise
Mister Zimmerman open up your eyes

Rabbit Hole

We are telling stories but the moral is not clear
Three pigs run from the wolf saturated in fear
The brickhouse is the bank in the metaphor
While cowardly clowns never frown on endless war

There are rabbits in the rabbit hole
While vampires lurk in the collective soul
There are rabbits in the rabbit hole
The iron bells rings as life takes its toll

Cthulhu is sleeping in the great depths beneath
Don't trust the dentist to take care of your teeth
The roulette wheel is spinning double zero winning
In the window Alice see the Cheshire Cat grinning

There are rabbits in the rabbit hole
While vampires lurk in the collective soul
There are rabbits in the rabbit hole
The iron bells rings as life takes its toll

The leaders feed upon the blood that we bleed
The highway to hell is paved with the wages of greed
Jesus turned water into wine and it tasted mighty fine
Gargoyles lurch on the church perch ain't that divine?

There are rabbits in the rabbit hole
While vampires lurk in the collective soul
There are rabbits in the rabbit hole
The iron bells rings as life takes its toll

I was thinking in the summer haze
When we were together it was better days
A sign on the road said detour ahead
I always thought that we would wed

Draw your last desperate breath death awaits in the tomb
Sorry to consume the tune in some gloomy gloom
Duty calls the angel falls I quote John three sixteen
Have Alice you were a secretary and a beauty queen

There are rabbits in the rabbit hole
While vampires lurk in the collective soul
There are rabbits in the rabbit hole
The iron bells rings as life takes its toll

She's A Demon With An Angel's Voice

She says baby the love is all in the song
Oh no she protests I do believe this is wrong
My neckline needs to plunge and my mini's too long
Who needs starving artists victory's to the strong?

She's a demon with an angel's voice
Money and money are her choice
In the inferno see Satan Sam rejoice
She's a demon with an angel's voice

It's a Black Sabbath with a dark sun rising
When it comes to the bottom line no compromising
Sex sells, hell burns, but one learns what they desire
I'll take the glory and I'll deliver the fire

She's a demon with an angel's voice
Money and money are her choice
In the inferno see Satan Sam rejoice
She's a demon with an angel's voice

She sings a cover to discover ample pop fame
Life is a party a regular snappy happy game
As long as the cash flows in everything's fine
Rule number one when all is done its mine

She's a demon with an angel's voice
Money and money are her choice
In the inferno see Satan Sam rejoice
She's a demon with an angel's voice

Charlie the archangel made a final pact
You can't have John but I'll give you Jack
She signed in blood never having a hint
Of the secret secrets written in fine print

There she goes whoring and scoring on stage
Time commits the dreadful crime called age
Some other ambitious slut struts in her shadow
When you're on top you can only drop to below

She's a demon with an angel's voice
Money and money are her choice
In the inferno see Satan Sam rejoice
She's a demon with an angel's voice

Sylvie

Blackbird was flying away on the winter breeze
I heard Mother Earth crying please, please, please
I ain't no pop star and I can't play guitar
But I am what I am and love will take you far

Sylvie look where life took us
Nailed to a cross just like Jesus
I guess we always get our due
Sylvie if I ever loved someone it was you

You found me when I was lost counting the cost
The fire of your heart melted my angry frost
Forgive and forget the past is something to build on
And soon Sylvie I'm afraid you'll be gone

Sylvie look where life took us
Nailed to a cross just like Jesus
I guess we always get our due
Sylvie if I ever loved someone it was you

And there ain't nobody gonna sing this song
With all this evil we can't even right a wrong
But still I put these words into cosmic verse
Sometimes blessings are the worst curse

You never had it easy and I guess neither did I
I saw you yesterday still saying the long goodbye
Sometimes in the pain you can't refrain from asking why
So take this song as a long overdue lullaby

Sylvie look where life took us
Nailed to a cross just like Jesus
I guess we always get our due
Sylvie if I ever loved someone it was you

And all of God's children wept in the acid rain
We'd laugh at the money except the bankers are vain
Sylvia you and I had fairy tale with no pretending
Who knows maybe there's a chance for a happy ending?

Sylvie look where life took us
Nailed to a cross just like Jesus
I guess we always get our due
Sylvie if I ever loved someone it was you

The Perfect Man

She's such a little girl in a big old world
Blessings and blasphemies constantly hurled
Some things make sense some she can't understand
Walking wide awake dreaming of the perfect man

Somebody gentle somebody kind
With a great body and wonderful mind
He'll be a miracle like sight to the blind
One in a billion he's sure hard to find

He's something special with a great big heart
A picture of grandeur a masterpiece of art
She's looking up and she's looking down
Searching bright lights and the shady part of town

Somebody gentle somebody kind
With a great body and wonderful mind
He'll be a miracle like sight to the blind
One in a billion he's sure hard to find

The dam is bursting the world rushing in
Saturday at the bar and the wages of sin
How is it possible to find your mister right
If you never give them a trial of delight

Somebody gentle somebody kind
With a great body and wonderful mind
He'll be a miracle like sight to the blind
One in a billion he's sure hard to find

Years they pass she wonders what went wrong
Life isn't anything like a rock and roll song
Loneliness is freezing in the rays of the dawn
In her searching to find innocence has gone

Somebody gentle somebody kind
With a great body and wonderful mind
He'll be a miracle like sight to the blind
One in a billion he's sure hard to find

These Days

Everybody's looking for the bigger score
They want it all and that starts with more
Jim's in on the in without a doubt
He finds himself always looking out

These days the words don't rhyme
I think that's a terrible crime
Here we go on a journey through time
These days the words don't rhyme

I spent the day hanging pictures with Joe
What's the future hey man I don't know
The past is shrouded in a myriad of lies
Love is the answer nobody denies

These days the words don't rhyme
I think that's a terrible crime
Here we go on a journey through time
These days the words don't rhyme

The going rate is about a buck a word
It's more for comedy or so I have heard
In Kuwait the toilets are made of gold
Somewhere along the way the dream got sold

These days the words don't rhyme
I think that's a terrible crime
Here we go on a journey through time
These days the words don't rhyme

I'm at a loss listening to the Boss sing
Wondering what tomorrow is gonna bring
If I win I'll be going down the Tennessee
With sweet Anna Spratley on my knee

These days the words don't rhyme
I think that's a terrible crime
Here we go on a journey through time
These days the words don't rhyme

Wandering

Don quit the band full of frustration
The road was endless with no destination
Hey I believe in love peace and joy
But I grew old said goodbye to the boy

Pack your bags it's time to go
Where were headed I don't know
Ain't even got time to take it slow
Wandering the universe to and fro

It was back in nineteen ninety eight
The world was teetering on the edge of hate
Four young men rocked the world with an amen
They said look to the skies He's coming again

Pack your bags it's time to go
Where were headed I don't know
Ain't even got time to take it slow
Wandering the universe to and fro

Well dreams they are the last thing to die
Whenever you're down give it one more try
In the end it's the pleasure of the road
And having a friend to share the load

Pack your bags it's time to go
Where were headed I don't know
Ain't even got time to take it slow
Wandering the universe to and fro

Sometimes prayers are answered with silence
Never give in fight on with defiance
You're not alone there are many who care
Wandering the wide road we'll meet you there

Pack your bags it's time to go
Where were headed I don't know
Ain't even got time to take it slow
Wandering the universe to and fro

When You're In Love

I had a dream it was blue and yellow
I gave a scream you had some other fellow
He was a banker wearing a green tie
He was a prophet proclaiming a lie

We never danced the night away
But baby today's a new day
My arms are open and strong
When you're in love nothing's wrong

The universe has a place of grace for us
A demon band plays with an angelic chorus
Seize the second and baby don't let go
There's something about love I need to know

We never danced the night away
But baby today's a new day
My arms are open and strong
When you're in love nothing's wrong

See the asteroids shining in midnight sky
Love and only love is the reason why
Your kiss of bliss is nothing to miss
I asked God in prayer please more of this

Alligator stew goes grand with skunk stew
If you've never been it's a sin so true
Surrender to the pretender call his bluff
A pair of one eye jacks should be enough

We never danced the night away
But baby today's a new day
My arms are open and strong
When you're in love nothing's wrong

Zapp Zapp Zapp

I was in a haze of a manic phase on the down
Don the landlord no longer wanted me around
Scumbags for money only care about number one
This is a song about the evil that is done

Zapp zapp zapp you're a greedy liar
Zapp zapp zapp hell is a burning fire
Zapp zapp zapp listen to the radio
You and me are the ones that know

You were so nervous trying to make the score
Ron next door describes you as a money whore
He who laughs with God they laughs forever
No do you think yourself either wise or clever

Zapp zapp zapp you're a greedy liar
Zapp zapp zapp hell is a burning fire
Zapp zapp zapp listen to the radio
You and me are the ones that know

They're bombing Yemen we're watching genocide
They burned the Amazon I've nowhere left to hide
Maybe I'll read Wonder Woman to ease the pain
Life ain't easy when you're temporarily insane

Zapp zapp zapp you're a greedy liar
Zapp zapp zapp hell is a burning fire
Zapp zapp zapp listen to the radio
You and me are the ones that know

Big Ben rings in London across the pond
Jesus is in heaven past the great beyond
This song will make a million in the banks
To a greedy liar I give you my thanks

Oh, you know how collectors are it must be fine
You know the evil that you claim as mine
There's peace in the valley the river flows clean
So so sorry if the truth comes out so mean

Zapp zapp zapp you're a greedy liar
Zapp zapp zapp hell is a burning fire
Zapp zapp zapp listen to the radio
You and me are the ones that know

Be Clean

We have enemies that we cannot see
You must understand this mystery
They bind the body they bind the mind
For too long have you been blind

Be clean be clean we must stay pure
Be clean be clean this is a war
We shall be slaves no more
Be clean be clean this is a war

They talk of COVID a vicious foe
There are more shadows behind the show
A secret voice telling you what to do
Some of you don't have a clue

Be clean be clean we must stay pure
Be clean be clean this is a war
We shall be slaves no more
Be clean be clean this is a war

Wash your hands try to learn about your past
The devil's shadow spell has been cast
Don't let them define your friend or foe
Seek you shall find ask to know

Be clean be clean we must stay pure
Be clean be clean this is a war
We shall be slaves no more
Be clean be clean this is a war

There is a reality hiding before your eyes
Rivers are polluted and above gray skies
A monster called greed rages in this place
Slay the beast with the righteous sword of grace

There ain't no magic pill that'll cure your ill
You must be strong and use your freewill
Money's only a piece of paper
Try to think you'll escape her

Be clean be clean we must stay pure
Be clean be clean this is a war
We shall be slaves no more
Be clean be clean this is a war

Come Back Home

We are sailing tall ships, small boats, jet planes all headed east
We are fleeing Babylon God will soon destroy the beast
A land of promise it is waiting for the children it lost
Now is the time to act there is no time to count the cost

Oh, lost pilgrim forever on the roam
I call to you come back home (come back home)
Return to the land that you have never known
I call to you come back home (come back home)

Torn from your mother's soft breast to toil in a stolen land
They raped your women and sold your soul do you understand?
Now's the moment for the red man to rise in their angry tide
The American dream with a loud scream it was crucified

Oh, lost pilgrim forever on the roam
I call to you come back home (come back home)
Return to the land that you have never known
I call to you come back home (come back home)

Freedom is waiting for those who are brave
Africa is a force Africa to save
We shall fight until we earn the grave
Freedom is waiting for those who are brave

Child the seas are full of those stolen from where they belong
Make the Exodus flee white Jesus the day's for the strong
See the sin of the white man real soon the depth will be repaid
Love, hope and peace are the foundations of tomorrow laid

Oh, lost pilgrim forever on the roam
I call to you come back home (come back home)
Return to the land that you have never known
I call to you come back home (come back home)

The plantation is still real and your slavery transformed
To the image of Africa I call you to be conformed
Burst free from your shackles they exist only inside your mind
With the story and false glory of money you are blind

Oh, lost pilgrim forever on the roam
I call to you come back home (come back home)
Return to the land that you have never known
I call to you come back home (come back home)

Conquer And Divide

Don't let them tell you who is your enemy
Haven't you yet learned your true history
With a voodoo gospel full of misery
They preach evil sermons of agony

Conquer and divide conquer and divide
Behind their twisted lies they hide
Conquer and divide conquer and divide
For our future we must stay unified

You are my kin we share the very same heart
Don't let them deceive and tear us apart
You are my brother Africa our mother
Dismiss hatred let's love one another

Conquer and divide conquer and divide
Behind their twisted lies they hide
Conquer and divide conquer and divide
For our future we must stay unified

With empty words they make us promises grand
But all they desire is to steal our land
We are weak alone but together mighty
Do not raise the cruel sword do not fight me

See the traitors the puppet kings
Songs of treason the vulture sings
Don't be fooled or even schooled
Emancipated let us not be ruled

Conquer and divide conquer and divide
Behind their twisted lies they hide
Conquer and divide conquer and divide
For our future we must stay unified

The sun is rising toward a righteous dawn
Our yokes of slavery soon to be gone
Side by side we will work for the good of all
Hear mother Africa answer the call

Conquer and divide conquer and divide
Behind their twisted lies they hide
Conquer and divide conquer and divide
For our future we must stay unified

Get Up And Live

Wake up get up the sun is rising in the eastern skies
Time you understand the message and open up your eyes
They've muddied the rivers and they polluted the skies
In the caverns of your mind so they planted their lies

Get up and live you only get one chance
Get up and live ask your sweetheart to dance
Get up and live life is a gift of grace
Get up and live make the world a better place

We are on a journey we're the people of one nation
In service to your brethren is the glory of salvation
So you were born in poverty and baptized in sorrow
That was yesterday my friend you still got tomorrow

Get up and live you only get one chance
Get up and live ask your sweetheart to dance
Get up and live life is a gift of grace
Get up and live make the world a better place

Some men they were born to sing the blues
And some men they walk the Earth with no shoes
And some men live in palaces grand
But all men are equal do you understand?
For God He is the creator of us all
And in His sight there is no great or small

The philosophy of equality is not a radical notion
Hand in hand sharing all we set the future in motion
You are a stone in God's temple a wonderful thing
You have reasons to rejoice you have reasons to sing

Get up and live you only get one chance
Get up and live ask your sweetheart to dance
Get up and live life is a gift of grace
Get up and live make the world a better place

Won't you walk with me as I go down the narrow and straight?
I promise you love I have forsaken the ways of hate
Look in the mirror my friend tell me what do you see
I see the secret in your eyes I see humanity

Get up and live you only get one chance/ Get up and live ask your sweetheart to dance
Get up and live life is a gift of grace / Get up and live make the world a better place

Lament For Libya

We can decide our destiny
We must fight until we are free
Don't speak your lies of deviltry
We understand our history

Libya jewel of the Mediterranean Sea
NATO the cruel sin of hypocrisy
Gaddafi a prophetic visionary
See the flames burning in agony

When we rise to emancipate
So gather the hawks of hate
Freedom or death is the choice
On to the grave I do rejoice

Libya jewel of the Mediterranean Sea
NATO the cruel sin of hypocrisy
Gaddafi a prophetic visionary
See the flames burning in agony

Libya a chapter in the book of pain
Written by bankers sadistically insane
Between man and gold, they decide
They take all and deliver genocide

Drops of rain fall from the sky
Rivers are raging swelling high
There are forces you can't deny
That is what we are you and I

Libya jewel of the Mediterranean Sea
NATO the cruel sin of hypocrisy
Gaddafi a prophetic visionary
See the flames burning in agony

Hear the ancients they speak no lie
Speak in whispers give a cry
Our words will echo around the Earth
From the ashes comes the new birth

Libya jewel of the Mediterranean Sea
NATO the cruel sin of hypocrisy
Gaddafi a prophetic visionary
See the flames burning in agony

Life Is What You Do

You can't slay the dragon with words polite
If you try you'll be a dinner delight
The crops don't grow from a good thought
There's war raging and a battle that must be fought

The word became flesh to show us the way
Life is what you do not what you say
For the cause of freedom there's a price to pay
Life is what you do so seize the day

Philosophy is something inside the mind
Fancy words razzle dazzle leaves you blind
Hope and prayer is never enough
We must walk the road as one no matter how tough

The word became flesh to show us the way
Life is what you do not what you say
For the cause of freedom there's a price to pay
Life is what you do so seize the day

If your neighbor's hungry give them some food
We all work united for the common good
Action is the key to it all
Climb the stairway to heaven don't be afraid to fall

In Africa the spirit's burning in a mighty blaze
We are headed for a golden age of better days
Talk the talk but walk the walk as well
We'll get heaven when we give them hell

The word became flesh to show us the way
Life is what you do not what you say
For the cause of freedom there's a price to pay
Life is what you do so seize the day

The future's open it depends on you
on all that you try on all that you do
We only have our chains to shed
Fight for our children the innocent must be led

The word became flesh to show us the way
Life is what you do not what you say
For the cause of freedom there's a price to pay
Life is what you do so seize the day

Sanitize

Wash your hands and cleanse your mind
Hatred and war are leaving us all behind
Embrace the fire let truth purify the soul
We are revolting against colonial control

Sanitize sanitize forsake the lies
Sanitize sanitize accept no alibies
Sanitize sanitize or creation dies
Sanitize sanitize tomorrow belongs to the one who tries

Trust in the ancient's old way
Are you radical willing to win the day?
Slavery's yoke chokes Africa's tender throat
The truth shall set you free that is far more than a quote

Sanitize sanitize forsake the lies
Sanitize sanitize accept no alibies
Sanitize sanitize or creation dies
Sanitize sanitize tomorrow belongs to the one who tries

COVID's the sign of the day
Death demands wicked wages we cannot pay
Look beyond the television see the real sin
United as family is the way we can win

Sanitize sanitize forsake the lies
Sanitize sanitize accept no alibies
Sanitize sanitize or creation dies
Sanitize sanitize tomorrow belongs to the one who tries

Headlines scream but her the whispering voice
To follow the dream one must make a choice
Resist the call to war think of those who are poor
There is a grand future we just need to open the door

I will die if so I must
If I fight today then tomorrow I can trust
I sing a song to inspire those who are lost
The time is for action we must stop counting the cost

Sanitize sanitize forsake the lies
Sanitize sanitize accept no alibies
Sanitize sanitize or creation dies
Sanitize sanitize tomorrow belongs to the one who tries

Silent Cries

The story of King Leopold is being retold
They barter innocent souls for the price of gold
And don't you know it's the same as yesterday
The powers that be simply look away

Can you hear out silent cries (silent cries)?
Congo the heart of Africa slowly dies
They say they care they speak many lies
Oh, why don't you answer our silent cries?

As long as they get their money let the people be damned
They're raping the women while stealing the land
For the wealth in the ground the armies are here
Forces of terror they deal the devil's fear

Can you hear out silent cries (silent cries)?
Congo the heart of Africa slowly dies
They say they care they speak many lies
Oh, why don't you answer our silent cries?

From the history of man the lessons are learned
As a human being you should be concerned
When your brother perishes in genocide
For the love of God you must choose a side

What would you do if it happened to you?
Tomorrow the nightmare could come true
The holocaust it never comes to an end
Until we embrace all humanity as friend

Can you hear out silent cries (silent cries)?
Congo the heart of Africa slowly dies
They say they care they speak many lies
Oh, why don't you answer our silent cries?

The river flows red from the blood of the slain
Greed is the evil deed that drives man insane
We must stop the tide peace can't be denied
In Congo once more the pure are crucified

Can you hear out silent cries (silent cries)?
Congo the heart of Africa slowly dies
They say they care they speak many lies
Oh why don't you answer our silent cries?

Song Of Praise

Listen hear birds sing sweetly a song of praise
Chirping a vision of better days
The melody is hope the words true
It's a song for me it's a song for you

Won't you come along and help sing our song?
One voice is weak many are strong
It is a song of victory to right every wrong
Won't you come along and help sing our song?

Our father in heaven watches with a smile
In His eyes our fight is worthwhile
A reward awaits after the trial
Face the terror and forsake denial

Won't you come along and help sing our song?
One voice is weak many are strong
It is a song of victory to right every wrong
Won't you come along and help sing our song?

Preacher man says don't you understand
Preacher man came and stole the land
Hypocrisy turning love to hate
See the evil the preacher man creates

But God is Love and his Way will come to pass
Dark skin doesn't make us second class
The fight for freedom in paramount
I ask you brother on you can we count?

Won't you come along and help sing our song?
One voice is weak many are strong
It is a song of victory to right every wrong
Won't you come along and help sing our song?

Listen family Africa will be free
For we shall rise it's our destiny
And God himself shall lend us a hand
Trust in Him you know He does understand

Won't you come along and help sing our song?
One voice is weak many are strong
It is a song of victory to right every wrong
Won't you come along and help sing our song?

We Are A People Proud

We are empty in the land of plenty there's no food on the plate
In the name of the God of love they delivered a world of hate
Promising friendship and freedom for all they made us slaves
Early to toil to earn the master's spoil we descend to early graves

We are not a colony we are a people proud
We demand our freedom clear and loud
A few greedy men are always a crowd
We are not a colony we are a people proud

The furnace has raged for long centuries do you embrace the flame?
My skin is like the midnight sky on high and I feel no shame
Africa's the place I embrace mother of civilization
Listen to the score once more I am sure we'll rise to a great nation

We are not a colony we are a people proud
We demand our freedom clear and loud
A few greedy men are always a crowd
We are not a colony we are a people proud

We were living in mighty tall towers while Europe was in caves
In the illusion of cruel confusion you made us slaves
Well seasons change my friend and it's time for terror to end
God has a purpose and God has a way there's no chance to defend

For Arica I fight I pledge my life and all
Freedom is my delight I answer the call
For Africa I sing a blessing forever more
We are a people proud of that I am sure

We are not a colony we are a people proud
We demand our freedom clear and loud
A few greedy men are always a crowd
We are not a colony we are a people proud

Let's celebrate in unity of the family of our home
To you who have wandered so far away I say cease to roam
Side by side hand in hand let us join our minds to the day
See in the east the rosy rays of dawn God's answer to what we pray

We are not a colony we are a people proud
We demand our freedom clear and loud
A few greedy men are always a crowd
We are not a colony we are a people proud

A Road Made For Two

Straight and narrow hate can wait
Fools in folly in endless debate
I will carry the cross of peace
These wicked wars may they cease

This is a road made for two
Baby that means me and you
I dream about the thing we'll do
This is a road made for two

I surrender to God's call
A humble man he will never fall
On the ground we walk heaven bound
Sweet songs so sweet is our sound

This is a road made for two
Baby that means me and you
I dream about the thing we'll do
This is a road made for two

Blue eyes blues skies all is well
Eden is bleeding you've created hell
A walk of faith trusting in grace
Love can save the human race

This is a road made for two
Baby that means me and you
I dream about the thing we'll do
This is a road made for two

Sunbeams daydreams life ain't what it seems
Harsh lessons whisper the failure screams
There is forgiveness when you change your way
After the night always comes the day

Secretes in the silent kiss
Mysteries of the apocalypse
Twilight's delight no shades of gray
Repent knees bent so you pray

This is a road made for two
Baby that means me and you
I dream about the thing we'll do
This is a road made for two

Bubbles Blowing By

His sin is gin and he's dealing again
King of clubs will kill if he doesn't win
Birth of a nation power equals salvation
Greed in blinding speed what's our destination?

Heaven is always high
Hardest question is 'Why?'
I'm willing to give one more try
See the bubbles blowing by

Lazarus is laughing inside his grave
Smile walk in single file better behave
I climbed the temple walls goodbye reservation
They're still picking cotton on the plantation

Heaven is always high
Hardest question is 'Why?'
I'm willing to give one more try
See the bubbles blowing by

And the madness is a cosmic merry-go-round
If you never were lost how can you be found?
Evangelicals tell grandiose stories of hell
Sell all you have give to the poor why not pray tell?

If love comes by never let her hand go
More than actors are putting on a show
The government shut down my latest Facebook post
God is in three persons welcome Holy Ghost

Heaven is always high
Hardest question is 'Why?'
I'm willing to give one more try
See the bubbles blowing by

Flying kites satellites weather balloons
Court jesters sing to kings their merry tunes
The knight got in a fight with the flashy drag queen
You may be old but you were once seventeen

Heaven is always high
Hardest question is 'Why?'
I'm willing to give one more try
See the bubbles blowing by

Clouds High In The Sky

Lola she was a lady and that's all you need to know
I did it cause they pay me she says after the show
Pride is like the tide it'll come and it'll go
The love of friends never ends see the river flow

Dreams are hard but dreams never die
In heaven blue clouds high in the sky
We can love if we really try
How I love you clouds high in the sky

In an oasis of social graces he took a drink
Every now and then comes a moment when you can think
Lola was on stage lovely in feminine rage
In the light her body tight her face showed her age

Dreams are hard but dreams never die
In heaven blue clouds high in the sky
We can love if we really try
How I love you clouds high in the sky

Doctors lawyers and engineers
Big money comes with massive fears
That's the trick of choosing careers
Nothing is really as it appears

Oh where can we run now they're burning down the Amazon
Soon maybe at noon all Mother Nature will be gone
Let's make love he said and tomorrow come what may
Lola chuckled they call it love when they can't pay

Dreams are hard but dreams never die
In heaven blue clouds high in the sky
We can love if we really try
How I love you clouds high in the sky

Lola stared into the night twas close enough to pretend
In the game there's more of the same around the next bend
Silently she slipped into the night with no shoes
Why the clouds high in the sky hang out with the blues

Dreams are hard but dreams never die
In heaven blue clouds high in the sky
We can love if we really try
How I love you clouds high in the sky

Love Is The Way

Jesus touches the leper making him clean
Day after day I repeat the scene
I try to fail but one day I'll prevail
Cause Jesus is the author grace is the tale

Night to day years pass by
Love is the way love is why
I say we all gonna die
Love is the way love is why

The Earth spins but tell me where are we going?
For all our labor nothing showing
Towers of Babel with the golden bull
I'm searching for a soul who isn't cruel

Night to day years pass by
Love is the way love is why
I say we all gonna die
Love is the way love is why

We're marching to Zion won't you come along?
Embracing all that's right forsaking wrong
If you're empty we've got plenty to share
Ain't it good to know that some people care

Night to day years pass by
Love is the way love is why
I say we all gonna die
Love is the way love is why

Songs to redeem the gospel of the good news
We all stumble when paying our dues
Your clay being formed in the Potter's hand
The way of the cross something to understand

Night to day years pass by
Love is the way love is why
I say we all gonna die
Love is the way love is why

No Greater Love

Castles of stone stand alone in my mind
Before I was grown I should have known what to find
I was searching high and low though I was blind
My greatest treasure was the pleasure of one who treated me kind

No greater love than to give it all
No greater love than to answer the call
On the cross I felt the loss of the fall
No greater love than to give it all

On the edge of a dream nothing seemed real
I sold all gave it to the poor such was the deal
Before love the vain pain was all I could feel
Tears of joy can destroy but boy meet girl has nothing to conceal

No greater love than to give it all
No greater love than to answer the call
On the cross I felt the loss of the fall
No greater love than to give it all

I searched for a poet looking about
Cruel chains remains lingering in the lusts of doubt
The key to set me free was made of pure gold
They insisted I resisted I stopped doing all I was told

No greater love than to give it all
No greater love than to answer the call
On the cross I felt the loss of the fall
No greater love than to give it all

In Genesis I heard God bless procreation
Love is the pathway leading to salvation
Adam and Eve both believe in sacred rhyme
Eating the apple wasn't the only crime

At the end of the road the journey ends
We were more than lovers the very best of friends
Go on be brave love saves my darling young bride
I'll cry at goodbye promise you'll meet me on the other side

No greater love than to give it all
No greater love than to answer the call
On the cross I felt the loss of the fall
No greater love than to give it all

Secrets

In the magic of love there I met you
We swore a sacred oath forever true
Now the river of time rushes you on
You're leaving me but you won't be gone

Secrets they hold power
Secrets see them seize the hour
Secrets bite and devour
Secrets an eternal shower

All the right words rhyme hear the church bells chime
I'm stepping out through the murky depths of time
An elusive dreams visits as I sleep
Oh what in life can we truly keep

Secrets they hold power
Secrets see them seize the hour
Secrets bite and devour
Secrets an eternal shower

Sing the melody of endless eternity
Embrace your friends in devout certainty
The king is calling you must answer the call
There is a Truth and that Truth is all

Penniless paupers extend their tin cups
Power that's absolute fully corrupts
They cling to money in elaborate graves
While the wiseman laughs cause Jesus saves

Secrets they hold power
Secrets see them seize the hour
Secrets bite and devour
Secrets an eternal shower

Story Of Glory

Have you heard the Word of Love supreme?
That heaven is more than a dream
There's a story of glory just for you
A story of glory every word true

Jesus died for sinners that's me
He broke the chains set us free
I owe it all to the grace of Calvary
Jesus died for sinners that's me

The good book take a look at mercy
A ticket to eternity
There's a story of glory just for you
A story of glory every word true

Jesus died for sinners that's me
He broke the chains set us free
I owe it all to the grace of Calvary
Jesus died for sinners that's me

A poor man who brought riches untold
I'll take Jesus you keep your gold
He's the Lamb of God and the Prince of Peace
His kingdom and power always increase

Jesus died for sinners that's me
He broke the chains set us free
I owe it all to the grace of Calvary
Jesus died for sinners that's me

Tell it to the children tell it to the old
See the faithful walking streets of gold
The Tree of Life with leaves to heal
A story of glory every word real

Jesus died for sinners that's me
He broke the chains set us free
I owe it all to the grace of Calvary
Jesus died for sinners that's me

The Mark Of God's Hand

The chill of the night dark and deep
But the saints of God do not sleep
Busy hands blessing their toil
Salt of the Earth never to spoil

The love in a smile
The joy of the trial
The light of our land
See the mark of God's hand

Forgiving each and every wrong
In persecution happy song
Gentle turning the other cheek
Knowing truth blessed are the meek

The love in a smile
The joy of the trial
The light of our land
See the mark of God's hand

Walking the path narrow straight
Embracing love forsaking hate
Rejecting all worldly pleasures
In heaven there lies our treasures

The love in a smile
The joy of the trial
The light of our land
See the mark of God's hand

Tomorrow is our grand reward
Victory in the cross not sword
Jesus the only name to save
Jesus who arose from the grave

The love in a smile
The joy of the trial
The light of our land
See the mark of God's hand

Through The Years

A Brooklyn baby maybe a little blessed
Hazy days wild and crazy always second guessed
Cheap gods hanging out saying dismiss all doubt
Took a while of hard trial to find what life's about

Smiles and tears through the years
Hope and fears through the years
Now as my journey's end nears
Nothing is really as it appears
Where has time gone through the years

Eighteen I saw in the mirror a real man
Stumbling and bumbling followed a fool's mumbling plan
The fire of my desire was to make love mine
Chasing the dragon there was poison in the wine

Smiles and tears through the years
Hope and fears through the years
Now as my journey's end nears
Nothing is really as it appears
Where has time gone through the years

The institute was nothing but a racket
I found freedom my reward a straightjacket
They slipped Thorazine in my juice for control
Crucified my mind but liberated my soul

Smiles and tears through the years
Hope and fears through the years
Now as my journey's end nears
Nothing is really as it appears
Where has time gone through the years

And the road is really a circle in disguise
Theories of men written in pen but lies
Love is the supreme dream we must achieve
There's power in the hour that you first believe

When I hit the road the cross my only load
Bombs are designed to kill that's why they all explode
Salute the flag boast and brag not on my time
See the light you'll know its right when all the words rhyme

Smiles and tears through the years
Hope and fears through the years
Now as my journey's end nears
Nothing is really as it appears
Where has time gone through the years

Tomorrow Never Came

Aces high deal from the deck of many things
Grace is why the real saint prays and sings
A king a queen something never seen
Heaven and hell with nothing in between

The day tomorrow never came
Tell your glory reveal your shame
We only got self to blame
The day tomorrow never came

On a cosmic high always asking why
Soldiers fighting see them kill and die
The spy is only loyal to greed
Billion dollar bomber babies in need

The day tomorrow never came
Tell your glory reveal your shame
We only got self to blame
The day tomorrow never came

One day the clock will finally unwind
Truth I say will rock even the blind
Deaf man do you hear nature's hand turn?
Fools are fools because they never do learn

The day tomorrow never came
Tell your glory reveal your shame
We only got self to blame
The day tomorrow never came

Trust the man just so he can steal
Lie like he can trust in the deal
Glory see that fate is always just
In retribution the honest will trust

Rapture is the cure of never more
Now tell the hell you were fighting for
Imagine no sin and we all win
In hellfire you won't see the devil grin

The day tomorrow never came
Tell your glory reveal your shame
We only got self to blame
The day tomorrow never came

When The World Is New

Walking hand in hand girl and boy
Life so new singing songs of joy
Love is a treasure none can steal
And love the essence of all that's real

When the world is new
And Love is true
There I'll meet you
When the world is new

Hey babe look at this photograph
Miles of smiles they're making me laugh
Yesterday a mystery lost
Sweet innocence the coin that we tossed

When the world is new
And Love is true
There I'll meet you
When the world is new

A place of grace where dreams were real
Playing games pure pleasure our deal
Book of life many lessons to learn
Rule number one you cannot return

When the world is new
And Love is true
There I'll meet you
When the world is new

The melody is wild and free but all is strange
I quote note for note but the lyrics change
You'll find out when you're older goes the command
Now that the years are here I still don't understand

Heaven were the days of my youth
Love's lesson the ultimate truth
I cling to the child in my heart
When the world is new living an art

When the world is new
And Love is true
There I'll meet you
When the world is new

With The End In Sight

There's something about Jesus don't you know
He's got power and glory sitting front row
Lord of Lords and the King of Kings
He humbles the proud as the pauper sings

I'm living trying to do right
I'm giving with the end in sight
Heaven forever is worth the fight
I'm living with the end in sight

Seven shades of blue tell me secrets true
Crying on the cross forgive what they do
Man of greed has his wicked deed
Only the gospel message shall succeed

I'm living trying to do right
I'm giving with the end in sight
Heaven forever is worth the fight
I'm living with the end in sight

The river is wide and the bridge so frail
Put your faith alone in the sacred tale
Spirits abound unseen unknown
In the way of the cross so we have grown

I'm living trying to do right
I'm giving with the end in sight
Heaven forever is worth the fight
I'm living with the end in sight

Winter's chill whips a freezing breeze
You have kept the faith be at ease
Close your eyes Sister Sylvia seek your peace
One day this wicked world will know release

Welcome me when I enter on high
In a land where joy could never die
I'm living with the end in sight
I see the Son rise so ends the night

I'm living trying to do right
I'm giving with the end in sight
Heaven forever is worth the fight
I'm living with the end in sight

Chlorophyl So Wonderful

It's green not money green but still green
Mother Nature she's the best babe I've seen
Say Betty Boozy on top of my face
What is the future of the human race?

Chlorophyl so wonderful a little pill
Chlorophyl so wonderful gives me a thrill
Synthetic dinosaur from ages long before
Chlorophyl so wonderful the universal cure

Trees swaying in the breeze full of leaves
Truth is the lies the ignorant believes
Plant a seed fight the greed and let it grow
Have hope for tomorrow you never know

Chlorophyl so wonderful a little pill
Chlorophyl so wonderful gives me a thrill
Synthetic dinosaur from ages long before
Chlorophyl so wonderful the universal cure

In the forest Frankie sings our song
Musical Mormons fighting all wrong?
Shooting an arrow on a moonless night
Wrong is wrong and sweet love is always right

Chlorophyl so wonderful a little pill
Chlorophyl so wonderful gives me a thrill
Synthetic dinosaur from ages long before
Chlorophyl so wonderful the universal cure

Extract black let the chemicals react
Your backs to the wall give a call out to Jack
I'm happy so happy yes I'm happy as can be
Slaughter the daughter of the chief Apache
Christ was crucified they hung him on a tree

Homegrown yeah baby open the door
I liked things better how they were before
But you delivered your notice to quit
And say brother that was the end of it

Chlorophyl so wonderful a little pill
Chlorophyl so wonderful gives me a thrill
Synthetic dinosaur from ages long before /Chlorophyl so wonderful the universal cure

Here Comes The Eviction

Donnie got some nerve he got papers to serve
The straight and narrow took a conservative curve
He's the owner driving the green mean machine
I wouldn't mind if he kept the place clean

Here comes the eviction the venal sin
Here comes the eviction the devils win
Here comes the eviction at least it's warm
Here comes the eviction I'll never conform

The love of money well the roots run deep
Say sweet honey hot hell what loot can we keep?
Here comes the hearse all life ends in final curse
For God so loved the world my favorite verse

Here comes the eviction the venal sin
Here comes the eviction the devils win
Here comes the eviction at least it's warm
Here comes the eviction I'll never conform

Money in the bank money in the bank money and more
Money in the bank money in the bank he's a money whore
Money in the bank money in the bank what will you buy?
Money in the bank money in the bank one day we all die

I heard many words saying birds fly for free
The penguins and ostriches love anarchy
His eye is on the sparrow please pay the rent
A ten million dollar bonus heaven sent

Here comes the eviction the venal sin
Here comes the eviction the devils win
Here comes the eviction at least it's warm
Here comes the eviction I'll never conform

Fantasy and dreams I only want a home
Reality seems I'm about to go roam
I've been hard in training for fifty-four years
Goodbye Sylvan Place no more laughter or tears

Here comes the eviction the venal sin
Here comes the eviction the devils win
Here comes the eviction at least it's warm
Here comes the eviction I'll never conform

It's A Synthetic Miracle

Your voice looks good in my twilight eyes
Devils and demons digitalize
I'll lose the battle to win the war
In an hour falls Babylon the whore

It's a synthetic miracle for real for real
It's a synthetic miracle don't you know the deal?
Dismal death steals the breath in this ordeal
It's a synthetic miracle nothing is for real

Fantastic plastic in the ocean
Poetry puts the love in motion
If I had a rhyme I'd fly away
Guilty of crime from day after day

It's a synthetic miracle for real for real
It's a synthetic miracle don't you know the deal?
Dismal death steals the breath in this ordeal
It's a synthetic miracle nothing is for real

Sinister Sam he cursed the great I Am
He heard the word was only a scam
The diet ends when you lose all your friends
The sweetest lover always pretends

It's a synthetic miracle for real for real
It's a synthetic miracle don't you know the deal?
Dismal death steals the breath in this ordeal
It's a synthetic miracle nothing is for real

The linoleum on the floor is secure
God and oil the impetus for endless war
Hocus pocus focus on the lovely assistant
They'll rob your job if you are not resistant

Chemicals you take that tranquilize
Gospel of greed only feeds more lies
Sylvia dementia took your mind
Come tomorrow the blind kills the blind

It's a synthetic miracle for real for real
It's a synthetic miracle don't you know the deal?
Dismal death steals the breath in this ordeal
It's a synthetic miracle nothing is for real

Putting It On Paper

As long as the sun shines and the grass grows
Abbot and Costello coming to blows
Who's on first what's worst has been broken
Here's your reservation our kind token

Putting it on paper we lie anyway
Putting it on paper night becomes day
Putting it on paper the American way
Putting it on paper we'll make you pay

Tonto was pronto at the gala ball
They said your red wait outside in the hall
A billion buffalo in shallow graves
The neon sign flashes Jesus saves

Putting it on paper we lie anyway
Putting it on paper night becomes day
Putting it on paper the American way
Putting it on paper we'll make you pay

It's green mean and yes truly obscene
Here comes the cavalry on the move screen
Gatling gun have some fun more dead Indjun
We're the best and that's how the west was won

Putting it on paper we lie anyway
Putting it on paper night becomes day
Putting it on paper the American way
Putting it on paper we'll make you pay

An anonymous drunk signs an X
We need something showing respect
Legal and binding sign on the line
Yours is mine and that's just fine

Alcatraz then shuffle to Wounded Knee
Fourth class citizen in this land so free
Names of pain remain soon to be forgot
There's a cold war now but it's getting hot

Putting it on paper we lie anyway
Putting it on paper night becomes day
Putting it on paper the American way
Putting it on paper we'll make you pay

Quoting Me

Give me liberty but put it in an injection
Live free the corrupt we won't even mention
Silicon chips slip as she slowly sways her hips
Cosmic Charlie spoke at the rally with Captain Trips

Quoting me so shall it be
Quoting me words are free?
Quoting me where the sky meets the sea
Quoting me a new reality

Jeff Hoey says this here is a Peace Action event
We all love Jesus but refuse to repent
Rude and crude the dude is supporting endless war
You can quote me on this when I say to you no more

Quoting me so shall it be
Quoting me words are free?
Quoting me where the sky meets the sea
Quoting me a new reality

It's a matter of technology say Eric real sly
I say what really matters is how many die
Hear the guided missile sing the song of evil
Sadly women and children are caught in the middle

Quoting me so shall it be
Quoting me words are free?
Quoting me where the sky meets the sea
Quoting me a new reality

The Montclair Local ran a front-page story
I made more money so honey please hear me
I said wait let's hesitate and avoid the hate
Explosions and gun fire cancelled the debate

We're having a cookout Bennet is to be the host
He's got good manners but he's no Holy Ghost
John three sixteen and then there's Acts two thirty-eight
All the well-fed sleep in their bed and the times too late

Quoting me so shall it be
Quoting me words are free?
Quoting me where the sky meets the sea
Quoting me a new reality

A Hand To Hold

Sylvia sits waiting in her chair
And God is still despite prayer
Yesterday gone tomorrow unsure
Somehow I thought there'd be more

I've got a hand to hold
Fire burns in the cold
A story to be told
I've got a hand to hold

Old and gray the hours wasting away
Crosses are cruel so they say
But I step out of the flow of time
To jot down this humble rhyme

I've got a hand to hold
Fire burns in the cold
A story to be told
I've got a hand to hold

Sometimes Sylvia remembers me
Mostly I'm a mystery
We're lost in space where are all the stars?
In a band playing guitars

I've got a hand to hold
Fire burns in the cold
A story to be told
I've got a hand to hold

In a world of greed we need to comprehend
That love is the only thing that has no end
Sylvia's hand in mine she holds on tight
Love, friend, companion my sweetest delight

A sad face stings deep inside my heart
Our vows to death do us part
True love it either dies or grows
So the river gently flows

I've got a hand to hold
Fire burns in the cold
A story to be told
I've got a hand to hold

A Poem

I got caught in a frost forever lost
Carousing with cats counting the cost
In Harlem I sung the blues in fading hues
David the shepherd recorded good news

I read a poem it was you
Every word rhymed true
I read a poem the sky was blue
I read a poem it was you

Shakespeare kissed on the lips without fear
I looked into heaven the stars were clear
The man in the moon sung his merry tune
We met in December and married in June

I read a poem it was you
Every word rhymed true
I read a poem the sky was blue
I read a poem it was you

Words of truth engraved on the asylum wall
Do you have the courage to answer love's call?
Preachers and teachers sublimely obtuse
A nation in frustration cries what's the use

I read a poem it was you
Every word rhymed true
I read a poem the sky was blue
I read a poem it was you

A black suit an orange tie a desire to kill
Very little money in trying to do God's will
That's why you're the only one for me
That's why you're a book of poetry

I read a poem it was you
Every word rhymed true
I read a poem the sky was blue
I read a poem it was you

A Rockabilly Hillbilly

The police were chasing the bee afraid of the sting
Boys go hand in your guns this is my own thing
I am the anointed I am the high king
He broke his heart falling off of the chart unable to sing

He's a rockabilly hillbilly from London
A rash of the Clash the city burning down
He's a rockabilly hillbilly looking for a clue
He's a rockabilly hillbilly maybe's he's you

Johnny Ace needed a bass cause Stagger Lee left town
Something was wrong he was wearing a frown
As it goes the egos couldn't fit in the room
In the corner of God's eye real sly Jimi jammed on a broom

He's a rockabilly hillbilly from London
A rash of the Clash the city burning down
He's a rockabilly hillbilly looking for a clue
He's a rockabilly hillbilly maybe's he's you

Wes came from Alabama banjo on his knee
This great land's free but only if you agree
An English man in New York God would be proud
Jesus was hip and took a trip to slip away from the crowd

He's a rockabilly hillbilly from London
A rash of the Clash the city burning down
He's a rockabilly hillbilly looking for a clue
He's a rockabilly hillbilly maybe's he's you

Here comes the B but an A or a C would be fine
I may be gay but I have a reality to call mine
Assata Shakur declared war on the racist pigs
On the corner of Fifth Avenue we got open gigs

So here I am thinking out loud inside of a song
When evil happens to you it's always wrong
Karma's a bitch when you're a comic book witch
When you shower in San Quinton pray hard you don't get an itch

He's a rockabilly hillbilly from London
A rash of the Clash the city burning down
He's a rockabilly hillbilly looking for a clue
He's a rockabilly hillbilly maybe's he's you

Baby Ken

Hey Baby Ken I wrote you a special song
You're a tiny baby who can do no wrong
One day soon you will grow into a man strong
Wondering just where in the world you belong

You measure faith in years
You measure hope in tears
Oh baby Ken the future nears
Let love conquer all your fears
Oh baby Ken the future nears

Sorry this world we gave you is such a mess
Let me wish you some good luck and may God bless
We tried our best but sometimes our best won't do
When the night is dark remember Jesus loves you

You measure faith in years
You measure hope in tears
Oh baby Ken the future nears
Let love conquer all your fears
Oh baby Ken the future nears

Good times bad times you'll be singing lonesome blues
Seems in chasing your dreams you'll be paying your dues
Never quit don't give up you just get one chance
When the music moves you take the time to dance

You measure faith in years
You measure hope in tears
Oh baby Ken the future nears
Let love conquer all your fears
Oh baby Ken the future nears

One day you'll be old maybe with a child or two
Keep the faith it's the very least you can do
Remember Jesus and his cruel crown of thorns
There was a special reason that you were born

You measure faith in years
You measure hope in tears
Oh baby Ken the future nears
Let love conquer all your fears
Oh baby Ken the future nears

Blessing

Looking for a seven for an inside straight
Hoping for heaven but I had too much hate
Marty the marine charged the machinegun nest
On the last day God said He's taking a rest

God country and that thing
Blessings oh I need a blessing
More gold to hold for the king
Hold everything where's my blessing?

Our Mother Earth treasures colored green and blue
There's nothing down here as wonderful as you
They raised old glory the flag was stained red
Sinners while living becoming saints once dead

God country and that thing
Blessings oh I need a blessing
More gold to hold for the king
Hold everything where's my blessing?

Marty can't forget the terrors of the war
No heat on the street he can't take any more
He'd trade tomorrow for some decent friends
Fighting a war in his head that never ends

God country and that thing
Blessings oh I need a blessing
More gold to hold for the king
Hold everything where's my blessing?

Scar on his face medals on his chest
Patriotism is the ultimate test
Thank you sir now get out of sight
God knows we all know it ain't right

The market went bull as Marty searched the trash
Ain't got a cigarette let alone hash
Turkey dinner be sure to pray for the poor
Careful in this world you'll get used like a whore

God country and that thing
Blessings oh I need a blessing
More gold to hold for the king
Hold everything where's my blessing?

Blizzards

Winter blues snow three feet deep
Missing you there's no more sweet sleep
I turn only the embrace the cold
Frightened by the fact I'm getting old

Blizzards blowing never knowing
My love is eternal as time
Blizzards blowing ever growing
My love in this eternal rhyme

Tomorrow it never comes
Rise and fall of endless kingdoms
I have the faith to pick up the pen
I have the faith you'll come around again

Blizzards blowing never knowing
My love is eternal as time
Blizzards blowing ever growing
My love in this eternal rhyme

Icicles life becomes death
Misty tears frozen on my breath
Searching the sky for a ray of hope
Searching my soul for a way to cope

Blizzards blowing never knowing
My love is eternal as time
Blizzards blowing ever growing
My love in this eternal rhyme

What were we to do young souls in an ancient place?
What were we to do full of love but void of grace?
Mountains of white destined to melt away
A kingdom of ice and snow vanquished by a sunny day

Winter witch laughs most cruel
I am sorry I played the fool
Lies are like snowflakes in the game
Two of them are never the same

Blizzards blowing never knowing
My love is eternal as time
Blizzards blowing ever growing
My love in this eternal rhyme

Champion Of The World

Golden gloves rusting ruby red glow
Bronx bombers bursting with words we know
King of the ring in da one man show
TKO motion flows sweetly slow

He's the champion of the world ladies and gents
A thriller killer who never repents
He's the champion of the world take a bow
Camera flash cash the moment is now
He's the champion of the world take a bow

All alone is all he's known in life
Mistress whore unsure about his wife
Muscles bulging gloves fit very tight
Hell is well headlines tell of the fight

He's the champion of the world ladies and gents
A thriller killer who never repents
He's the champion of the world take a bow
Camera flash cash the moment is now
He's the champion of the world take a bow

Crying misty tears behind the stage
Four blunt corners of cruel iron rage
Money comes money goes foe after foe
A mighty man with a mighty blow

He's the champion of the world ladies and gents
A thriller killer who never repents
He's the champion of the world take a bow
Camera flash cash the moment is now
He's the champion of the world take a bow

Never been to Vegas how about Atlantic City?
Rockettes on power jets kicking back pretty
I saw a plastic island Texas oil style
You see kings of things if you open your eyes

Bank books empty signing autographs
The jokes on me and nobody laughs
Lift the flame at the Olympic game
Napalm orange really ain't to blame

He's the champion of the world ladies and gents

A thriller killer who never repents
He's the champion of the world take a bow
Camera flash cash the moment is now
He's the champion of the world take a bow

Dreams For Sale

See in the front row the banker and his ho
With season passes they're at every show
If you meet 'em they really ain't bad to know
That's if you catch 'em before the blow

Don't you know they got dreams for sale?
Life is hard and you don't have to fail
They're singing life's wondrous tale
Don't you know they got dreams for sale?

Movie stars and electric guitars mix
Don't blink or think the climax it comes quick
She smiles wide it's a natural reaction
Good or bad she just loves some action

Don't you know they got dreams for sale?
Life is hard and you don't have to fail
They're singing life's wondrous tale
Don't you know they got dreams for sale?

Police look the other way money rules
And who would want to rock this ship of fools?
Things are grinding away and life marches on
Soon all signs of God will be long gone

Don't you know they got dreams for sale?
Life is hard and you don't have to fail
They're singing life's wondrous tale
Don't you know they got dreams for sale?

Skyrockets and pistols in his pockets
Watch out around live electrical sockets
The zeppelin is sinking into the soggy sand
Under a raging moon who will understand

Divorce is messy and force sometimes used
If there's fame she'll claim to be abused
Best of friends only ends with a farewell kiss
I love you but I can't take more of this

Don't you know they got dreams for sale?
Life is hard and you don't have to fail
They're singing life's wondrous tale
Don't you know they got dreams for sale?

Dungeons

Nothing left but these dreams full of holes
A million people with a billion goals
Spinning grinning winning and all sinning
Near the end but I'm just beginning

These dungeons halls are freezing cold
Searching up and down for some gold
I love you baby am I being too bold?
Dungeons after dungeons and I'm getting old

I've been searching for sweet treasures Green
Trying to go places I've never been
Peace on Earth is something we understand
Then why do I got a sword in my hand?

These dungeons halls are freezing cold
Searching up and down for some gold
I love you baby am I being too bold?
Dungeons after dungeons and I'm getting old

Song lyrics are like maps on the wall
Even the lonely hear loves precious call
The rouge robbed the party of everything
All that's left is this sad song to sing

The dungeons halls are freezing cold
Searching up and down for some gold
I love you baby am I being too bold?
Dungeons after dungeons and I'm getting old

The dragon breathes fire flies in clouds gray
Princesses are looking for heroes to win the day
But me I'm just a pauper looking to survive
Suckered by swindlers with sweet sounding jive

One of these days I'm calling it quits
Give up my fantasy of platinum hits
I'll write poetry to the chosen few
At least I'll be under skies true blue

The dungeons halls are freezing cold
Searching up and down for some gold
I love you baby am I being too bold?
Dungeons after dungeons and I'm getting old

Empty Coffins

Queen of the dream yesterday don't belong
Been in the scream crucifying my wrong
Sinful sharks like a dog barks in greed
In the Land Of Plenty so many in need

Did you love me when the song turned sad?
When life went all wrong and I burned mad
Empty coffins they wait for us all
Empty coffins they beckon and call

Endless war rages money men to blame
Burning cities refugees full of shame
Soldiers kiss their wives maybe goodbye
Don't you know brother we're fighting for a lie

Did you love me when the song turned sad?
When life went all wrong and I burned mad
Empty coffins they wait for us all
Empty coffins they beckon and call

I'm betrayed by friends cheated by strangers
A world of illusion I see dangers
Do your best then try to take a rest
Happiness is a never ending quest

Did you love me when the song turned sad?
When life went all wrong and I burned mad
Empty coffins they wait for us all
Empty coffins they beckon and call

You're standing at death's door ready to leave
There's something better I gotta believe
Where is true Love when you need God most?
Where is my true Love when she's only a ghost?

Did you love me when the song turned sad?
When life went all wrong and I burned mad
Empty coffins they wait for us all
Empty coffins they beckon and call

Endless Night

Our band was in the club playing the last song
We had the melody right but the chords wrong
She stood there counting money with a grin
Humming how I love the wages of sin

Religion is God's philosophy
Is love ever a reality?
I want to believe but something ain't right
I hope for day in this endless night

Down in the alley we loaded up the van
There sat a junkie next to a garbage can
A seductive smile simmered on her face
I asked does emptiness equal grace

Religion is God's philosophy
Is love ever a reality?
I want to believe but something ain't right
I hope for day in this endless night

Neon glow advertising the show tonight
You have as long as you live to get it right
Sipping whiskey while waiting at the bar
Somehow we forgot our bass guitar

Religion is God's philosophy
Is love ever a reality?
I want to believe but something ain't right
I hope for day in this endless night

The promoter and the manager were whispering back stage
I looked into the mirror my face was showing its age
I'd get off the merry go round but I'm addicted to the sound
I've been searching a life time and I don't know what I've found

Time melts as we laugh over when we used to fight
The sun never rises in this endless night
Dreams of better days haunt inside my mind
I'd trade it all for a woman kind

Religion is God's philosophy
Is love ever a reality?
I want to believe but something ain't right
I hope for day in this endless night

Fantasy

Sturdy dark wood sails unfurled
Before you lie the secrets of the world
Girl meets boy and boy meets girl
In the oyster the rare black pearl

Fantasy is free to a certain degree
I guess that would be you and me
Fantasy serves the god of anarchy
Fantasy conquers reality

Welcome to the ogre's cave
Use your napkin politely behave
Only Jesus can truly save
You'll need to know that in the grave

Fantasy is free to a certain degree
I guess that would be you and me
Fantasy serves the god of anarchy
Fantasy conquers reality

You drew your trusty magic sword
Golden doubloons your reward
Wipe the blood off of your blade
Say you won the treasure in fair trade

Fantasy is free to a certain degree
I guess that would be you and me
Fantasy serves the god of anarchy
Fantasy conquers reality

You're the hero and so ends the game
Story of glory you've earned your fame
In the twist of the mist it's all the same
A new age a new rage what's your name?

Fantasy is free to a certain degree
I guess that would be you and me
Fantasy serves the god of anarchy
Fantasy conquers reality

Fighting Fire

Ain't nobody likes to lose that's for sure
Unless they're singing the blues with some whore
Crushed by the weight of some big thighed brunette
Live life so when you die you ain't got a regret

I ain't gonna fight fire with fire I'll fight fire with water
It was pure heaven making love to the devil's daughter
They're lining up the armies for sensational slaughter
I ain't gonna fight fire with fire I'll fight fire with water

I was singing the blues in east Memphis
I asked George where I could find more of this?
He said roll the dice and hope for the best
When your crazy righteousness is an eternal quest

I ain't gonna fight fire with fire I'll fight fire with water
It was pure heaven making love to the devil's daughter
They're lining up the armies for sensational slaughter
I ain't gonna fight fire with fire I'll fight fire with water

They cut down almost all of the Amazon
Now the future and the past both are gone
Chemtrails are darkening the blue-sky gray
You have the winning hand but we're all gonna pay

I ain't gonna fight fire with fire I'll fight fire with water
It was pure heaven making love to the devil's daughter
They're lining up the armies for sensational slaughter
I ain't gonna fight fire with fire I'll fight fire with water

I build on the past my pain becomes a spark
The fire burns and look I'm out of the dark
Caught in the superego unable to let go
I'll catch you sweetheart after the show

I wanted to write a song with no cliché
It hurts right now but soon I'll be okay
Fighting fire well sir that's a noble cause
Breaking all the rule trying to obey the laws

I ain't gonna fight fire with fire I'll fight fire with water
It was pure heaven making love to the devil's daughter
They're lining up the armies for sensational slaughter
I ain't gonna fight fire with fire I'll fight fire with water

God Knows

We all want happy lives and our dreams to come true
We want beautiful wives wonderful children too
God knows there's something wrong on Earth
They were trying to kill Jesus right after his birth

They wanna tell me I'm wrong
They wanna tell me I don't belong
That the world was made for the strong
But God knows I'll sing my song

Love's a mystery but you can't deny the cross
Reality's take and take never wanting loss
Slow down pilgrim think at least twice
Who are these new found friends giving you this advice?

They wanna tell me I'm wrong
They wanna tell me I don't belong
That the world was made for the strong
But God knows I'll sing my song

I walked the walk speaking things that were hard
Talked the talk silver bracelets were my reward
On a fifty-one fifty fuzzy static inside my mind
I'm a child of the sixties God they left me behind

In Palestine they're killing in God's holy name
Where is love why do we tolerate such sick shame?
Love your enemy turn the cheek
Words become weapons see our politicians speak

They wanna tell me I'm wrong
They wanna tell me I don't belong
That the world was made for the strong
But God knows I'll sing my song

This song's over before it even had a start
Can you see in my soul read the chart of my heart?
Honesty's a lesson to learn
The fire of desire rages higher and it will burn

They wanna tell me I'm wrong
They wanna tell me I don't belong
That the world was made for the strong
But God knows I'll sing my song

Graystone Hustle

Slow day gray in every way
Love always has a price to pay
When dreams and life begin to clash
You know the master thief insists on cash

Hustling in Graystone
Hustling all alone
Blue in dorm sixty-two
Hustling in Graystone

You stole my heart without concern
Youth means you have lessons to learn
Storms arose who knows where you went
At one time the devil was heaven sent

Hustling in Graystone
Hustling all alone
Blue in dorm sixty-two
Hustling in Graystone

I won't bother to mention your name
I ain't one to point fingers of blame
Still I'm sure you'll feel the shame
Only because I'm riding high in the game

Brother you'd better watch your back
It don't matter you hang with Jack
Take the pills gotta play the part
Cure the mind while they kill the heart

Hustling in Graystone
Hustling all alone
Blue in dorm sixty-two
Hustling in Graystone

Stigma of forever begins
Here's a cross now pay for your sins
Addicted to the yellow pill
Jesus dying on the hill was God's will

Hustling in Graystone
Hustling all alone
Blue in dorm sixty-two
Hustling in Graystone

Hell

She's a preprogrammed blonde with long red hair
I'll tell the truth but I wouldn't dare
I have albums numbered one to three
I sing of the glory of misery

And I stayed a little while in Hell
I prayed with a smile all was well
I always got my soul to sell
Lord have mercy it's hot as hell

On the radio the deejay chatters
Proficient in nothing that matters
I was walking the narrow and straight
Sad to say I lost the way love faded to hate.

And I stayed a little while in Hell
I prayed with a smile all was well
I always got my soul to sell
Lord have mercy it's hot as hell

Back to the zinger of our pop singer
Backstage fat mice full of lice linger
Darling your beautiful let's go to bed
You can use your body or use your head

And I stayed a little while in Hell
I prayed with a smile all was well
I always got my soul to sell
Lord have mercy it's hot as hell

Circles of miracles secrets time will tell
God is grace heaven His place what of hell?
Is it okay if I laugh it is okay if I cry?
The hardest question sweetheart is Why?

After the encore they always want more
She's plenty high price but still a whore
Businessman robbed me with a zip zap
Ben you're an ugly slob and a piece of crap

And I stayed a little while in Hell
I prayed with a smile all was well
I always got my soul to sell
Lord have mercy it's hot as hell

Hey Carly

I went to the ocean and I found it blue
Searched the heavens I hadn't a clue
Trying to tell someone I love you
It's the hardest thing for me to do

Hey Carly where's your smile
Hey Carly it's been a while
Hey Carly sing me your song
Hey Carly stay strong

When you ain't got joy what is life
The butcher ain't the only one with a knife
She's a cover singer in a band aid band
Playing in the night clubs across the land

Hey Carly where's your smile
Hey Carly it's been a while
Hey Carly sing me your song
Hey Carly stay strong

I searched the bottle and found the needle
She was there dancing in the middle
Death on the cross takes its sweet time
When you're the law stealing ain't a crime

Hey Carly where's your smile
Hey Carly it's been a while
Hey Carly sing me your song
Hey Carly stay strong

In western Kansas the band played all night
I kissed her at sunset and it felt right
I asked Neil if what I thought was real
But he didn't know so I took the deal

Hey Carly where's your smile
Hey Carly it's been a while
Hey Carly sing me your song
Hey Carly stay strong

Hey Sylvia

I'm bleeding the red blood flows from the heart
I'm needing to know why you had to part
Sylvia life's song always comes to an end
I was happy to call you lover and friend

Hey Sylvia time to say goodbye
Hey Sylvia forgive me as I cry
You're a good woman and faithful wife
The best thing I had in this life

On this Earth it's rare to find someone kind
Legions of the lost following the blind
On the radio a song about love true
Sylvia I'm singing this song just for you

Hey Sylvia time to say goodbye
Hey Sylvia forgive me as I cry
You're a good woman and faithful wife
The best thing I had in this life

The pick plucks the strings upon this old guitar
We all dream of being some famous star
What really matters when it's time for you to leave?
There's a better place oh yes I do believe

Hey Sylvia time to say goodbye
Hey Sylvia forgive me as I cry
You're a good woman and faithful wife
The best thing I had in this life

I've been up I've been down that's for sure
I'm been rich I've been poor wanting more
I wandered the crooked trail in the midnight hail
I lived long enough to talk about my tale

Hey Sylvia I really do love you
Hey Sylvia I promised to be true
Goodbyes are tough when you're saying the last one
It's seems that our song of life had just begun

Hey Sylvia time to say goodbye
Hey Sylvia forgive me as I cry
You're a good woman and faithful wife
The best thing I had in this life

I Got Me A Sign

Let the rains fall and life renew
May the gray pains pass to blue
I died in dorm sixty-two
Only love is a lesson true

I got me a sign and I'm holding it high
I got me a sign look at me defy
Kings and queens practice a lie
I got me a sign and I'm holding it high

Money is a madness supreme
Hear the marine's dying scream
Was this life only a dream?
Is anything just as it seems

I got me a sign and I'm holding it high
I got me a sign look at me defy
Kings and queens practice a lie
I got me a sign and I'm holding it high

I awake as secrets unfold
There's much more to life than gold
You learn things as you grow old
Lesson one don't do as your told

I got me a sign and I'm holding it high
I got me a sign look at me defy
Kings and queens practice a lie
I got me a sign and I'm holding it high

The game never ends in a tie
The hardest question is Why?
Let me say I got me a sign
And I'm out there holding it high

I got me a sign and I'm holding it high
I got me a sign look at me defy
Kings and queens practice a lie
I got me a sign and I'm holding it high

I Shall Rise

Meat and bones dollars and cents he takes a chance
Here's a dollar baby do you do more than dance?
Sparkling eyes tomorrow dies in yes and no
Let's make the trick quick I gotta do a show

I've been cheated by men full of greed
They take and take but have no need
But I shall rise you can't keep me down
I shall rise you can't deny my crown

My past of a fool fuels the rocket to fly
I declare beware I ain't gonna take a lie
Look hear mister I got my fighting shoes on
Have no sad tear sweet sister my life ain't gone

I've been cheated by men full of greed
They take and take but have no need
But I shall rise you can't keep me down
I shall rise you can't deny my crown

On La Rue Avenue there's a comic store
Batman and the Joker fight in eternal war
Can you sleep at night sir that's the real score?
It's easy to get high but it's hard to soar

I've been cheated by men full of greed
They take and take but have no need
But I shall rise you can't keep me down
I shall rise you can't deny my crown

Scum of the Earth Jesus died for you
What is your worth one and one is two
The calculus of capitalism is pain
Like a crook you took from the insane
Let me explain you're a carnal crook vain

There's a cop waiting to stop your red corvette
You're a real prince but even the kings regret
I'm going in the dungeon to find my gold
Life is a tale and the future's still untold

I've been cheated by men full of greed
They take and take but have no need
But I shall rise you can't keep me down/ I shall rise you can't deny my crown

In The Morning Light

She kissed me sweet as honey
Grabbed my heart took my money
And the part I find funny
Is she was there
Like solemn prayer
An angel of white in the morning light

I want to understand
To hold somebody's hand
Life is more than the band
I think I understand

Poets search the vast beyond
Whispers and hushes never gone
Solemn words we lean upon
Written with care
And who was there
An angel of white in the morning light

Answers never come fast
Good things never seem to last
Choose the future or the past
The die it has been cast

Faith are words of oaths sacred
Embracing love not hatred
Reasons why we live and die
Hear the soft cry
Answering why
An angel of white in the morning light

Jenny

Jenny's seventeen the queen of the scene
She lives in fantasy she wishes for the dream
Jenny's been to places we've never been
Hear her parents as they fight and scream

Jenny Jenny Jenny you're loved by so many
A quarter for a kiss and a hug for a penny
You are a ripe field in the in the Land of Plenty
Jenny Jenny Jenny you're loved by so many

God damn child you had have better behave
You're gonna send your old man to an early grave
He hits the bottle everythings black
Jenny's on the run never coming back

Jenny Jenny Jenny you're loved by so many
A quarter for a kiss and a hug for a penny
You are a ripe field in the in the Land of Plenty
Jenny Jenny Jenny you're loved by so many

The whispers of rumors in the high school hall
Nobody understands cause Jenny had it all
An empty seat like a blessing without grace
They say the police are on the chase

Jenny Jenny Jenny you're loved by so many
A quarter for a kiss and a hug for a penny
You are a ripe field in the in the Land of Plenty
Jenny Jenny Jenny you're loved by so many

In the big city the streets ain't paved with gold
Wondering what to make of all the lies she's told
She's meat for a dog and pleasure for a pig
Jenny cries sometimes life is just big

She ain't got a future nothing to last
Hell is always a gamble the die has been cast
Looking ahead while she's looking behind
All Jenny wanted was something real kind

Jenny Jenny Jenny you're loved by so many
A quarter for a kiss and a hug for a penny
You are a ripe field in the in the Land of Plenty
Jenny Jenny Jenny you're loved by so many

June

Flower stores bring about flower whores
It ain't only the early bird who scores
Hear the bees buzz in one last song
Does anybody know when we went wrong?

This is a tune but it ain't about June
See the sun kissing the moon
At night I write the sacred rune
This is a tune but it ain't about June

Turning over in my grave Jesus saves
Down in Atlanta they slaughter the braves
Marched them out west on the Trail of Tears
Genocide for Pilgrim pride is our fears

This is a tune but it ain't about June
See the sun kissing the moon
At night I write the sacred rune
This is a tune but it ain't about June

I'm going to play you some of my best stuff
You may be a cool fool and taffy is really tough
Listen to me Mister Down Town Ken Brown
Kneel before the Lord and accept the crown

Back to the story June was in a grove
In life it seems we have something to prove
I can be a funk star just watch me move
A little grease to release what I got to prove

This is a tune but it ain't about June
See the sun kissing the moon
At night I write the sacred rune
This is a tune but it ain't about June

Theft by deception is a crime I must mention
Hell is the ultimate house of detention
Yet another miraculous mention in my rhyme
Of Ben Zapp and his heinous evil crime

This is a tune but it ain't about June
See the sun kissing the moon
At night I write the sacred rune
This is a tune but it ain't about June

Living

It all ends it all begins in her smile
They say life is more than survival
Jane says "Baby let me take you high"
Suddenly it doesn't matter why

Laughing loving living
Sin will never win if you're forgiving
Ecstasy is the art of giving
Laughing loving living

At the train station summer is here
A kiss goodbye I give a cry in fear
Valleys and hills do you comprehend
This may be goodbye but is it the end?

Laughing loving living
Sin will never win if you're forgiving
Ecstasy is the art of giving
Laughing loving living

I work the soil my hands full of grace
In every flower I see Jane's face
In the heat I taste the sweat of my brow
Praying hard that tomorrow was now

Laughing loving living
Sin will never win if you're forgiving
Ecstasy is the art of giving
Laughing loving living

There she is with her wonderful grin
Her arms wide open shouting take me in
Faithful and true Jane that's why I love you
The sun is shining and the sky is blue

Laughing loving living
Sin will never win if you're forgiving
Ecstasy is the art of giving
Laughing loving living

Love Is More

Have you been cheated? know how the fire feels?
Been on the down side of some dirty deals?
The machine gun echoes the bombs burst in pain
A war of man ego and greed equally vain

Love is more than a warm feeling
Rich man makes a living by stealing
He got two decks from which he's dealing
Love is more than a cold feeling

Starless skies a child cries for peace on Earth
Fact or fiction the diction of Jesus's birth?
Cathedrals of stone stand alone in death
What matters is what happens after your last breath

Love is more than a warm feeling
Rich man makes a living by steeling
He got two decks from which he's dealing
Love is more than a cold feeling

You weren't even welcome the first time
You got the money the fruits of your crime
But I got a song telling of your wrong
Heaven is full of sinners but you don't belong

Love is more than a warm feeling
Rich man makes a living by steeling
He got two decks from which he's dealing
Love is more than a cold feeling

I beat the house on my wonderful cruise
On the Titanic seems we all lose
I've got them World War 3 blues
In China they're paying their dues

Deny yourself and carry that old cross
The dollar bill will never be my boss
I'm searching for a secret never found
Take everything mister because I'm heaven bound

Love is more than a warm feeling
Rich man makes a living by steeling
He got two decks from which he's dealing
Love is more than a cold feeling

Love Is The Cure

The bridge is low and my flute out of tune
She smiles saying Love comes too soon
Terry the troll eats frogs and fish
Say hey what you trying to accomplish?

There was a door to before
We had a chance to end the war
But they went for the ultimate score
I ask for love Cause love is the cure

I waged peace turning the other cheek
Willy the hillbilly took the time to speak
The Blue Ridge Mountains got some soul
They stole our heart along with the coal

There was a door to before
We had a chance to end the war
But they went for the ultimate score
I ask for love Cause love is the cure

The diet starts tomorrow goes the song
Even a child knows right from wrong
I'm running in the fields where daisies grow
God is Love tell me what's more to know

There was a door to before
We had a chance to end the war
But they went for the ultimate score
I ask for love Cause love is the cure

Help me Jesus what else can I really say
Words are empty when you can't even pray
I was lost in lust until I caught the train
You lose more than your mind when you go insane

There was a door to before
We had a chance to end the war
But they went for the ultimate score
I ask for love Cause love is the cure

Love Is Whenever I'm With You

Searching an infinite sky asking why
Did God perchance hear my lonesome cry?
I reached for the stars in futility
In the echo of guitars you discovered me

New and blue searching for a reason to due
Is it true that the sky reveals a clue?
Love is whenever I'm with you
I count my many blessing they're few
Love is whenever I'm with you

The drain of the complain drove me insane
Silver and gold told an offer vain
Tossing the dice the best advice was love
In the call of the fall I gave my all to above

New and blue searching for a reason to due
Is it true that the sky reveals a clue?
Love is whenever I'm with you
I count my many blessing they're few
Love is whenever I'm with you

Strumming sweetly the reward of the chord
There was something special in the Word
I held your hand it helped me become strong
I could count on you whether I was right or wrong

Tragedy is a trip one would rather not see
Up and down receive the crown of reality
Ask of me there is nothing I won't do
Love is whenever I'm with you

New and blue searching for a reason to due
Is it true that the sky reveals a clue?
Love is whenever I'm with you
I count my many blessing they're few
Love is whenever I'm with you

Love Is

I ain't looking for a lover to make me smile
Laughter is lost in the song of survival
I need a saint to carry her old rugged cross
I need a sinner who's acquainted with loss

Love is a card dealt to all
Love is a lonely desperate call
Love is being willing to take a fall
Love is love love is all

Where Mathew went wrong I haven't the slightest clue
He loved his money I must say that was true
Materialism's the wisdom of this golden age
And the carnal choir sings from the same page

Love is a card dealt to all
Love is a lonely desperate call
Love is being willing to take a fall
Love is love love is all

The mirror of life are the eyes of an angry wife
You can't sail the ocean without surges of strife
Sylvia the devil has come and taken your mind
Dementia the disease has left you far behind

Love is a card dealt to all
Love is a lonely desperate call
Love is being willing to take a fall
Love is love love is all

And Deborah called just to say hello
Somebody from somewhere I happen to know
Lovers and friends who pretends to be fine?
Take a look at the hook you'll find in this line

And I cry and I giggle and I sing a dirge
Legions of lustful ladies itching with an urge
I haven't recovered from the fright of the first fall
I lie in bed half dead waiting for that call

Love is a card dealt to all
Love is a lonely desperate call
Love is being willing to take a fall
Love is love love is all

Love's A Mystery

You say I'm no good I ain't like your mamma
You say I'm a dirty girl but still you wanna
Listen mister you ain't the only one looking for fun
I'll be out the midnight door when the deed is done

Love will come and love will go
Love's a mystery none can know
Hear the wild wind blow
Love's a mystery none can know

In the heat of the street you gotta compete
You got lonely lustful wolves looking for fresh meat
I got a degree majoring in sexuality
You have that true love at first sight fatality

Love will come and love will go
Love's a mystery none can know
Hear the wild wind blow
Love's a mystery none can know

I'm a free bird so I'll flap my wings and fly
Out the door you won't see me no more no goodbye
Strings are meant for puppets and I won't let me be tied down
Be tough live long enough and I might come back around

Love will come and love will go
Love's a mystery none can know
Hear the wild wind blow
Love's a mystery none can know

My heart is as empty as my hands
Wiseman or fool nobody understands
Love's a mystery think that through
Love's a mystery more than me and you

Once there was a dream but it died in a scream
He made promises words are things you can't redeem
Cheated and robbed lies are the most dangerous of weapons
My chambers are empty but I'll stick to my guns

Love will come and love will go
Love's a mystery none can know
Hear the wild wind blow
Love's a mystery none can know

Marilyn

Hey sister it's been a long long time
Have I told you that I've learned to rhyme
Though profound I found love is no crime
Hey sisters it's been a long long time

Hey Marilyn how have you been
I'm at heaven's door let me in
Is missing you a sin
Hey Marilyn how have you been

I heard a song on the radio
It brought me to a time long ago
You were so good to me don't you know
I heard a song on the radio

Hey Marilyn how have you been
I'm at heaven's door let me in
Is missing you a sin
Hey Marilyn how have you been

I'm down on Earth messing around
One gotta be lost to be found
My lips pray but I make no sound
I'm down on Earth messing around

Hey Marilyn how have you been
I'm at heaven's door let me in
Is missing you a sin
Hey Marilyn how have you been

What is the meaning of this mixed-up maze?
Lost in the haze of the latest craze
And they say that we have seen our better daze
What is the meaning of this mixed-up haze?

I guess you're an angel with wings and all
Beware doll cause you can always fall
In glory it don't matter big or small
I guess you're an angel with wings and all

Hey Marilyn how have you been
I'm at heaven's door let me in
I missing you a sin
Hey Marilyn how have you been

Merry Go Round

Love is a promise we should all keep
Love's a mystery an ocean deep
Sorry baby that I made you weep
You ain't the only one losing sleep

I found myself on the merry-go-round
Like a slave to my emotions I was bound
Endless searches but nothing ever found
Take my hand on this merry-go-round

Ain't no stopping for once life is real
What are the rules I gotta know the deal
Without you I'm empty with you I'm whole
The more I take the less I control

I found myself on the merry-go-round
Like a slave to my emotions I am bound
Endless searches but nothing ever found
Take my hand on this merry-go-round

In the dream I never heard the scream
I'm searching for power to redeem
The climb is without end I see the view
All Earth's kingdoms are nothing without you

I found myself on the merry-go-round
Like a slave to my emotions I was bound
Endless searches but nothing ever found
Take my hand on this merry-go-round

At the carnival riding on the Ferris wheel
I snook a kiss and a little feel
Decades before I explore my memory
I know the truth and I am far from free

I keep saying tomorrow will be fine
I keep saying that you'll soon be mine
Between weddings and funerals my dear
The grace of your face fills me with fear

I found myself on the merry-go-round
Like a slave to my emotions I was bound
Endless searches but nothing ever found
Take my hand on this merry-go-round

Your heart will confess yes your mind says no
In endless circles on the race we go
Riding the merry-go-round till life's done
Riding the merry-go-round never one

I found myself on the merry-go-round
Like a slave to my emotions I was bound
Endless searches but nothing ever found
Take my hand on this merry-go-round

Money

I got a Ferrari red hot and quick
Love me but do not scar me in the trick
If you're a gold digger well I'm your mine
Furs, jewels, Champaign I'll be treating you fine

Be my baby honey I got plenty of money
When make jokes are bad laugh like they're funny
You can be my private Playboy bunny
Be my baby honey I got plenty of money

A beautiful girl hanging on my arm
Luscious legs lovely breasts wonderful charm
In London we'll have some tea with the queen
You'll be the hit of the Hollywood scene

Be my baby honey I got plenty of money
When make jokes are bad laugh like they're funny
You can be my private Playboy bunny
Be my baby honey I got plenty of money

My private Lear jet it's got a back seat
After making love some lobster to eat
As long as the stocks rise there's no worry
Come on sweetie life's a constant hurry

Be my baby honey I got plenty of money
When make jokes are bad laugh like they're funny
You can be my private Playboy bunny
Be my baby honey I got plenty of money

Well sorry my dear this is your worst fear
It's magic time so go and disappear
You're a blonde and a red hair walked on by
Live is short I'll give someone else a try

Be my baby honey I got plenty of money
When make jokes are bad laugh like they're funny
You can be my private Playboy bunny
Be my baby honey I got plenty of money

Our Last Goodbye

Salt melting in the rain whipped by an iron chain
You're leaving again you softly explain
We've been here my dear endless times before
But today baby you walked out the door

Who's going to play guitar as I sing?
Who's going to sit next to the king?
We promised our love would never die
But darling today is our last goodbye

It was love at second sight you treated me right
Cooking me breakfast after love through the night
We laugh we cried we shared our secret dream
You were my perfect match so it did seem

Who's going to play guitar as I sing?
Who's going to sit next to the king?
We promised our love would never die
But darling today is our last goodbye

Well years roll in like the waves of the mighty sea
You get so low you question reality
I never told you what you meant to me
And now you're saying you wanna be free

Who's going to play guitar as I sing?
Who's going to sit next to the king?
We promised our love would never die
But darling today is our last goodbye

A dog and a cat and miles of memories never to forget
Now all the tears and the smiles only point to regret
You're throwing the dice but it's a crooked game
But I ain't got nobody but myself to blame

I should have written this love song while in my prime
Taking your for granted is my biggest crime
Life is like a poem that doesn't rhyme
Questions only answered inside of time

Who's going to play guitar as I sing?
Who's going to sit next to the king
We promised our love would never die
But darling today is our last goodbye

Pretend

I knew the man who knew the man who played the bass
On the very best album featuring Johnny Ace
Robert you were the angel that fell from grace
We always thought that you would save the human race

Should I laugh or should I cry
What's it matter we all gotta die
The song it never really does end
Now don't pretend you were my friend

I went out with Natasha's sister last night
We had a big fight arguing over who was right
Blues is the universal language of our pain
I was a big spender but I learned money's vain

Should I laugh or should I cry
What's it matter we all gotta die
The song it never really does end
Now don't pretend you were my friend

I would have dreamed bigger but I was awake
We'll ask Mister Myron just how much pain he can take
We can pretend that everything was just fine
But it ain't your sanity hanging on the line

Should I laugh or should I cry
What's it matter we all gotta die
The song it never really does end
Now don't pretend you were my friend

So here you are with guitar playing to yesterday
I guess in this mess we all got dues to pay
Have you ever written a song about being free?
Cry out in vain the chain that binds is agony

A pilgrim marching to the crusade's front line
Mania's found in the profound lesson of divine
Don't pretend that there's isn't a wrong or right
As God speaks with thunder I wonder about night

Should I laugh or should I cry
What's it matter we all gotta die
The song it never really does end
Now don't pretend you were my friend

Promises

In another world when time was under my feet
You were my girl wedding bells chimed sweet
Naïve to believe that we would never grieve
Prophets priests and poets are paid to deceive

Promises for forever sad when it ends
Lovers lose not even friends
Promises for forever me and you
Promises for forever words untrue

I still cannot say where on the path things went wrong
You had our children I had my song
Second guessing is a way of constant pain
Life's greatest mysteries I've found none to explain

Promises for forever sad when it ends
Lovers lose not even friends
Promises for forever me and you
Promises for forever words untrue

I went north you went south the kids found living hell
Innocence the price virtue to sell
I've lived that dark scene every day of my life
Divorce with force you were no longer my wife

Promises for forever sad when it ends
Lovers lose not even friends
Promises for forever me and you
Promises for forever words untrue

Was I too selfish or blinded in my need?
Did I care too little pursuing futile greed?
Maybe it was fate blame it on a bad sign
I wish today that I could still call you mine

Are you happy when life hits hard can you still smile?
When you look behind is it worthwhile?
The meaning of life is love there is no doubt
But what love really is I can't figure out

Promises for forever sad when it ends
Lovers lose not even friends
Promises for forever me and you
Promises for forever words untrue

Searching

This body of dust pays for my lustful blues
That's you and me on the Sunday evening news
Leslie taught me love was more than you feel
In this world below only faith is real

I'm searching for the way to go
Sometimes fast sometimes slow
Wondering what I don't know
I'm searching wandering to and fro

I was writing horror books with romance hooks
Giving wimpy pimps my fair share of dirty looks
I always feel dirty getting into the mood
I'm not evil but I ain't any good

I'm searching for the way to go
Sometimes fast sometimes slow
Wondering what I don't know
I'm searching wandering to and fro

Daemon went to prison searching for a fix
All the cops are crazy criminals doing tricks
They lied to me when I was a child small
Didn't tell the truth on anything at all

I'm searching for the way to go
Sometimes fast sometimes slow
Wondering what I don't know
I'm searching wandering to and fro

I'm wise enough to tell my right from wrong
But baby I'm a child and I ain't strong
Jesus walked on water I believe that's true
But what does that matter to me and you?

I went to church with Bert playing silly games
Nicole I love you with all of my soul says James
If I was a saint I'd paint a picture true
God loves all sinners that means me and you

I'm searching for the way to go
Sometimes fast sometimes slow
Wondering what I don't know
I'm searching wandering to and fro

Streets Of Gold

We're gonna see a miracle I heard the voice through the door
It's a simple line they've used so many times before
In the hospitals the preachers aren't ever found
Put your money in the plate and yes your heaven bound

It's more blessed to give than receive
That's the word why don't you believe?
I'm anointed my words drenched in fire
Streets of gold are my only desire

The Mercedes Benz is a necessity that's for sure
I'm close to Jesus Christ why I deserve so much more
God revealed it all to me in inside of a dream
We gotta all pull together as one big team

It's more blessed to give than receive
That's the word why don't you believe?
I'm anointed my words drenched in fire
Streets of gold are my only desire

Late in the evening he slips out he's fighting a righteous war
Preaching the good news to both the drug dealer and the whore
I don't know why I care I mean who is without sin
At one time I had the fire but that was way back when

It's more blessed to give than receive
That's the word why don't you believe?
I'm anointed my words drenched in fire
Streets of gold are my only desire

He gives the eye to the ladies in the choir
With some help he could lead them higher
He quotes the Bible but still he is a liar
Streets of gold are my only desire

Sometimes between here and there he pauses to think about his life
He blames society or maybe he picked the wrong wife
The preacher ain't a fool he can quote the holy book
Walking on the streets of gold you'll never find a crook

It's more blessed to give than receive
That's the word why don't you believe?
I'm anointed my words drenched in fire
Streets of gold are my only desire

Tell Me

Messing up messing down just like a clown
Messing around on the other side of town
We're bound on that train to some other place
There are tales of terror stories of grace

Did I say that I love you?
Tell me what I could do
To make your dreams come true
Did I say that I love you?

Well fools they only bet on a sure thing
If they can't have the ace they'll go for the king
I fled with the queen as they lusted
In poker the joker cannot be trusted

Did I say that I love you?
Tell me what I could do
To make your dreams come true
Did I say that I love you?

The comic man came by to sell me joke
Honey and butter were the words that he spoke
But I got a song and life is fine
Liars and losers laughing at this line

Did I say that I love you?
Tell me what I could do
To make your dreams come true
Did I say that I love you?

I saw a vision of an angel shining bright
She came and kissed me in midnight flight
But the words on my lips were concealed
Take my hand secrets soon to be revealed

Answers are useful only to questions
Tell me the secrets that nobody mentions
Lie down in the tall grass here's my kiss
Forever's a long-time forever's this

Did I say that I love you?
Tell me what I could do
To make your dreams come true
Did I say that I love you?

The Dead Can't Give No Praise

Promoters pimping pretty petite pop stars
Lip synching songs preprogrammed guitars
Grant got the coffee pot out to change the line
Don't worry they'll rob the story just fine

Barb watches eyes of wonder
Love is the spell she's under
Barb kicks back in heaven these days
Cause the dead can't give no praise

Steal a little well then whose really to know
After all music makes up the show
Live and die laugh and cry ride the circle round
All the matters is where your soul is bound

Barb watches eyes of wonder
Love is the spell she's under
Barb kicks back in heaven these days
Cause the dead can't give no praise

Massive money to count the party's rocking
All the better the story's shocking
Headlines reveal us everything but what's real
Life goes on long after you make the deal

Barb watches eyes of wonder
Love is the spell she's under
Barb kicks back in heaven these days
Cause the dead can't give no praise

We worship the idol bow to the golden calf
You want mercy and grace then just laugh
Winds of war are swirling in a hurricane
Generals and bankers chasing promises vain

Night is long and dark and we all need to sleep
I pray to the Lord my soul to keep
Mysteries abound where are the answers found
Needles on plastic make magical sound

Barb watches eyes of wonder
Love is the spell she's under
Barb kicks back in heaven these days
Cause the dead can't give no praise

The Final Fantasy

Got lost on Traci in a two-minute affair
Signs to the west signs to the east signs everywhere
Little crosses of gold hanging down on your neck
At least one of the thieves showed Jesus some respect

Welcome to the final fantasy
Love is only love if it's free
Picture perfect just you and me
Welcome to the final fantasy

Billionaires and empty prayers greed's the legal crime
In the psychiatric wards I put in my time
A better world a perfect girl an ideal place
I still have some hope to spare for the human race

Welcome to the final fantasy
Love is only love if it's free
Picture perfect just you and me
Welcome to the final fantasy

In sin I'm shedding skin like a beetle in pain
The sweet source of my dreams I cannot explain
I just know it's so that love is never in vain
Now if only I wasn't lonely and insane

The groovy movie took a hot twist of my wrist
Lieutenant Salt gave a call I couldn't resist
So what is real beyond the squeal of sex appeal
If the cards aren't marked then don't bother to deal

Welcome to the final fantasy
Love is only love if it's free
Picture perfect just you and me
Welcome to the final fantasy

Cheated and mistreated they flogged the Son of God
Money honey ain't funny with that chastening rod
Thirty pieces of silver that the high priest paid
The fast last words of Goliath "I ain't afraid"

Welcome to the final fantasy
Love is only love if it's free
Picture perfect just you and me
Welcome to the final fantasy

The Man Who Had It All

Missing you baby is the devil's fire
Cause you're like heaven only higher
In Vegas you never see the house lose
Baby I'm a winner singing the blues

I'm the man who had it all
But paradise took a fall
Now whom I supposed to call
I'm the man who had it all

Life don't come with a map nobody knows
We go whichever way the wind blows
While on the road we met in a dark place
You were a fountain and I drank your grace

I'm the man who had it all
But paradise took a fall
Now whom I supposed to call
I'm the man who had it all

Your smile, your hello, your peculiar style
Somehow life became worthwhile
I shared my secrets told you my dreams
And into the night I revealed my screams

Maybe I was selfish maybe I was cruel
Whatever the reason I was the fool
I'd trade my gold records and guitars
To find you again in one of these bars

I'm the man who had it all
But paradise took a fall
Now whom I supposed to call
I'm the man who had it all

When you hear this song on the radio
Remember that I'll always love you so
My arms are open to take you back in
Oh baby forgive me let's start again

I'm the man who had it all
But paradise took a fall
Now whom I supposed to call
I'm the man who had it all

The Road

Eleven in heaven dancing with seven
Say your prayers and don't forget amen
I'm drowning in what could have been
Draw a card pick your favorite sin

On the road you walk as far as you can
On the road you'd better have a plan
The road will make a boy a man
On the road you walk as far as you can

At the crossroads baby I took a hard right
I followed the winding road all night
At dawn the memory was gone
Life's only real choice is to go on

On the road you walk as far as you can
On the road you'd better have a plan
The road will make a boy a man
On the road you walk as far as you can

Eating oatmeal finding out the doubt is real
Trying to write a verse you'd want to steal
Second guess what a mess I smile
If you look you'll find something worthwhile

On the road you walk as far as you can
On the road you'd better have a plan
The road will make a boy a man
On the road you walk as far as you can

Silver or gold it doesn't matter what you're walking on
You take a step and the moment is gone
Once we strolled along your hand in mine
I told you a lie it was my favorite line

So here we go hoping for a brand-new dream
Needle to my heart sewing the seam
On the auction the last bid wins
Seven kisses eleven God grins

On the road you walk as far as you can
On the road you'd better have a plan
The road will make a boy a man
On the road you walk as far as you can

The Way Of The World

The way of the world is wicked with greed
The way of the world cuts you till you bleed
The way of the world takes more than they need
The way of the world it plants its evil seed

You can't walk this road if you ain't got no gold
You can't walk this road if you ain't sold your soul
The banker counts his money thinking he's cheated God
But her comes the specter of death with staff and rod

The way of the world they think that they are strong
The way of the world let me tell you they're wrong
The way of the world I'll never sing that song
The way of the world seems like I don't belong

You can't walk this road if you ain't got no gold
You can't walk this road if you ain't sold your soul
The banker counts his money thinking he's cheated God
But her comes the specter of death with staff and rod

The way of the world they'll cheat you till you die
The way of the world they traded truth for a lie
The way of the world there is no alibi
The way of the world here the lonely one cry

You can't walk this road if you ain't got no gold
You can't walk this road if you ain't sold your soul
The banker counts his money thinking he's cheated God
But her comes the specter of death with staff and rod

Love is something genuine and real
Love is striving for the ideal
Love is the strength that I feel
Love is the winner of the deal

The way of the world it is wicked and cruel
The way of the world they play the devil's fool
They way of the world the dominate and rule
The way of the world they play the devil's tool

You can't walk this road if you ain't got no gold
You can't walk this road if you ain't sold your soul
The banker counts his money thinking he's cheated God
But her comes the specter of death with staff and rod

This Is The Hook

Who are these singers singing songs on the radio?
Where are they from what do they know?
I used the play the bass in dream number two
The sky was auburn and the feelings blue

This is the hook money on the line
This is the hook money is divine
Lustful eyes covet all that's fine
This is the hook make it mine

The blind are hunting down the blind
God's first lesson was teaching us to be kind
But truth be told we left God long behind
Now the goal of the soul is how much gold can we find

This is the hook money on the line
This is the hook money is divine
Lustful eyes covet all that's fine
This is the hook make it mine

I saw a Vrock demon gnawing on my lover's heart
His fangs were sharp his devouring a form of art
The blood was red let it be said blood is red
There are some visions I can't shake out of my head

This is the hook money on the line
This is the hook money is divine
Lustful eyes covet all that's fine
This is the hook make it mine

Ancient mariners singing a pop song
Even proud poets get life wrong
These words set up the hook
The hook makes you take a second look

I took calculus and chemistry instead of band
I guess now some of you finally understand
Engineers building weapons of war be damned
You in lofty ivory towers this ain't your land

This is the hook money on the line
This is the hook money is divine
Lustful eyes covet all that's fine
This is the hook make it mine

True Love

Words are letters who have made friends
And as it begins so it ends
Tell me the story of a broken heart
Tell me of true love never to part

In the world of fairy tales
True love never fails
Righteousness prevails
True love never fails

The knight went to the castle wall
To the fair princess went his call
I shall slay the dragon for your pleasure
And buy your true love with the treasure

In the world of fairy tales
True love never fails
Righteousness prevails
True love never fails

In the kingdom darkness prevailed
And our hero sadly he failed
The good lady met legions of fine men
But the princess would not love again

In the world of fairy tales
True love never fails
Righteousness prevails
True love never fails

She sits in her tower looking lost
A legend at the highest cost
Her beauty and charm far beyond fair
To her good knight no one could compare

In the world of fairy tales
True love never fails
Righteousness prevails
True love never fails

Waitress

Kriti is pretty on the marble floor
Takeout is tough with an open door
In black funeral black tells me a tale
Jonah ran and found the belly of the whale

She's the waitress God bless her soul
She's the waitress Loves rock and roll
Smile all the while her back aches
She's the waitress got what it takes

Poetry is her dream while on her lunch hour
The menu is new feeling blue power
Excuse me honey does that come with fries
Why don't you love me I'll hear some poisoned lies

She's the waitress God bless her soul
She's the waitress Loves rock and roll
Smile all the while her back aches
She's the waitress got what it takes

Two burgers extra mayo diet coke
Truth of the youth can you please guess at the joke

Montclair House Diner on Holy Avenue
From my booth in the back with a view
Dreams sacrificed on the altar of paradise
Six-gun shooters ain't no Whooters vice

She's the waitress God bless her soul
She's the waitress Loves rock and roll
Smile all the while her back aches
She's the waitress got what it takes

And Kriti will run to the edge of time
Lost with Frost searching for today's rhyme
A balancing act she juggles the meals
In the shadow of the cross Satan makes no deals

She's the waitress God bless her soul
She's the waitress Loves rock and roll
Smile all the while her back aches
She's the waitress got what it takes

What Really Matters?

I lost my mind on La Rue Avenue
When up became down what was I to do?
Who slipped a trick inside of my drink?
I'm trying hard but I cannot think

What really matters is it money?
In the grave cold cash is funny
What really matters maybe love?
What are the things you think of?

Brenda Bops never stops singing the blues
Big Tiny smiles bringing only bad news
Go Gizmo Go welcome to the show
You don't know the things that you don't know

Two-minute warning Ezra chapter ten
The sermon's over can I get an amen?
East Orange Hospital Zeal felt shame
Wagging a wicked finger of blame

What really matters is it money?
In the grave cold cash is funny
What really matters maybe love?
What are the things you think of?

Daddy didn't know that he lived a lie
All the best things in life money can't buy
That don't mean that the people don't try
Lay down a funny twenty to get high

What really matters is it money?
In the grave cold cash is funny
What really matters maybe love?
What are the things you think of?

Poets and profits are oceans apart
Here I am starving carving out my art
I cut the turkey breast in the shape of a heart
Every lover discovers there's time to depart

What really matters is it money?
In the grave cold cash is funny
What really matters maybe love?
What are the things you think of?

When I'm Down

I was a blind man on a moonless night
Loving the lust trusting the blissful blight
Kissing cockroaches cause such was the way
A dragon of agony too awful to slay

Don't kick me when I'm down
Don't laugh I ain't a clown
Help me to lose this frown
Don't kick me when I'm down

A prophetic poet lost in free verse
All I had was ego my fateful curse
I said let me write a number one tune
Zombie accountants can never come out too soon

Don't kick me when I'm down
Don't laugh I ain't a clown
Help me to lose this frown
Don't kick me when I'm down

Searching the church for answers never found
Eagle on his perch heavens secret sound
Could music be the trick to being free
The key of discovery is you loving me

Don't kick me when I'm down
Don't laugh I ain't a clown
Help me to lose this frown
Don't kick me when I'm down

Reggae rockers quarterback say thanx to blockers
Storm troopers shooting machine gun shockers
Up in the sky death is dealt to the masses below
They threw the world series say it ain't so

And tomorrow brings hope if you make up
Kiss the sun hello coffee in the cup
The hunger isn't bad if you keep your mind
I was only searching for a lover good and kind

Don't kick me when I'm down
Don't laugh I ain't a clown
Help me to lose this frown
Don't kick me when I'm down

When You Get There

Crawling in the gutter with roaches and rats
Wizards and witches cooking gizzards in vats
Spin the wheel deal the cards kiss Lady Luck
Demons are angels messing around in the muck

Falling down hanging on air
They offer a hope and a prayer
I wonder if they are aware
You'll know it when you get there

Love was a rumor a word heard often vain
Money is the means that drives mankind insane
They're starving in Africa that's how it goes
Politicians holding power putting on shows

Falling down hanging on air
They offer a hope and a prayer
I wonder if they are aware
You'll know it when you get there

One of these days I'm going to try to rise
I'll speak only the truth and defy the lies
Measure me for a cruel cross of my own
Seeking death strung out on meth my how you have grown

Falling down hanging on air
They offer a hope and a prayer
I wonder if they are aware
You'll know it when you get there

Here comes the winner see him lie cheat and steal
He'll deceive so well all of his words will seem real
Lessons are hard they teach you to guard the heart
In every Broadway show you know to do your part

Hell and heaven we hold both inside our hand
I tell you the truth the youth don't understand
I'm guilty lead me to the fountain pure
It's a one-way trip when you walk through death's dark door

Falling down hanging on air
They offer a hope and a prayer
I wonder if they are aware
You'll know it when you get there

When Your Manic

When you got the right to choose the baby's gonna lose
We're free in America to pick our own blues
The comic book guy will cheat you when you're high
From infinity to here we're all going to die

You'll panic when your manic watch you're right
You'll panic when your manic here comes the fight
In between Thorazine and the pop scene there's the pill
You'll panic when your manic and make the kill

Going crazy you ain't lazy soaring in the sky
Giving it all away cause money's just a lie
In my mind I find a reason to be kind
We got pop stars with guitars the blind leading the blind

You'll panic when your manic watch you're right
You'll panic when your manic here comes the fight
In between Thorazine and the pop scene there's the pill
You'll panic when your manic and make the kill

Silver bracelets are the reward after the grand chase
I was only trying to save the human race
Into the blue ambulance taking a short ride
Playing the game blame the shame for crucifying my pride

You'll panic when your manic watch you're right
You'll panic when your manic here comes the fight
In between Thorazine and the pop scene there's the pill
You'll panic when your manic and make the kill

Tony came by to say that's the man
Chaos and anarchy my only plan
I promised to be faithful and true
Oh Sylvia darling I still love you

Writing lyrics so I can get on the radio
Every day I say life's a radical show
Ken and Lauren they had themselves a baby boy
I sing to the king it brings rivers of endless joy

You'll panic when your manic watch you're right
You'll panic when your manic here comes the fight
In between Thorazine and the pop scene there's the pill
You'll panic when your manic and make the kill

With You On My Mind

Every word brings me to you
Each note sings of love true
There is beauty in loss
Good things have their cost

I sing with you on my mind
Yesterday's moments kind
I sing with you on my mind
Living in years behind

Your kisses of pleasure
Devotion above measure
You were my greatest treasure
Believe me you'll never leave me

Circles lead me round and round
You hear their echoes in the sound
The love in you that I found
A memory beyond profound

I sing with you on my mind
Yesterday's moments kind
I sing with you on my mind
Living in years behind

Your gentle late-night caress
Kind ways always to bless
Filling my empty thirst
Putting others first

I sing with you on my mind
Yesterday's moments kind
I sing with you on my mind
Living in years behind

God's greatest miracle in my life
Sylvia so sweet my wife
I cry during the long goodbye
A cross to carry is why

I sing with you on my mind
Yesterday's moments kind
I sing with you on my mind
Living in years behind

Words

Winners and losers x's and o's
The wind she comes and the wind she blows
He bottled laughter a decent share
And sold it at the town's local fare

Words on the paper come alive
Words of healing to help us survive
Politicians' words simply jive
Words are heard we march and drive

There was the brass money on a leash
Hippies were rioting for world peace
Penny spent a dollar to be made
Local loser looking to get laid

Words on the paper come alive
Words of healing to help us survive
Politicians' words simply jive
Words are heard we march and drive

Well money talks with words that entice
God's good but we disdain His advice
Our hero's walking his lady home
In territory previously unknown

Words on the paper come alive
Words of healing to help us survive
Politicians' words simply jive
Words are heard we march and drive

Aunt Sally had a book of rock and roll heroes
You get the same sum as you multiply with zeroes
Aunt Sally used to be a groupie hard core
Score after score she never found what she was looking for

You're only a loser until you win
Talk about the pleasures of sin
Pressures building without and within
Innocence we can never return again

Words on the paper come alive
Words of healing to help us survive
Politicians' words simply jive
Words are heard we march and drive

Yellow

Headed out west until concrete became dirt
Words of the best poets confessed my same hurt
The radio played a song I didn't know
When love is laid strong it's hard to let go

She was a blonde naturally dyed
With a golden cross crucified
Yellow is the color of the stars
Yellow is melody of my guitars

I saw the sun set on the deep blue ocean
Judgment is done while we keep true emotion
Seagulls' song so strong over the crashing waves
To whatever we serve we become slaves

She was a blonde naturally dyed
With a golden cross crucified
Yellow is the color of the stars
Yellow is melody of my guitars

I sought redemption in a lab making meth
For a formidable fee we dealt double death
I found religion while at a garage sale
If you never try well then you never fail

Checking out the checkout girl I was wrong
I offered salvation in the form of song
The witch queen of the dream had a crystal ball
You only want nothing when you got it all

She was a blonde naturally dyed
With a golden cross crucified
Yellow is the color of the stars
Yellow is melody of my guitars

I recall how I held you in the cold night
There is something deeper beyond wrong and right
Mysteries and wonders why did I let you go?
You were everything you were my yellow

She was a blonde naturally died
With a golden cross crucified
Yellow is the color of the stars
Yellow is melody of my guitars

<u>A Question</u>

Holy Father bursting through the sky
Repent, I was sent so that they might not die
But the man in pain was labeled insane
The sin of what could have been
Was drowned in a shot of gin

A WALK IN THE PARK

Valley Avenue on a sunny day
Love eternal the message of the way
A foolish kingdom my thing?
Heaven is what tomorrow will bring

A walk in da park & it ain't even dak
A walk in da park & it ain't even dak
CiVilization has long lost the mark
A walk in da park & it ain't even dak

Hi meet me I'm a friendly guy
Tameeka was a mystery know why?
One day I say she'll moan and cry
I make promises and love, none can deny

A walk in da park & it ain't even dak
A walk in da park & it ain't even dak
CiVilization has long lost the mark
A walk in da park & it ain't even dak

So baby if you're ready for Heaven's try
I know you got wings can they fly?

Blue Bird No, No

It's a sad song
You'd know if I didn't tell you
We all can see
This broken reality
Children
These are the wages of sin
God have mercy on you & me
Forgive us, sweet Jesus

Child
Can you smile?
When you learn
It'll be your turn
But the time is now
And somehow
The tears must dry
And nobody die
In nuclear war's curse
Or something worse
Child

And the Blue Bird sings No, No, No, No
I forgot life is not a television show
Promises are to be kept If we can
While failure makes us a man or woman
I was told Ice was cold
Now bold and old
I agree with quandary
Before you draw another breath
Recall above all
Silence equals death
The moral of the rhyme
It's a crime to speak at the right time

Brawls

Hey Tyrone toss a bone with meat and juice
All alone hear my moan the universe turns loose
First and last present and past you gotta resist
Thirst for righteousness without a fist?

COINTELPRO is the foe brand
A higher power gives a call
Fight to be a man brawl
Damn Damn Damn Give it your all
Spades & Shades fades into brawl

Gandhi and King had this thing of turning the cheek
When they're young and pull the tongue you gotta speak
Scream and yell give 'em hell but please don't draw their blood
This time brother fire instead of flood

COINTELPRO is the foe brand
A higher power gives a call
Fight to be a man brawl
Damn Damn Damn Give it your all
Spades & Shades fades into brawl

All the red King's armies and all the black Queen's men
Couldn't disarm a thermonuclear weapon
We had the Soviet Union with fascism
So what are u, please us some wisdom

COINTELPRO is the foe brand
A higher power gives a call
Fight to be a man brawl
Damn Damn Damn Give it your all
Spades & Shades fades into brawl

Sometimes you draw a fist before a gun
A song I sing is we shall overcome
History is a lie Christ the only Lord
While heaven is the greatest reward

COINTELPRO is the foe brand
A higher power gives a call
Fight to be a man brawl
Damn Damn Damn Give it your all
Spades & Shades fades into brawl

Broken (For Tiffany)

We met in East Orange Hospital
Both coming in handcuffs and all
Talked and walked with Rosa too
Soon the gray walls turned a deeper blue

I was broken now I am strong
I ain't jokin' I ain't wrong
I was broken broken now I belong
I was broken this is my song

The preacher man preached always non-stop
Bishop the guard was really a cop
Started searching for world peace
All killing and hatred to cease

I was broken now I am strong
I ain't jokin' I ain't wrong
I was broken broken now I belong
I was broken this is my song

Thriller killer at the nursery park
Devils & demons come out after dark
Striving for heaven just to miss the mark
Sing sweetheart your wing is broken my lark

God have mercy on the sinner's soul
I was a savior of rock and roll
Jesus He is God's sweet lamb
The question is about the I am

I was broken now I am strong
I ain't jokin' I ain't wrong
I was broken broken now I belong
I was broken this is my song

<u>Broken</u>

Earth
Love turns gray
Home?

Sex
42nd Street
Linda Lovelace Lust

Science
Haiku for two
Bonzo dunks over Jordan

East Orange Church of Christ
Love friends & Love
Jesus

Angry voices in the psych ward
Shouting!
We're all right

Sandinista
Reading & writing
Ortega over death squads

CIA
BIG MOUTH
WICKED DEEDS of woe

Cry Freedom (To Trudy My Nurse)

By John Kaniecki

Cry freedom, cry and wail
Awesome, awesome is your tale
Steven Biko the former saint
With rainbow colors so you paint
Cry freedom, shout the scream
Never sleep, never doubt the dream
Words they fail
Actions prevail
Cry freedom I shall cry along
Together the better in melodic song
Righteousness, bliss & sweet lover's kiss
Evil is wrong
CRY FREEDOM CRY!
Live or die, **Love is why!**
The chorus before us
Jesus
Messiah on the cross
His gain our loss?
Cry freedom cry
NO MORE TO CRUCIFY
Cry freedom cry
Truth tells no lie

<u>Hair</u> (For Rosa Linda)

Ummm here I sit getting my hair did
In the psychiatric ward doing my bid

Ever since I was a young crazy Indian
I regretted all the white man had done

I got friends over here I got friends over there

Hair! Everybody falls down and says a prayer
Wounded Knee don't say you care
On the cross of Calvary, I was there. -Aware – aware – aware

Lobotomies are friendly if you're a sociopath
Led Zeppelins sail unless they're struck by God's wrath
Hippies with LSD wore and adore their long hair
If Angel Dust is a must well then take care

Hair! Everybody falls down and says a prayer
Wounded Knee don't say you care
On the cross of Calvary, I was there. -Aware – aware – aware

Piano Solo

Full Orchestra on Synthesizer

Silence for 3 seconds

Acapella
The prettiest of hospitals is still a prison cell
Raging turmoil fiery lashes in hell
Take your meds don't overdose we'll doctor up the chart
Survive the psych ward be still my beating heart (my beating heart)

Hair! Everybody falls down and says a prayer
Wounded Knee don't say you care
On the cross of Calvary, I was there. -Aware – aware – aware

I went down on the preacher he was full of lines of hate
Goaded me to argument foolish debate
Steven's Tech mohawk warned the evil cult to wait
Fuck parental guidance it's a little too late

Hair! Everybody falls down and says a prayer
Wounded Knee don't say you care
On the cross of Calvary, I was there. -Aware – aware – aware

The nurse with braids was extremely nice but at a price
Sagacious words of wisdom of sacrifice
I ain't chasing the dreams of yesterday anymore
Yesterday's virgin tomorrow's whore? Really

Hair! Everybody falls down and says a prayer
Wounded Knee don't say you care
On the cross of Calvary, I was there. -Aware – aware – aware

It's a new day Miss Telesford a new day praise the Lord
Jesus loves you and that's mainlining the Word
The sun glistens in your soft ebony hair
Press the dreaded red button if you choose to record
A moment of reflection some honest prayer

Hair! Everybody falls down and says a prayer
Wounded Knee don't say you care
On the cross of Calvary, I was there. -Aware – aware – aware

Locks On The Door

Went for a walk talked to everybody
This is America bold and free
Kept away from the children and the sin
Dice loaded exploded playing to win

Locks on the cage in East Orange City
Silver shines in rage so pretty
Locks on the cage free us all
Locks on the cage to God we call

Cutting nails life when we don't try hard
Madam President hello I'm you're guard
Let's get Bridget inside of this story
And of course, God's horse full of gold glory

Locks on the cage in East Orange City
Silver shines in rage so pretty
Locks on the cage free us all
Locks on the cage to God we call

Leonard P a friend to humanity
Mumia what is your reality
I'm in E.O. they got locks on the cage
Alive at five five I'm turning the page

We're singing new songs in Uganda grand
Aleena Zahir can you now understand?
Future and past the first and the last
I was released when the dice were cast

Locks on the cage in East Orange City
Silver shines in rage so pretty
Locks on the cage free us all
Locks on the cage to God we call

Love At First Sight Is Always Right To Tameeka

Love at first sight is always right
You're a dark delicious delight
With softer brown eyes
I'm the luckiest of guys

Me & you with a view
It's a dinner for two
How much I love you
It's a dinner for two

You said you had no other man
I'll do the best I can
Please don't break my heart
Please don't tear our love apart

Me & you with a view
It's a dinner for two
How much I love you
It's a dinner for two

Ms. Angie

Hey Ms. Angie they stole your name
Life is merry but not a game
Rolling Stone gather no moss
With songs sung at utmost cost

Hey Mick you're pretty sick you go through lovers quick
A tiny stud potato dud got cocaine on the prick?
Excuse me to criticize blind eyes selling no alibies
The devil's deal I Am your real catch me in some lies

Ms. Angie is the name my dear
Speak it correctly speak it clear
Ms. Angie is the name my dear
Try learning a little fear

Who plays guitar we really didn't know the bones?
Message I meant to be sent is talent was in Brian Jones
On the border give an order a line drawn in the sand
On a quest to our best it's now call Grandmother's land

Ms. Angie is the name my dear
Speak it correctly speak it clear
Ms. Angie is the name my dear
Try learning a little fear

The orphanages were a holocaust site
For royalty & rich men's delight
Wild horses they now run the plain
Gold makes you crazy not totally insane

I got satisfaction when Keith's finally clean
Roger Waters David Gilmour welcome to the Red Machine
David sits silently contemplating what could have been
Crying and not trying was not the ultimate sin

Ms. Angie is the name my dear
Speak it correctly speak it clear
Ms. Angie is the name my dear
Try learning a little fear

Not Eating With Tinker (Ivelesse Princess)

Those two ladies are names of sisters from the Church of Christ who ministered to me in a dire time of need. In the hospital I cowrote this song lyric with Ivalese (?) whom I called Prince. We laughed a lot writing this lyric. And while I wrote the majority of the lyric it would have been impossible without her inspiration. Tinker is the name of Prince's dog.

A blue clown dancing in a synthetic suit
The orange cat sat just so cute
No food on the table no refrigerator
Forgive me Lord for being a hater

Today I'm not eating lunch with Tinker
She's too deep a thinker
Today I'm not eating lunch with Tinker
The night sky is a spilled bottle of an inker

The path beyond I see a white butterfly
In a green clover patch on high
The barbecue grease gave release to some juice
Love's glory the story both tight & loose

Today I'm not eating lunch with Tinker
She's too deep a thinker
Today I'm not eating lunch with Tinker
The night sky is a spilled bottle of an inker

At the Last Supper Judas cut out early
Some of us are so worldly
But Tinker she really loves to Rock Roll
And you know my dog Tinker got some soul

Hatred in Haiti starving in Darfur
Between you and me what our resources are for
Machine of madness fueling endless war
Greedy Wall Street executives lusting for more
No thanx to the banks while the general in ranks
Orders a rear charge by the army tanks

Today I'm not eating lunch with Tinker
She's too deep a thinker
Today I'm not eating lunch with Tinker
The night sky is a spilled bottle of an inker

Patient's On Strike

IN ORDER TO CREATE A MORE PERFECT UNION
WELLTHAT'S ALL WE NEED TO SAY

The static on the radio was a t.v. show
A long before cable or the satellite buzzing go
The staff decided on our where and when
Even how to say the final amen

We the patients went on strike
Did all the tricks we didn't like
Like riding standing on a motor bike
We the patients went on strike

Paper and pencil good luck on a pen
You wait thirty minutes then ask again
Talk about Jesus then preach some Zen
Old folks don't know seven eleven

We the patients went on strike
Did all the tricks we didn't like
Like riding standing on a motor bike
We the patients went on strike

We cursed the guards and giggled with the staff
Blessed in verse our better half had a great laugh
All sides surrendered rendered to a higher healing
Bibles out no doubt that Love is more than a feeling

We the patients went on strike
Did all the tricks we didn't like
Like riding standing on a motor bike
We the patients went on strike

Quiet Room

A walk in the park ended in the dark
Twelve arrows and not a one hit the mark
Searching peace in a semi manic daze
Sweet release let's give God virtuous praise

In the quiet room hear the screams
In the quiet room nobody dreams
Maximum security no release
Next step call the police

Arrived in chaos confusion supreme
A dollar napkin for the white whip cream
How to know the blood would flow from my head
Writing this song nothin' wrong enough said

In the quiet room hear the screams
In the quiet room nobody dreams
Maximum security no release
Next step call the police

Cali dreaming palm trees sway in the breeze
Life so different my life is at ease
Kids playing under mother's watchful eye
Dad's singing marines fight to live or die

Scars and Thorazine a thing of ancient past?
Prophets praying will the darkness last
A dark room eyes contrast a crazy cast
Here and now future trumps the past

In the quiet room hear the screams
In the quiet room nobody dreams
Maximum security no release
Next step call the police

Random Words

I wish I had a cheeseburger
With fries on the side
I don't like spice & vinegar
Served with suicide
Maybe the revolution has really
Been won
But here my dear the victory
ain't done

Ketchup and blood mingle as one
Jesus in agony on the cross yes, he won
You're an angel an angle can't spell
It's a place of grace but sometimes hell

Utilize every single piece of paper you got, waste not/Dreams' shadows shine over memories forgot /We make love, we make war, we make love, in this score./I find myself every day/And the price to pay/Sometimes nothing is supreme/Then I awoke from the dream./With sweat on my brow and in the moment of now/Where oh where is your hair/Sacred substance for a prayer/No hash or LSD just me and ultimate reality/Book chapter & verse for blessings or curse./Times grow better times grow worse. X

Raven

Angels may fly to celestial heights
Of glorious colors mostly whites
But ravens, dark and grim
Are merely shades and shadows of Him
Tall Scarecrow talk of living hell
Of all of the intricate moments tell
Raven
Nevermore only for the poor?
Poe some moral whore
But who am I to count the score?
Jesus & Jesus alone
Pick the meat from the bone
Dark wings, lice stings, see what tomorrow brings
Blessings from the King of Kings
Fly Raven fly, fly and cry, cry Raven cry, fly
Heaven is low
But don't you know
Heaven is low

Showdown @ The Slowdown

Doc X had respect for private sex
The voodoo Jew cut the chicken's neck
Pop the valium baby be a doll
God's golden kingdom full of rock & roll

Here we go wearing a frown
It's a showdown at the slowdown
Freaks and geeks gather downtown
It's a showdown at the slowdown

Jack the popper loved a teeny bopper
He just knew nobody could stop her
So he flew to Hawaii and the sun
So hey praise the Lord a victory won

Here we go wearing a frown
It's a showdown at the slowdown
Freaks and geeks gather downtown
It's a showdown at the slowdown

Keep going this song's played out of tune
Tell me when is January June?
A blackish dog barked and I am the moon
What can I say I ended too soon

Here we go wearing a frown
It's a showdown at the slowdown
Freaks and geeks gather downtown
It's a showdown at the slowdown

Jesus at the cross
Was it a loss?
He rose from the dead
Enough said

Sick Psych (Punk Song)

Silver bracelets a key will set you free
Our Lord is not a God of anarchy
Where Charles Manson and I go Whoooh
Whoooooh I Am the wind see me blow

I like sick psych
Ride a motor bike in the acid rain
I love sick psych
A chart with no heart is vain
Sick psych sick psych

The song never ends but you will make some friends
Strong breeze don't sneeze see how the hard oak bends
Gentle calm atomic bomb the world ends
Scared to prayer see now how the wobbly knee bends
IWW! IWW! F-YOU! IWW!F-YOU! These words are true

I like sick psych
Ride a motor bike in the acid rain
I love sick psych
A chart with no heart is vain
Sick psych sick psych

We hold these words sacred a feather pen
Sign for the divine f your holy AMEN
Hypocrites and parasites delight in red
Someplace somewhere Miranda rights ain't fed

I like sick psych
Ride a motor bike in the acid rain
I love sick psych
A chart with no heart is vain
Sick psych sick psych

Hoops to jump through red white and blue
In the carpenter's belt a solitary screw served
NAIL HIM, Let them dream on Haldol in a shot glass
SICK PSYCH Sin enters in will you pass
Mossad blew up the buildings two with
England and old CIA too

I like sick psych/ Ride a motor bike in the acid rain
I love sick psych
A chart with no heart is vain/ Sick psych sick psych

Silent Spy

Hey she stated "I'm with the CIA"
I demand my rights and back pay
Dressed in blue thinks she has a clue
But brother mother that just won't do

She's the silent spy with a big mouth
Her specialty is figuring doubt
Double Agent on the way out
She's the silent spy with a big mouth

Getting her blood pressure taken big deal
Life is life so let's make it real
Puppet governments wicked crime
Change is coming now is the time

She's the silent spy with a big mouth
Her specialty is figuring doubt
Double Agent on the way out
She's the silent spy with a big mouth

Pinochet playing in the Chile snow
Thatcher coveting S.A. blow
Red is the color of the saint
Eradicate poverty and paint

She's the silent spy with a big mouth
Her specialty is figuring doubt
Double Agent on the way out
She's the silent spy with a big mouth

The Cage

Went to the liquor store & bought some cigarettes
Got some lotto tickets and lost all our bets
Cruisin' in our Caddy down Chancellor Avenue way
Street was dark as heaven on its bluest day

We're all hanging in the cage
We're all feeling some rage
It's time to turn the page
We're all hanging in the cage

Saw lights flashing in the mirror they're blue and red
Hoping praying to God we don't wind up dead
Got some weed and open Hennessy stashed in the back seat
Here's where the good hood & suburbia meet

We're all hanging in the cage
We're all feeling some rage
It's time to turn the page
We're all hanging in the cage

New York City pretty skyline
Sinatra's music twas never mine
Shakespeare my dear is still here
Maybe in a moment I'll disappear

FBI told many a lie at Wounded Knee
Pine Ridge Reservation we're still far from free
Olivia Benton a name of fame in fantasy
Justice & Love is our new reality

No justice no peace
Know justice know peace.

The Door

The door is my wall
On to the void
Future never destroyed
Roger, Roger Reaching out to all
Major Tom did the switch a rou
Jack Rankin too
Doors they open doors they close
Visions & secrets nobody knows
Cosmic rays as a river flows
Build a door to ward of titanium steel
Love is real……………

The Lock

Paupers & Kings tomorrow brings
Love & Hoped Love & Hope it sings
But tonight ain't right
So you're locked in tight
Locks rock------------Not!
Locks rock------------Hot!
Locks and it is never forgot
Cause when you try the door
You can't leave no more -The Guard
Waging wicked (?) war
With a smile of pleasure
Give a quadruple measure

The Double Deal With Zeal

SYLVIA DIED – JESUS WAS CRUCIFIED – LOVE CANNOT WILL NOT BE DENIED

I knew you we're a Jew from the look of you
I too hold the Holy Torah to be true
Searching for wisdom Love is an ending quest
With Jesus is heaven there is all of the best

The double deal with Zeal this is real
Men who listen have potent sex appeal
The double deal with Zeal try to steal
The double deal with Zeal this is real

The scent of a good woman who can forget?
Tameeka baby don't have any regret
My touch when Boom Boom on the Honey room bed
Only neutral blood will happily be bled

The double deal with Zeal this is real
Men who listen have potent sex appeal
The double deal with Zeal try to steal
The double deal with Zeal this is real

Mr. lawyer pretend is a never friend
A fighter in the cause against unjust laws
My job finished but the fight never to end
Take the brief moment of silence to pause

The double deal with Zeal this is real
Men who listen have potent sex appeal
The double deal with Zeal try to steal
The double deal with Zeal this is real

Sir we're going to program your barber nice
After all recall the God damns ticks and lice
Red, green, yellow or perhaps none at all
Whatever it is it's your head but our call

Stevie darling, I hope you decide to stay
Seven seven seven it's coming your way
Once Jesus was the only word I knew
But that's what the twenty four elder do its true

The double deal with Zeal this is real/ Men who listen have potent sex appeal
The double deal with Zeal try to steal/ The double deal with Zeal this is real

The Noisy Nurse

The video tape that none can escape
No sodomy and there's no rape
Forgive and forget no regret
Love is always my favorite bet
Leslie did you hear the lullaby
Bitterly weeping asking why
Hoping wishing that you could die
Well honey maybe I ain't your guy

The Nice Nurse

We put a hatchet in the skull of for nurse Ratched
And twist their arms with an electric rachet
Figaro figaro figaro fiddler fiddling on the roof
Where is Jesus I can't see any proof
Dressed in white heaven's delight
Red & yellow black & white
Thank God they got one thing right
I'm tired of the war tired of the fight
Throw loving arms around me
Know loving charms surround me
Agony's reality
Sweet Jesus come and rescue me

The Sun Rises - Dedicated to Tiffany

My paper napkin was tragically lost
Dancin' in moonlight at maximum cost
Blowing in the breeze your hair fell down
Cheek caressed cheek I kiss your crown

Night might reign in pain but the sun rises
Do you delight in pleasant surprises?
Night might reign in pain but the sun rises

There were miracle words on that paper
You escaped I never heard a whisper
A story of love a story of blue
The precious memory of you

Night might reign in pain but the sun rises
Do you delight in pleasant surprises?
Night might reign in pain but the sun rises

Alone on the beach twilight highest of highs
Slashing the cold see the sun rises
Love may be love in disguise
But love never tells any lies

Night might reign in pain but the sun rises
Do you delight in pleasant surprises?
Night might reign in pain but the sun rises

Tiffany

Tiffany in any disguise Jesus hears your cries
The world is full of lust and dies on our lies
But this is a happy song so please be strong
Sing "na na nah" and we all get along

Aztecs worship the fiery ball
You're the one you're the one
Hear in the shadows my ancient call
Finger and tongue you're the one

Hey woman I caressed you breast under open skies
We made love & the stars above heard our cries
Back in West Virginia paradise is green
Come on Baby you're a beauty queen

Aztecs worship the fiery ball
You're the one you're the one
Hear in the shadows my ancient call
Finger and tongue you're the one

Men they come and men they go
You ain't a whore I won't say so
But I Am the god of this melody
Tiffany the Truth shall set you free

Honestly

The orchestra becomes the latest grand marching band
Woodie Guthrie covers consuming the land
Our friend Rosa Linda we recall all the rest
When you're ready darling fly to my nest

Aztecs worship the fiery ball
You're the one you're the one
Hear in the shadows my ancient call
Finger and tongue you're the one

Where's Tupac?

Timothy didn't need a clue in pain
Clearly dearly together and both sane
Chaos in the crowd speaking much too loud
In comes the Hells Angels speaking you proud

Where's Tupac when we need the truth?
Where's Tupac when they betrayed our youth?
Hip Hop didn't stop with Buddy Holly
Santa Clause was always red and jolly

Crazy lazy or just out of your minds
I have seen the light and boy how it blinds
Eastside Newark my eyes are watching you
Purple is red and of course much worse blue

Where's Tupac when we need the truth?
Where's Tupac when they betrayed our youth?
Hip Hop didn't stop with Buddy Holly
Santa Clause was always red and jolly

All heroes fall recall Elvis Presley
Even Old Neil faces eternity
Quit the crime isn't that now crystal clear
Nineteen Sylvan place drop by for some cheer

Jesus is my savior Jesus is my hero
Numbers are everything numbers are zero
Tupac shall return he's got much to learn
The sky is high and the fire's gonna burn

Where's Tupac when we need the truth?
Where's Tupac when they betrayed our youth?
Hip Hop didn't stop with Buddy Holly
Santa Clause was always red and jolly

A 1st poem

Oh Nicolle,
I love you with all my soul.

James!

Facing Eviction

One hundred and fifty dollars raise in rent
Greed is an evil deed better repent
Food and shelter they should be a right
Facing eviction one hell of a fight

Facing eviction life's a bummer
Facing eviction thank God it's summer
Faction eviction I'm an overcomer
Facing eviction life's a bummer

The wild wind blows in comes the storms of living
Plenty of taking so little giving
Money over people could you explain
Chasing the dollar everything is vain

Facing eviction life's a bummer
Facing eviction thank God it's summer
Faction eviction I'm an overcomer
Facing eviction life's a bummer

Goodbye to my neighbor on the second floor
Come August first she'll be there no more
After twenty years ripped from her home
Thrown out on the streets to wander and roam

Facing eviction life's a bummer
Facing eviction thank God it's summer
Faction eviction I'm an overcomer
Facing eviction life's a bummer

Landlord what will be your reward a coffin of gold
Get ready to meet your maker you're getting old
Jesus said in Mathew twenty-five about the least of these
Capitalism is a sinister sickly disease

A juggernaut crushing the weak and the old
Life is a story what is being told?
The haves they have more than they could use
Facing eviction and singing the blues

Facing eviction life's a bummer
Facing eviction thank God it's summer
Faction eviction I'm an overcomer
Facing eviction life's a bummer

Three Doors Down

Apollo shot a golden arrow through the nymph's heart
I'm an artist and that means I create art
I'll be the biggest rapper I'll wear that golden crown
Yes I can says the man living three doors down

The hand of fate three doors down
I can scarcely wait three doors down
Rap hip hop soaring to the top
I'll keep on going I'll never stop
One day I'll be the talk of the town
I believe it's true three doors down

He was walking by and we talked about things of life
Exchanging truths they were cutting as a knife
We laughed we cried we gave a bitter sigh asking why
Agreeing quickly that life's a sickly lie

The hand of fate three doors down
I can scarcely wait three doors down
Rap hip hop soaring to the top
I'll keep on going I'll never stop
One day I'll be the talk of the town
I believe it's true three doors down

We gave Jimi praise thinking on days we never knew
With stars above brotherly love grew and grew
People are people God's hand deals luck and circumstance
I believe the brother has a hell of a chance

The hand of fate three doors down
I can scarcely wait three doors down
Rap hip hop soaring to the top
I'll keep on going I'll never stop
One day I'll be the talk of the town
I believe it's true three doors down

BOOKS BY JOHN KANIECKI

Poet To The Poor – This book is probably John's finest work of poetry. It includes much of his early writings when the muse was close. John combines poetic technique of rhyming, imagery, rhythm, and such with a heart for social consciousness.

More Than The Madness – This is John's memoirs dealing with his successful struggle with mental illness. This is a book of humanity showing life's up and downs. This informative book is full of exciting drama.

Without The Music – This is a book of song lyrics taking over 25 years to compile. The book depicts John's best and details some of his earnest efforts. This book is ideal for musicians looking for words or for those seeking poetic thrills.

Story Of The Scarecrow – Young Anne McFry is fleeing her satanic past on her way to New York City and her dreams of being a musical star. But the ride on the Greyhound Bus is infused with terror in the form of the Scarecrow.

I Should Have Been A Rock Star – A full length novel. Don Calandri is abducted on his way to a statics test by Nellie Watt. Don gets caught up in a cosmic contest. Naturally, his buddies at home claim he was kidnapped by a satanic cult so they can collect money and score with chicks. But they didn't count on the real devil worshipers getting so indignant. A book full of wonder and humor.

From Chaos To Cosmos – Short science fiction stories. The different topics and styles depict a creativity and imagination that is only bound by the English language.

Polishing The Fragments – When God shatters your life what do you do? Why you polish the fragments. A poetic book of suffering, hope, and persevering in the love of life.

Can I Get A Witness? – A guide to the art of witnessing. A practical guide on how to share one's Christian faith. Full of scripture and John's stories.

Dark Matters – Three science fiction novellas. Nazis exiled on a distant planet, a post-apocalyptic world full of horrific religion, and a college student caught up in some devious psychological experiment.

Murmurings Of A Mad Man – A book of poetry written with strict meter and rhyme as a mad man naturally would. 100 poems detailing John's stay at Graystone psychiatric hospital. Crazy Horse, Joe Hill and Woodie Guthrie star as John's id, ego and superego.

The Hustle – John's second book of song lyrics more voluminous than his original effort. Again, great for bands seeking words or readers appreciating poetic beauty. This book has been renamed **The Big Book of Song Lyrics.**

A Day's Weather – Poetry from John's early days. This work takes a look at the weather of a day each nuance expressed in poetic verse.

The Lost Cantos Of John Kaniecki – Another work of John's earlier days. This book is full of rhymed metered work which will bring a pleasant smile.

Words For The Future – A group of science fiction stories. A reprint of "Words Of The Future" with extra stores thrown in for good measure. Oozing with creativity and excitement.

In The Mind Of Magoo – Poor Walter Magoo is trapped inside a dead husk of a body. Worse yet his mind is alive with grandiose visions that he cannot share. The warlock's past is quickly catching up to him. A horror story with many tales.

Letting It Out – Prose poems capturing a snapshot of time. This book is a revolutionary work with logical words that uplift and inspire.

Seven Rings Of Saturn – A poetic experiment that is out of this world!

Bells and Whistles Thorns and Thistles – The poetic exploits of Edgar the banker as he commutes to work via the train. Later he heads to the rural outlands. Edgar is chasing his identity as his demons are chasing him.

Coming Soon

Myroniac – What's worse than a maniac? A Myroniac! A book of horror set in Chipowanock where the CIA and Mafia have a thriving heroin business. Two Myrons are being encouraged to kill by their wicked psychiatrist who once worked on Shadow Corps, the military's effort to make a perfect killer.

Story Of Satan's Siren – The story of Anne McFry goes on. Anne seeks revenge!

Fallon's Fight – The story of Fallon of Freetown. A simple young man thrust into a brutal world. This is an unparalleled book of fantasy with unique twists and turns.

FeatherLeaf Speaks And Other Prophetic Visons – The follow up to Poet To The Poor. This book delivers more great poetry with both social conscious and poetic flair using traditional technique.

Welcome to the Dream!

In your hands is *The Big Book of Song Lyrics*. If you have gotten to this page, well, thank you very much. I hope you found the poetic journey inspiring, meaningful and profitable.

Creating this book has been a labor of love, one that you too can partake in. Please take the liberty to utilize this book to the fullest. Take the song lyrics and make songs, it is the purpose of the book. Just be sure to give me a credit and the royalties due.

John Kaniecki can be reached at the following email address.

peacepoems@mail.com

Hope to see you down the line!

Made in United States
North Haven, CT
20 September 2024